THE HISTORIOGRAPHIC PERVERSION

MARC NICHANIAN

TRANSLATED, WITH AN AFTERWORD, BY GIL ANIDJAR

THE HISTORIOGRAPHIC
PERVERSION

COLUMBIA UNIVERSITY PRESS *New York*

Columbia University Press

Publishers Since 1893

New York   Chichester, West Sussex

Copyright © 2009 Columbia University Press

La perversion historiographique copyright © 2006 Lignes-Léo Scheer

Library of Congress Cataloging-in-Publication Data

Nichanian, Marc, 1946–

[Perversion historiographique. English]

The historiographic perversion / Marc Nichanian; translated, with an afterword, by Gil
Anidjar.

   p.   cm.

Includes bibliographical references and index.

ISBN 978-0-231-14908-2 (cloth: alk. paper)

   1. Historiography—Political aspects.   2. Genocide—Historiography.   3. Historiography—
20th century.   4. Massacres—Armenia—History.   5. Holocaust denial.   6. Witnesses.
I. Anidjar, Gil.   II. Title.

D13.2.N5413 2009

907.2—dc22

                                                                                          2009000793

Casebound editions of Columbia University Press books are printed on permanent
and durable acid-free paper.

Printed in the United States of America

c 10 9 8 7 6 5 4 3 2 1

References to Internet Web Sites (URLs) were accurate at the time of writing. Neither the author
nor Columbia University Press is responsible for Web sites that may have expired or changed since
the book was prepared.

To Grigor Hakopyan (1959–2005), in memoriam

CONTENTS

THE HISTORIOGRAPHIC PERVERSION

INTRODUCTION

THE NAMES AND THE ARCHIVE

THIS BOOK SPEAKS OF TRUTH IN HISTORY AND OF THE MODERN status of testimony in relation to the genocidal events of the twentieth century. It is a collection of four studies written over the course of the last few years, practically under the sway of circumstances. Its conclusion is a reflection on shame. Such disparate writing does not diminish, I think, the consistency of an interrogation, the contours of which I attempt to draw once again in this introduction.

1

Genocide is not a fact (*Le génocide n'est pas un fait*).

Genocide is not a fact because it is the very destruction of the fact, of the notion of fact, of the factuality of fact.

Hereby are two propositions related to the word (and perhaps to the reality of what we call) "genocide." If these two propositions can be inscribed in this way at the beginning of a book, without further precautions and without preliminaries, it is because their appearance is simple. They are somehow provocative, no doubt, but they do not give the impression of concealing shimmering false bottoms or otherwise labyrinthine and hidden layers. They do not require a technical vocabulary to attain a coherent and immediately accessible formulation. Indeed, before I wrote them here, they had already been enunciated by others in an equally explicit, hardly more inflected or indirect, manner and truly in a style so smooth that it was not even noticed. Here, for instance, is the form taken by the first proposition in Jean-François Lyotard's work: "With Auschwitz, something new has happened in history (which can only be a sign and not a fact)."[1] The same author enunciates the second proposition as explicitly and, we shall see later, in more or less the same terms as those I have adopted in my own opening. Of course, the use of an emblematic name ("Auschwitz") may slightly alter the terms of the problem, but it does not change the substance of what must be thought and brought to language, which is the following: that something has occurred in history that may not have occurred as fact. Or worse: that something has occurred as the very negation of the fact as such. This is what I will have to repeat in a number of ways and tones. For how—one will obviously be forced to ask—can something occur, how can something take place *in history* if it does not do so as a fact? Or, in a more ambitious manner: what is, henceforth, history? What is historical "reality"? What is a fact? How is it that there can still be for us, after all and fortunately, stable and indubitable facts at the same time as there are facts that have overthrown our very idea of factuality? Such questions, one might say, are all too general to be interesting! Perhaps. Such is perhaps the fate of the kind of gesture I am attempting here. As a result, at any rate, these questions and the two propositions that have brought them about will have to emerge (or reemerge) under our eyes out of a local interrogation or out of a sense of personal discomfort. They will have to impress themselves on us out of a particular historical situation. And here I speak of my own historical situation, of course—my task being to convince you that it is also unfailingly yours.

But the simple appearance of the two propositions inscribed at the outset is, in truth, completely fallacious. These propositions are resolutely contrary to common sense. That is why they must reemerge under our eyes and impose their contradictory or paradoxical necessity through logical aporias or out of a tale of beginnings. They must also be rendered explicit in a specific way, one that will at times be philosophical, and properly so. I myself have needed years—an entire life, as it were—to be capable of writing these simple words *genocide is not a fact*. Indeed, we must understand what this means: if genocide is not a fact, there can be no question of using the word *genocide* to designate or describe a fact. There simply cannot be a "fact" that could be qualified as "genocide." At the very least, historical truth will not suffice for it. Instead, we find ourselves in a space where *historical authority is already contested*. More elements are needed: a truth grounded in law, a truth grounded in memory, a truth grounded in artistic representation (and whatever else, God only knows!). And none of these do much to improve the business of truth. My opening words therefore demand some preliminary clearing, or something of the sort, in order to appear in all their blinding (or doubtful) evidence. Such spadework is not merely an individual endeavor. Its very possibility is largely related to contemporary circumstances, to conceptual advances of the time, as well as to almost fortuitous events, such as those that have provided the pre-text of my first two chapters, themselves responses to "affairs" that did not earn the privilege of reaching the front pages or at least to have their own Émile Zola. Nonetheless, these affairs have altered what we believed we knew heretofore of intellectual probity—and of truth in history. These are both affairs that have occurred in France, under our own eyes, in our present time. First, in 1994, Bernard Lewis, a world-famous American historian, was summoned by a French civil court for something else, God forbid, than a petty crime. Instead, it was because of the doubts he had expressed concerning the reality of a genocide, namely, that of the Armenians of the Ottoman Empire. In short, a state court was asking a historian to give an account of his conception of truth in history. What a scandal! Then, in 1999, another historian of the Ottoman Empire, Gilles Veinstein, declared his candidacy for a position at the Collège de France.

On that occasion, he also became the object of a campaign (deemed by many to be libelous) caused by an article he had written, which was, indeed, tantamount to denial. He had signed and published it five years earlier, on the occasion of the first affair, no doubt to come to the rescue of his colleague and friend, Bernard Lewis. The latter—this was the first affair—was having troubles with French law. Between these two dates, and, more precisely, in 1998, the members of the French parliament had adopted a laconically formulated law declaring that the Armenians of the Ottoman Empire had been the victims of a "genocide" in 1915 (the quotes around *genocide* are mine, and I will explain them in due time). What did the politicians and legislators know about this? Justice and law were allowed to intervene in an affair that should have been resolved strictly among historians. Indeed, what a scandal!

At the time, these two affairs had set in motion, as if by spontaneous generation, an army of historians, precisely, and that on both sides of the Atlantic. The second affair drew more attention because the integrity of the French university was on the line. It was the occasion for a campaign of signatures in favor of the defendant, a campaign that involved the helping hands of many French intellectuals. And since what was at stake was truth in history and the factuality of the fact (before the entire matter became a contest, that is, between the rights of the historian and the rights of the judge and of the legislator), it became possible for me to understand what the historiographic perversion is. Most important, the two affairs made it possible for me to understand that an event could fail to be a fact and that new categories were necessary in order to think the "genocides" of the twentieth century together with the unsettling events that have accompanied and followed them. What was required, therefore, was at the very least a work of explanation, as well as an attempt to provide a circumstantial account, without which the propositions I have enunciated at the outset would remain absolutely inaudible. But one also had to draw conclusions from these propositions, something that it is now our task to comment upon and explore. Such conclusions, or consequences, concern not only the nature of the event (whether historical or not) but also the modern status of testimony (what is sometimes called the testimony of the survivor) and, following a slight displacement caused by the fallout of the blast, the crisis of representation and the tear of the image (*la déchirure de l'image*), so often confused with the destitution of the fact. On this aspect of representation, of testimony and of the image, I will ask for the reader's patience—until the final chapter.

And yet, at the outset, even before I am to elaborate on the contextual and personal origins of the proposition "genocide is not a fact;" before I can announce or promise an explication in a philosophical mode, or observe the conflict of representation in its relation to the destitution of the fact, two remarks are clearly necessary. These remarks emerge from the use I have made, right from the beginning, of the expression "emblematic name" regarding the name of Auschwitz. It is the name of an irreparable, a "non-negatable negative," a destruction that cancels itself as destruction, a name "without name," the name of an "experience of language" or of a "para-experience"—all these qualifiers and many more were suggested or used by Jean-François Lyotard in 1980, over the course of a conference in which he inaugurated his own reflections on the question of the emblematic name, before these reached their final formulation in the masterwork that is *The Differend*.[2] This early presentation was followed by a debate, the abridged transcription of which contains the following statements (the names of the participants are capitalized):

> NANCY: "There would thus be a specific difference between Auschwitz and other situations that are apparently comparable." DERRIDA and LYOTARD seem to have agreed that other names than Auschwitz, equally impossible to link or elaborate upon [*aussi inenchaînables*], are nonetheless commanding that links be made. LACOUE-LABARTHE asks that these names be specified. NANCY sees the specificity of Auschwitz in that "there, the end of man is a project in itself and not the trial of another project" (313).

One does not know what the other situations were that are here deemed "apparently comparable." What followed in the debate seems to indicate that the "Soviet camps" were taking a non-negligible place in the minds of the interlocutors. In any case, no explicit mention is made of other genocides of the twentieth century. What was here in question was the singularity of Auschwitz, and I have no intention of commenting further upon this at the moment. I merely want to point out that the very use of the emblematic name governs the interrogation concerning the necessity of "comparing" different ways of putting to work "the project of the end of man" (since any enunciation on singularity, whether it is uttered with a tone of vehemence or with that of circumspect examination, does presuppose a comparison prior to any specific formulation). Were there other possible names for this very project? Were there no such names? One does not know. One only knows that Lyotard was, if "with reservations," in favor of a multiplication of models (this is what he declares later in the debate while responding to an injunction made by Jean-Luc Nancy). The discussion was never revisited, as far as I know, and we will therefore never learn anything more about such imaginable alternative models or about other names-without-name. Similarly, we shall obviously know nothing of the form that a reflection on names and models could have taken in response to Lyotard's "reservations."

My second remark is the logical consequence of the first, but it is much more complex. The use made of the emblematic name by Lyotard, but also by Theodor Adorno before him and by European philosophers in general (in the United States we know that intellectuals use the word "Holocaust" as a proper name and not as an emblematic one), is predicated upon the assertion of a specific difference that introduces and carries, is presupposed by, the entirety of Lyotard's considerations on the *differend*. Let us say it very simply: it is the difference between the generic name ("genocide") and the emblematic name ("Auschwitz"). Lyotard himself never uses the generic name and rightly so. He shows very clearly the perspective from which his usage is the right one: the emblematic name designates "that which has no name in speculative thought, a name of the anonymous."[3] Further, and even more clearly for the benefit of disgruntled people, Lyotard adds:

> Why say that this anonym [*cet anonyme*] designates an "experience of language" . . . ? Is this not an insult to the millions of real deaths in the real barracks and gas chambers of the real camps? One can guess what benefit a well-governed indignation might reap from

the word "reality." What is hatching under this indignation is the egg of the dispenser of justice. With its realism, however, such indignation is an insult to the name of Auschwitz.[4]

Now that I read it again, twenty-five years later, this passage still appears to me quite impressive after all. Let us say it again with Jean-François Lyotard then. It is the realism of the fact that constitutes an insult to the emblematic name. The latter, we recall (and Lyotard himself will do so two years later), is the name of a sign and not the name of a fact. Inversely, however, the realist insult of the fact explains and justifies the philosophical refusal to use the generic name. Would this constitute an insult and an injury for any other name and for any other "fact"? Of course not. It is precisely because genocide is not a fact that any use of the word "genocide" to designate an event that occurred in history is a shame and an ignominy. It is the shame and the ignominy of "realism." And there is nothing philosophical about that, believe me. I will come back to the issue of shame—I will most certainly not forget it. And since this second remark has now taken a personal turn, I wish briefly to add the following words to the chapter narrating the emergence and history of names: there is also a history of the name in the case of the extermination of the Armenians of the Ottoman Empire. At the very beginning, around 1919, the proper name of the event was rather *Yeghern*, which, in its common form, more or less means "pogrom" and was already the word one used to designate the planned series of massacres of 1895 in Eastern Anatolia as well as those of 1909 in the Adana region. The word has a respectable etymology (*that which was*, that is, *the Event*, par excellence). But terminology was not fixed, and other words were also used as proper names. In the familial context, the most current name was *Ak'sor*, which, as a common name, means "exile" or "deportation." And then, from 1931 on, another name appeared as proper name: *Aghed*. It is the common word for "catastrophe," which became a proper name by way of its capitalization. Why 1931? Because in this year, in Cyprus where he lived, Hagop Oshagan began to use it systematically in order to designate the event. He was writing his novel then, *Mnatsortats* (That which remains or The survivors), and it was not long before he would be perceived as the greatest writer of the twentieth century in the Armenian language. Of course, the word "genocide" had not been invented yet. But, aside from this, everybody knew perfectly well what was meant by an extermination project conducted to its systematic conclusion with sufficient perseverance. Among the survivors, no one needed to be persuaded of the fact that they had been the collective targets of such a project. It is only today, under the pressure of a politicization of the event, that the generic word (capitalized this time) is used as if it could designate the event as a proper name. In English, therefore, we now have "the Armenian Genocide," or simply (and in an ever more absurd manner): "the Genocide." It is the supreme insult, the realist insult that an entire people of survivors inflicts upon itself at every moment.

But why this aside on the proper name? Precisely because a generic name cannot be made to function as a proper name, but also because none of the proper names I've just mentioned could ever play the role of emblematic name.[5] The passage toward an emblematic use of the proper name only occurred when, in the wake of Hagop Oshagan, the word *Aghed* was translated into French and when the word *Catastrophe* began to serve as the proper name of the event—this time with the clear consciousness that such usage signified a kind of defusing of the realist insult and a curtailment of desperate efforts at refutation. Such a passage only occurred in a restricted circle of intellectuals, of course. It corresponds to my own use of the word *Catastrophe* dating from the first essay I have dedicated to these issues.[6] My aside on the proper name is therefore part of a personal history, part of my own dispute with the names. There lies what is ultimately the only adult decision for which I can publicly account. The rejection of the word "genocide" was an attempt to part with the realist insult, with refutation and negation as collective destiny, and with the historiographic stranglehold (*mainmise*) as such (a stranglehold that forbids any consideration of the event outside the coordinates of the fact). As for me, it is only today that I am able to name the injury, the despair of refutation, and the historiographic stranglehold as such. One will understand, in any case, that the insult of which Lyotard speaks, that this insult addressed to the emblematic name was more than familiar to me. The decision simply and purely to ignore the generic name was, for me, at the heart of a reading practice that was aimed at examining the treatment of the Catastrophe. And if I had to use a generic name, I would always suspend it within quotation marks, as I am doing here from time to time. Needless to say, such marks do not by any means signify a denegation.

To ignore, to defuse and reject, to suspend within quotation marks: these are expressions and practices that result from the radical distinction between the Catastrophe (which demands that one asks the question of its representation—possible or impossible) and the "genocide" (the historians' object, the last word of refutation, its categorical and renewed stake). Once the distinction was made (and for me it remains inaugural, a kind of ontological difference), one could begin to ask about "the style of violence," that is to say, as much about the limit-experience of the Catastrophe within language and about what these have to say about the event, about the very nature of the violence at play in the setting to work of the genocidal will (*la volonté génocidaire*). Only literature could take this experience to its conclusion. This is the way of seeing things that remains current for me. I renounce none of it. Hence, after this long aside on the name of the event, I find myself able to return to my second remark concerning the use of the emblematic name in Lyotard. We have seen that it says nothing or knows nothing of other, "apparently comparable," situations in the twentieth century, even if it leaves open the possibility of "other models." It thus cannot serve as an emblematic name for all these situations and all these models. Nor does it permit to ask whether such a thing is conceivable. As for me, I do not possess any emblematic name. It would seem, therefore, that I am unable to claim, repeat, or reproduce that which took place with the philosophical use of the emblematic name "Auschwitz." I have no means to register or record, by way of a simple name, what took place in the event, to inscribe that which, at the outset, locates the event beyond the reach of the historiographic grasp and provokes, in historiography as a discipline, a crisis from which it will have difficulties recovering (and about which it hardly cares, of course): the putting under question of the factuality of the fact. Later, I will refer to this in a more explicit, if also more complex, manner as the circular destruction of the conditions of possibility for destruction to become a fact. In this account, "Catastrophe" is not really an emblematic name. Clearly, the Catastrophe does not belong to the domain historians have assumed as their task to explore by way of archives and testimonies. This is because, for all intents and purposes, the Catastrophe was defined, it was constituted, by the rigorous exclusion of factuality and refutation—and so it was long before my own decision on the matter. At the very least, it was so defined in the confrontation of the survivors with testimony, the encounter of the writers with the impossible representation of the event. Were I to say, "The *Catastrophe* is not a fact; it has nothing to do in particular with the refutation of negationisms,[7] nor with the affirmation of the referentiality of the fact," this would not constitute a functioning enunciation. At most, it would be an analytic statement, one void of all substance. In this context, I would further add that the very name of Catastrophe, *Aghed* in Armenian, is merely the future name of the event. It is rarely used as a proper name, as I have already said, nor is it ever used as a substitute for the absent, emblematic name. Catastrophe, *Aghed*, is the name by which the event comes back to us from the future. Following Derrida, one should even use the future anterior here: it will have come back to us.

In such a situation, in which the emblematic name *remains to be produced*, it is my initial proposition—"genocide is not a fact"—that governs and directs me. It forces me to leave behind questions about the literary or testimonial treatment of the Catastrophe, to abandon for a time the representation and the "style" of catastrophic violence. For the very first time, it forces and obligates me to occupy myself with what historians, jurists, and lawmakers have called genocide and with what they do when they refute the negation of the event by producing proofs or passing laws. "We will bring no proofs," wrote Maurice Blanchot. It is perhaps time to know why.

2

During the two affairs I have mentioned above, and through the press campaigns that surrounded them, there were university professors who, motivated by interests that are of no concern to us here, inaugurated a kind of unanswerable negationist discourse. Accordingly, by signing the petitions then circulating in support of Gilles Veinstein, an entire segment of the French intelligentsia calmly affirmed that there was no negationism involved in denying the attributes of genocide to the interpretation of the extermination of the Armenians of the Ottoman Empire (while insisting, explicitly but *against all logic*, that the facts were verified and that it was, indeed, a genocide). They did not know how to make the difference, therefore, between the fact and the event (or worse: between a fact and a "brute" fact). They did not see the perverse role played by renowned historians. These historians had managed to render the negationist refutation irrefutable! It was the modern nature of the genocidal will that was at stake. My first chapter, "The Law and the Fact" ("Le droit et le fait") is a barely modified version of what I wrote in 1995 as a reaction to the verdict rendered by the Paris court in the trial conducted against Bernard Lewis. Under certain conditions, I argue, "only law can establish a fact." This sentence, written ten years ago, called for a reflection on the institution of the fact as such, in its greater generality as well as in its always possible *destitution*. For it just so happens that the genocides of the twentieth century have managed the tour de force that consists in actualizing that possibility. Since then, perverse historians have done even better in following this trend to the extent that they have wagered on the originary destitution *of the fact* (which was willed and produced by the genocidal will) in order to cast doubt on the reality *of the facts*. The genocidal will, in other words, is that which wants to abolish the fact in and through the very act that establishes the fact. There is here a phenomenon singular to the entirety of the twentieth century, which is the genocidal century because it is the century of the archive.

At the end of his essay on the "force of law," Derrida writes of "the system of mythical violence" such as was brought to its most extreme consequences by the Nazis. Of this system Derrida explains that "at the same time, it kept the archive of its destruction . . . and (at the same time, therefore) it produced a system in which its logic . . . made possible the invalidation and therefore the effacement of testimony and of responsibilities . . . ; in short, it produced the possibility of the historiographic perversion."[8] Derrida is here commenting on the archive of the destruction, which is in the process of occurring. He is also and simultaneously (I say it again now) commenting on the destruction of that which constitutes the condition of possibility for any destruction to become a historical fact in the eyes of civilized humanity: the archive. There is here an exemplary and complex circularity that has long escaped perception. But what does it matter, one will ask, whether this is now perceived? Unless I am mistaken, a few years after writing the lines I have just quoted, Derrida himself signed one of the petitions that circulated in favor of Gilles Veinstein. The year was 1999. In my second chapter, "Amputation and Imputation," I try to understand how such things are possible. For the past twenty years, many people have spoken about the historiographic perversion in relation to the genocidal phenomenon— so have many among European philosophers, at any rate (in the United States, the situation is hopeless, in spite of Hayden White). And yet, in all appearances, something remains to be said on the genocidal will and on the destruction of the fact that brings historiographic thought to crisis in its entirety, producing the phenomena of perversion that we now know.

Moreover, and since this is also the year in which Europe officially begins negotiations with Turkey (with a view to admitting it as a member of the Union, and with total disregard for the moral significance of that state's refusal to recognize its own past), it is high time, it seems to me, to conduct a reflection on the motivations and operations of the genocidal will, which *nowhere* appears as clearly as it does here. And let us not forget either that Turkish intellectuals themselves have had to suffer the wrath of the regime and the heavy pull of the state's negationist tradition when they organized a conference in Istanbul (the conference was twice forbidden by none other than the minister of justice himself before finally taking place at the end of September 2005), where, for the very first time, they all proclaimed a historical truth as if it was also a historiographic truth (to them, and to everybody else, historiography is the guarantor of historical truth). At any rate, there is here a true revolution. There must be a circulation of ideas between them and us ("us,"

Europe, or "us," intellectuals of "diasporism"). Such circulation of ideas presupposes a sound understanding that what is at issue is not only a matter of honest talk opposed to a state nationalism hardened in its positions. The genocidal will (essentially a philosophical will) requires more. It requires a reflection on the very notion of fact (and not only, sociologically, on the manner in which the memory of the events is constituted for civilized humanity). It requires a reflection that concerns itself with our consensus around this notion, the consensus holding that facts must be founded on testimony and guarded by historiography. I would add, as a matter of confession, that I have signed a petition last year, one calling on the French government to oppose the entry of Turkey into Europe, as long as no mea culpa was made by that state. This was no doubt a serious error on my part. On the contrary, I want Turkey to be recognized for what it is and what it already was at the beginning of the twentieth century: as European in spite of everything. This should put an end to a number of illusions and to hypocrisy as well with regard to morality. It should also enable underscoring that which ensures the cohesion of Europe, say, in the Homeric tradition that begins (does anyone remember this?) in Asia Minor with the Trojan genocide: the forgetting or the systematic ignorance of the *genocidal will* (but there was no archive then, there was only epic, and that is the whole difference). The historiographic perversion is European or it is not. By way of a strange coincidence—I say this in passing—it was in 1999, the year of the Veinstein controversy in France, that the trans-European debate took place on the American intervention in Bosnia. Was the genocidal will suddenly perceived then? Perhaps. Was there however a law justifying the intervention? Of course not. The only justification was moral. And yet, as Habermas put it at the time in an article written in favor of military intervention, such violent and illegal intervention was anticipating on a law to come and found its justification in this anticipation. The entire problem of Western consciousness (and conscience) confronted with the genocidal will was thus posed in that debate and particularly in the response of Habermas, who was taking into account as much as he could the antihumanist critique of humanitarian intervention and concluded by rejecting this critique. Minimally, such things tell us to what extent the reflection on the genocidal will and on the crisis of historiographic representation is necessary and urgent.

However one understands all this, it is high time to conduct a resolutely antihumanist reflection on the genocidal will in the twentieth century and on the historiographic crisis linked to this peculiar will. This reflection must engage the Armenian example, but, in reality, it must also be a pure reflection, one *without example*. It is also high time to reflect without the burden of worn-out clichés on the duty of memory (as if survivors had any choice but to remember, generation after generation, the founding catastrophe) and to do so without empty, allegedly political, claims for recognition. It is high time, finally, to conduct a reflection capable of thematizing the tear of representation, the destitution of the fact, and capable at the same time of distinguishing one from the other, in order to understand better how the two operate together.

Between the two (and here I am shifting registers), which is to say, between the tear and the destitution, between representation and fact, there was always testimony, taken hostage, neither knowing where to turn nor where to go. Did it have to embrace literature or the claim for recognition? Representation or document? The emblematic name or the generic name (that is to say, realist shame, desperate refutation, the historiographic stranglehold)? Chapter 3 (where I attend to the insufferable 1991 debate between Hayden White and Carlo Ginzburg on truth in history) and chapter 4 (on the rapport of art to testimony in the proximity of Catastrophe) both return in more detail to the question of the historical status of this very peculiar rhetorical production that is testimony. Seemingly, it is here, in the significance and good use of testimony, that the debate about truth in history and about the realist presupposition of historiography has been concentrated for the last few years. This aspect of things was not explicitly treated by Lyotard at the time, and it deserves to be lingered upon, especially because of the way shame, such as produced by the realist insult, is directly related to the documentary and probative function attached to testimony from the outset. I will explicate this in three points, briefly, while omitting explicit references to the texts I allude to (I will provide these at a later stage) and while leaving for later my commentary on the idea of art as a rewriting of "the event-without-witness" thematized by Shoshana Felman in an extraordinary 1989 essay on testimony.

A. In February 1917 Zabel Essayan, a woman and writer who had miraculously escaped the roundups of April 1915 in Istanbul, published the first authentic testimony to reach us from the hell of deportation. She was transcribing the words of a survivor and added a short preface in which she announced that it would be indecent to submit them to a literary treatment of any sort. In August 1931, in the interview conducted in Cyprus in which he invented the name *Aghed* as the proper name of the event and announced that his project was to "approach the Catastrophe," Hagop Oshagan declared at the same time that he did not know whether he would be able to write the last part of his novel (which was supposed to address the deportation as a historical fact, no doubt in a realistic manner), since he did not have access to the necessary archives. He was therefore obliged to "limit" himself to the form of the novel. Oshagan did not pronounce the word "archive," but that is what he implied. "What will be minimally needed is a topographic study, the reading of thousands of narratives and of hundreds of volumes, of testimonies, prior to being able to write [the final part]." This declaration has obsessed me for years. I come back to it here, one more time, at the end of a long journey. The writing of the Catastrophe was in need of testimony—that, at least, is clear. But it is equally clear that the task to be confronted was also something that I would provisionally call a sublimation of testimony. One had to liberate testimony, as it were, from its realist and documentary function, to draw it out of the sphere of refutation. Literature did not intend to speak reality. Its intention, its function, its task—was the redemption of testimony. Of all this, Oshagan was only able to enunciate the project. Another generation was needed, and more than half a century, for that project to be completed, if upon entirely different premises. In the meantime, these writers, the greatest of the century among the Armenians, expressed their readiness to become the secretaries of testimony and, in truth, of the archive, to the point that they themselves chose to inflict the fatal blow on literature.

Here is, at different levels, the power of the archive activated by the catastrophic event. Yet, and inversely, it is also the case that the power of the archive is what has made possible the genocidal will as such.

B. In 1991 the historian Carlo Ginzburg was leading the charge against Hayden White in an article entitled "Just One Witness."[9] The problem as Ginzburg saw it was the following: carried away by his "relativist" critique of historical discourse and by his insistence on the generalized rhetoricity of this discourse, White had apparently reached the conclusion that the "reality" of the event is dependent on the force of its interpretations. Truth in history was becoming a matter of power, pure and simple, or, let us say, a matter of dominant representation. In his quite violent reaction, Ginzburg quoted Renato Serra, the Italian essayist who, at the beginning of the twentieth century, was responding to Benedetto Croce's theses. Serra had maintained a correspondence with Croce in which he put under interrogation the very relation of fact to testimony, making the latter independent from all realistic use, from all documentary usage, from all archive. How could Ginzburg manage to enlist Serra in his own, fiercely antirelativist struggle? This is what we shall try to understand. But Ginzburg was also capable of quoting Lyotard ("With Auschwitz, something new has happened in history, which is that the facts, the testimonies . . . the documents . . . all this has been destroyed as much as possible"),[10] while doubting that there occurred anything new at all. Hayden White defended himself poorly from this and other attacks mounted by an ad hoc court of historians. We must therefore begin anew, putting aside the notion of relativism, which is only the other face of the presupposition of reality. Here the status of testimony was made to intervene in an essential manner, but in order to serve a demonstration intent on denying the crisis of historiography in the face of genocidal crimes.

C. Giorgio Agamben also invokes the concept of archive in his attempt to reestablish a philosophy of the subject that would take into account the most extreme dereliction of man in the experience (if it is one) of the "Muslim" in the Nazi camps. This is what occurs in Agamben's *Remnants of Auschwitz*. The book concludes with an indictment of the archive in the name of "Levi's paradox." It is indeed from Primo Levi that Agamben learns about the *Muselmann* as the complete witness, but also as a witness who, nonetheless and precisely, cannot testify for himself. Of this paradox, Agamben claims logically that it contains "the only possible refutation of every denial of the existence of the extermination camps." It is to the extent that "it is not possible to bear witness" to Auschwitz, to the extent that the survivor "speaks only on the basis of an impossibility of speaking," that Auschwitz "is absolutely and irrefutably proven."[11] Agamben proceeds here, first of all, with a systematic rebuttal of the idea of testimony as refutation, as the constitution of an archive. There is no room for refutation or, rather, there is no room for the historiographic style of refutation. We find ourselves indeed at the very limits of which Lyotard was speaking, there "where historical knowledge sees its competence impugned."

In each of these cases, one can see that testimony is quartered between the realist option and the emblematic option. In Ginzburg the very idea of such a quartering is purely and simply denied. Yet, in order to deny it, it had to be considered in the first place. The Armenian writers knew nothing of the emblematic option—and this is their problem, of course. They were locked in a structural and sterile opposition between the *documentary* and the *literary* use of testimony. They were prisoners of the circular logic of the archive. This logic is very general. It is genocidal logic: that of the realist illusion, which is truly a transcendental illusion. It is the logic of shame, the logic of injury of the emblematic name. It seizes testimony at the very moment it is uttered and instantly puts it at the service of historiographic refutation. That is why Agamben opposes it with another kind of refutation, which remains (and fabulously so) a refutation nonetheless, that is to say, the bringing forth of *proof*, something that will never cease to astonish us. We shall have the opportunity to voice this astonishment on many more occasions.

1. THE LAW AND THE FACT

THE 1994 CAMPAIGN

1

THE SYSTEMATIC AND RADICAL EXTERMINATION OF THE
Armenians of the Ottoman Empire during the years 1915–1916 is finally, or so it seems, on the current agenda. It has been eighty years since
the event.[1] For the survivors and their descendants, it never ceased being current. Not for an instant. If it is so today, it is only for "civilized
humanity" and for the duration of a trial and a judgment. The trial is
that which brought before a French civil court the famous historian of
the Islamic world and of the Ottoman Empire Bernard Lewis. He was
summoned before the law for having "contested the existence of the
Armenian genocide or, at the very least, for having banalized the per-
secutions and sufferings that were inflicted upon the Armenian deportees." In an interview published by the daily *Le Monde*, Lewis had been

asked the following question: "Why do the Turks still refuse to recognize the Armenian genocide?" To which he had answered: "Do you mean the Armenian version of this history?" Later, in a detailed response to the "heated reactions" occasioned by the unanticipated position he had taken, and while deploring the sufferings inflicted and endured, which he described as "having been a horrible human tragedy, which marks the memory of this people, as that of the Jews was by the Holocaust," he attempted to reduce the dimension of this tragedy to that of a natural catastrophe ("famine," "sickness," "abandonment," "cold weather"). He further added: "There is no serious proof of a decision or of a plan on the part of the Ottoman government regarding the extermination of the Armenian nation." This last statement constituted the culmination of his argumentation.[2] All it was about was a deportation that had turned out badly. The verdict of the high court of Paris has just condemned Bernard Lewis, and one could trust, according to good logic, that the condemnation responds to the main charges brought by the plaintiff, that is to say, precisely to the accusation of negationism.[3] An examination of the verdict, however, reveals that such is not quite the case. This examination will serve as an illustration of the situation—one of literal madness—in which survivors find themselves when confronted with an enterprise of systematic, repeated, and universal denegation. It will serve to indicate the limits of judicial action against negationism, in particular within the context of national law. On the opposite end, when an international court has already been seized to adjudicate crimes against humanity committed in Bosnia, when, almost fifty years after the 1948 Convention, the creation of a permanent international court is finally announced, a critical interrogation of the limits of law, of the necessity and conditions of its application, is perhaps not superfluous. One must acknowledge, after all, that each of the extermination projects conducted over the course of this century has been—among other things, yet perhaps essentially—a challenge directed at law. It is in this perspective that I want to consider the reaction of the judicial apparatus confronted by the latest wave of negationism, which extends and confirms one of these extermination projects, itself conceived and perpetrated more than eight decades ago.

Bernard Lewis's negationist intervention was not an isolated phenomenon—far from it. It was part of a negationist wave, the outline of which is well defined if exceedingly subtle. Over the course of 1994 a number of more or less notorious historians and political scientists, not to mention a few philosophers who did not want to be left behind, renewed the attack with similar arguments. The thesis of a quasi-natural catastrophe and of a deportation evolving badly under conditions of total war was thus elaborated by Jay Winter, an American historian, in the same newspaper on 3 August 1994. In this strange article, which endorses and narrates the entirety of the facts, while prefacing that narrative with a provisional declaration ("This deportation was not a decision of genocide, although it was synonymous with death for those who were elderly, sick, or disabled. . . . What did transform the war crime into a genocide was the context of a total war, which inexorably turned deportation into extermination, following the ill treatments and the deprivations").[4] Perhaps the translation is faulty: there was no decision to perpetrate genocide—the war crime became a genocide. Yet everybody knows that "genocide," even before it signifies mass murder, presupposes precisely and indeed implies *the intention and decision* to exterminate. How, then, could a war crime transform itself into a genocide? It is a pure contradiction in terms, something that does not seem to seriously bother the author and the newspaper that publishes him. Further on, Winter goes over the argument again:

> The criminal character of the deportations was established after the war. . . . The crime was the systematic deportation, the humiliation and murder of an entire community. The massacre of children shows that the crime was intended to erase the next Armenian generation, as well as the present generation. And yet . . . this extermination was, as it were, "makeshift [*artisanale*]." . . . The ideological preparation for the extermination was superficial. . . . The deportation was therefore not a genocide as such. . . . What

the Turks inflicted upon the Armenians in 1915 and in the years that followed was not motivated by race criteria.

All this looks strikingly similar to Freud's kettle logic. The crime is recognized in its entirety ("to erase the next Armenian generation, as well as the present generation") and a moment later it is reduced and assimilated to "population movements . . . unavoidable in times of war." All the elements of the genocidal will are found and yet it is not a genocide, because . . . Indeed, because of what precisely? Because the extermination was makeshift, the ideological preparation superficial, and there was no racial hatred. So many bizarre arguments, all of which keep returning like so many commonplace motifs in negationist literature. Once and for all: refutation serves no purpose. No, what is interesting is the entire ensemble of contradictions in which each author takes comfort. The principle is to recognize all the allegations, and even more if need be—all but the essential. Bernard Lewis's arguments are identical. There was no "hate campaign," deportation "was not total," and, besides, the Ottomans had always used the practice. Finally, the most important argument: "these events must be considered in the context of a conflict, no doubt unequal, but involving real stakes, and an authentic concern on the part of the Turks, even if this concern was greatly exaggerated, if not entirely unfounded."[5] There was a motive, in other words, a *motivation*, whether real or imagined. And all the rhetorical precautions, all the circumvolutions, will not change a thing. The arguments about a state of mutual belligerence and, ultimately, the motives of the crime are those that recur with the most constancy through this kind of literature. And the reader may wonder about the use of such arguments or about what they aim to show precisely, what interests they serve, with what goal in view they are put forth. Along with the reader, I ask myself the same questions.

One can laugh at the kettle logic to which the authors mentioned are condemned. One can also be offended when knowing that this new negationist wave only extends and seals eight decades of systematic denegation on the part of the Turks, of which I shall have more to say. In the process, it invokes an argumentative relay of unfathomable consequences: the claim regarding the uniqueness of the Jewish catastrophe. For Jay Winter, as for all the new negationist wave, this issue constitutes an explicit reference. The makeshift extermination, the superficial ideology, the absence of racial hatred—these are the reverse side of everything designated by the proper name of *Auschwitz*, as one could easily surmise, but without quite establishing whether these arguments ground uniqueness or whether uniqueness provides their justification, their hidden mechanism. The same goes for Bernard Lewis, who repeatedly enumerates his arguments in order to prove that "the comparison with the Holocaust is biased, however, on many important aspects," even if no one had thought of proposing such a comparison.[6] There is here a double perversion of the negationist approach, which gravely perverts the very term said to be incomparable with its own comparison. This should minimally draw the attention of those who believe in the uniqueness of the Holocaust, strained by the unethical use to which it is put by its unworthy defenders. The stakes could not be higher.[7]

3

What does the judgment of the Paris high court say? In its conclusions, it asserts explicitly that its authority does not enable it to "evaluate or state whether the massacres perpetrated between 1915 and 1917 upon the Armenians constitute or not a crime of genocide, such as defined by Article 211-1 of the new penal code." Indeed, historians, and not the courts, are supposed to adjudicate and decide upon these polemics as well as determine the nature of an event. The court will therefore not pronounce itself on said nature. Clearly, it must have some general idea on the matter, but this idea or intimate conviction does not ground the condemnation. Why, then, does the court issue a condemnation? Why does it not grant the historian the full right to adjudicate the facts according to his professional understanding? To this, the court answers: "It is by occulting the elements contrary to his thesis that the defendant has been able to assert that no 'serious proof exists of the Armenian genocide.'" In so doing, the historian was at fault; he was lacking in his "duty to objectivity" and thus renewed "the pain of the Armenian community." But, in reality, it is all too evident that suffering caused cannot serve as a criterion for judgment on the part of a historian. This is only a subsidiary argument, therefore, which the court invokes in addition to its main claim. This claim can be summarized in one sentence: *the defendant has not proven the lack of proof.* The court cannot judge the nature of the historical events. But it can judge the irresponsibility of a man, whether historian or simple citizen, in a matter "so sensitive."

One must, however, admit that the idea of an occultation by a historian of "elements contrary to his thesis" is quite astonishing. For one could thereby conclude that, had he not so occluded these elements, he would have had the right to maintain, in all impunity, "a different opinion" from that of the plaintiff. This is quite precisely what the court says. There are three such "contrary elements." First, the conclusions of the UN subcommittee on the question of prevention and repression of the crime of genocide (1985); second, those of the "permanent tribunal of the peoples," heir of the Russell Tribunal (1984); finally, those of the European Parliament (1987). All have recognized the reality of genocide as such. And yet, the high court clearly asserts: "Bernard Lewis had the right to contest the value and the significance of such affirmations." He had the right, in other words, to pursue his negationist enterprise, and justice would have had nothing to say. Furthermore, there is nothing to sustain the claim that his was a negationist endeavor. And the court does not dare to say so. The law does not allow it. Must one deduce from this that the law does not posit the fact, or, on the contrary, must one believe that the fact is never posited (and thus that no judgment could ever be pronounced on it) *as long as the law has not adjudicated it*? A fact must first of all be validated as such, in one way or another. But, then, it is completely legitimate to ask about the current procedures whereby facts are validated. And the genocidal will has contributed some good to this century insofar as it has brought men of good will to this—in all appearances, philosophical—question, a relevant and extremely grave question. Indeed, Jean-François Lyotard's work *The Differend* addresses this very question and finds its point of departure in the negationist phenomenon. I will return to this in due time. But, in order to be just with the high court of Paris, I must also add that it does visibly hesitate on the matter of "validation" of facts. The court seems to admit that the converging evaluations of "international organizations" carry a certain weight, and not only as "contrary elements" to Lewis's thesis but also *as a legitimate validation of the facts themselves*. It never says this explicitly, however (for it would be contrary to its initial principle according to which the decision regarding the nature of the event does not pertain to its competence).[8]

4

Where and how does the validation of fact occur in the human community? When my father died, I was not there. I have not seen him die. I have not *known* his death. Only later, an inscription on a tomb has assured me of his death. Forty years earlier, when my grandparents were crushed, together with their families, at the very beginning of the deportations (my ancestors did not make it to the desert), no one saw them die. I mean: no living being. And yet I know how one of them died under the blows of an axe; how another was taken from a group of women where he was hiding; how an aunt was given to a Muslim dignitary in order for her sisters to survive (and there is also shame. Who has ever spoken of shame among these survivors?). Yes, I know in more or less elaborate details the place where each of them has died, the way in which they were raped or murdered. The great family narrative, in all decency, assured me of this throughout my childhood. Yes, they are dead. The story is their grave, and it will remain so forever. I am, by the way, convinced that, inversely, every grave is a narrative. I shudder at the thought of families in which a deathly silence ruled instead of narrative as grave. But this is another matter—the matter of mourning. Here I am speaking of the validation of facts. Sometimes, even silence is the best narrative. Narrative validates the proximate facts. Distant facts are validated, it seems, by the media, the archives, history. In every case, validation presupposes a consensus. The human community knows a "fact" because the latter is carried and posited by narratives, themselves assumed to be truthful. Such validation by way of a narrative strengthened by consensus is doubled by the modern recourse to the archive. As long as one does not analyze this modern doubling of narrative by the archive, one cannot understand anything of the genocidal phenomenon. All philosophical digressions on the question of validation will fall flat. For there is one case, and one case only, in which consensus no longer works, in which the usual mechanisms whereby positing and validating are ensured no longer function. Then the door opens onto madness for those who found themselves at the murderous center of a fact that is not one. There is no genocide except there, where the scene of validation, the scene upon which "facts" acquire "reality," is governed by the archive. That is why there is only genocide in the twentieth century. And that is why historians are today doubly responsible. They are not only responsible for the facts and for determining their nature. They are also responsible for their *reality*. One should, above all, not read this as a paradox. This modern doubling of narrative by the archive, heavy with consequences of all kinds, along with its possible perversion—this is what Hagop Oshagan denounces when he writes, "After all, history is but a succession of denials."[9]

I know the precise circumstances of the death of my family members, but also of hundreds, of thousands of individuals. Over the course of decades, survivors have narrated, they have written and published, they have asked for and gathered testimonies from those—mostly women—who did not know how to write, who would not have written anyway. "Each had a tragic, atrocious story to tell." And yet, were I to know all the details of all the deaths, there would remain one fact that could never find validation by such means, that of the "crime of genocide." For these are individual deaths, collective deaths, massive deaths. This could even be the Catastrophe. But it is never "genocide." Moreover, no survivor's memory, no testimony, whether direct or indirect, from the victims or from a third party, could ever serve as a proof without appeal of the genocidal intention and decision. In the Armenian case, as in the Jewish case, we know that the perpetrators did not publish, nor did they leave behind them, any official or hidden document that would announce their intentions and their decisions! In the Armenian case, one must know that they have done even better: they have put to work the genocidal machine as a denegating machine, true to modern exigencies regarding validation by way of the archive, exigencies that were, of course, diverted and perverted but thereby, and for the first time, confirmed and revealed.[10]

No work by any historian can counter this, since everything began with a perversion of the archives. The work of historians, which proceeds by descriptions and cross-verifications and concludes by producing a plethora of probatory and converging arguments, will always be placed—*rightly* so and *by law* as it were—under interrogation. This is more or less what the high court of Paris asserts. It is therefore natural for the historian to consider "maintaining a different opinion." But this is also the only case in which he should not have *the right* to maintain such an opinion. Because the genocidal machine is, in its essence, a denegating and negationist machine; because those who invented it had already perfectly understood everything about the coming reign of the archive, consequently its operations can never become a *fact*. For a fact is that in the face of which no "different opinion" can ever occur. Here there cannot even be a question of opinion. The genocidal-denegating machine is dedicated to destroy *the very notion of fact*. Such is its most radical finality. It is, in other words, the first philosophical machine of the twentieth century.

When the first survivors, in 1918 Aleppo, were coming to see Andonian in order to narrate their atrocious journey,[11] they were not doing so to add their contribution to the great family narrative that was about to constitute Armenian memory for the next eight decades. They were rather, and literally, hallucinating. One can also surmise that, as they were reduced to the state of walking corpses, mostly women and often illiterate, they were not in the mood to philosophize. And yet, they all knew, already and from the outset, that by the end of this programmed extermination, it was the validation of the fact, as such, that would become the primordial question, the object of a debate without end. They knew that the machine that had crushed them was not only a genocidal machine (they had no doubt in this matter: the goal pursued was *the extermination without remainder of their people*) but also "a philosophical machine." At the exit from the black box, it was the reality of the "fact" that became problematic. What they did not know was that, before be-ing arrested (in 1918–1919), the leaders of the Young Turks and those of the Special Organization were about to destroy all their archives. They did not know that the trials of 1919 in Istanbul, conducted by Turkish military courts under the pressure of English occupiers, would in fact conclude that there was "in existence a plan aiming to exterminate the Armenian people," but also that, by 1922, the issues of the official Turk-ish journal covering the period of the trials were going to vanish in their entirety—and with them the very minutes of those trials.[12] They did not need to know this; they did not need to know the details of the denegat-ing enterprise that was about to be masterfully organized, on the basis of the original denegation, at the heart of the very event. In what fol-lowed, they proceeded superbly to ignore these details. But they did know that they had gone through the mill of the philosophical, geno-cidal, and denegating machine. They wished for their testimonies to be *archived*, so that the word *fact* could preserve some sense for civilized humanity. And they were wrong. They were powerless. Their obses-sion, which aimed at the *archivation of testimonies*, had only one conse-quence, a truly catastrophic one: the disowning of their memory; the transformation, grave, and never to be undone, of the "mnemogenic" narrative into a discourse of proofs. They had to prove their own death.

5

The fact itself was therefore a questionable object, contingent on var-ied opinions. The fact itself being subject to opinions, all that remains are considerations on the nature of the event. Which is precisely what the modern discourse of negationism that shifts gear on the genocidal machine asserts. Such considerations can be debated, revised, put to the test. Any historian has the right to participate. Archives are missing. There are opposing theses. The historian cannot but defer his judgment. And this is how the genocide of the Armenians becomes a case study for historians, demonstrating that there are, in all obviousness, situations of *undecidability* with regards to the nature of the event.

I repeat: when coming out of the black box, there is no fact, no "reality" of the fact. No great narrative, no consensus that can establish or reestablish this reality. Here, when the responsibility of the historian extends beyond the decision regarding the nature of the fact, when it concerns essentially the "reality" of the fact, which is to say, then, its validation, *only law can posit the fact*. French law has drawn the conclusions perfectly from this state of affairs with the passing and implementation of a law against all negation of crimes against humanity committed during World War II. Only law can put an end to the contradictory opinions of historians or those claiming to be. This is why I was saying at the beginning that all genocidal projects of the twentieth century have been first of all challenges to law. In some exceptional circumstances, law has taken up the challenge.

For the reader to measure the stakes involved in this discussion, which touches upon the relation of *justice* and of *law* to the "task of the historian," as well as the stakes of this quasi-philosophical and paradoxical conclusion ("only law can posit the fact"), I will quote here a few lines from Robert Maggiori, who states very clearly what the problem is that has occupied us here. "It may seem shocking that a historian of such stature as Bernard Lewis, offering his own reading of the massacres of Armenians by the Turks, could find himself brought to justice, as if the courts were capable of determining the relevance of a certain historical vision or the interpretation of historical facts."[13] What Maggiori gives voice to is his indignation. Any consideration of historical facts must be conducted serenely within the framework of the appropriate discipline. There is a true scandal in the attempt to resolve in a court of law a debate that should take place among specialists and experts. Maggiori explains his indignation, which has nothing to do, he says, with the idea that research must be "totally free." Here is his explanation: "To write that the Nazi genocide is not a historical reality and to deny the existence of gas chambers is a criminal offense. What about refusing to call 'genocide' the massacre of the Armenians? Can it be a matter of penal justice?" I interrupt the citation. What is clear is that the author is addressing the "nature" of the facts. Maggiori shares this concern with the high court of Paris and the modern discourse of negationism. I believe that I have demonstrated abundantly, however, that it is not qualification but rather *the factuality of the fact* that is in question. I add here the reminder that the penal proceedings engaged against Bernard Lewis were concluded, as it were, inconclusively. Maggiori continues: "One must decide on the *intentions*. Those of the negationists of the Nazi genocide are clear. Those of Bernard Lewis are not: must one suppose that his work as a historian is overdetermined by political or ideological concerns, capable of giving credit to lies?" This last sentence does make explicit the reason for Lewis's negationist discourse, even if it does not assert its essence. And yet it waxes ironical. One could not seriously believe this, it says. Personally, I do not see why the intentions of a Faurisson are any clearer than those of a Lewis (not to speak of their respective interests). Besides, the civil court has decided on the matter: there are concerns that, unknown to us, have "given credit to lies." I conclude the citation: "Who will adjudicate? A *Historikerstreit*, a dispute among historians, who would review the truth of the facts? Or else a tribunal, duly authorized to sanction 'the offense to the victims'?" Here too, the same court has decided: the court can adjudicate on the responsibility of historians, but the historians must decide on "the truth of the facts." One can thus see the difficulty of the matter. The question, as Maggiori raises it (and as the civil courts consider it) is only just if one restricts oneself to the "qualification" of the events. But I will not cease to repeat: in the genocidal and denegating will, it is not the qualification of the events that is in question. That is what we are expected to believe today—the ultimate goal of negationism. In the last resort, what is at stake is the factuality of the fact, its reality. At stake is the universal procedure of validation. But the events have been invalidated from the start, in their very eventiality. *That is what constitutes the genocidal fact.* Today, perverse historians play with this originary invalidation, they wager on it, they repeat it and extend it. What court could ever judge such perversion? One must therefore correct the paradox. In such a situation, only law posits the fact, but it can only do so on the condition that it takes the full measure of the denegation at work in the genocidal act itself. Historians are not helping—that is the least one can say. *The essence of genocide is denegation.* Genocide is destined to annul itself as fact.

We will see later that the extermination of the Armenians of the Ottoman Empire has become a case study for undecidability on the part of historians, a model for the "brute fact." That is what I want to conclude this chapter with. In February 1994 the same newspaper that had welcomed Lewis's declarations published the text of a lecture by Eric Hobsbawm on the task of the historian.[14] In this lecture there is a passage that foreshadows the entire finality of the ongoing debate. Hobsbawm wants to bring his audience (apprentice historians of Eastern Europe) to the recognition that the historian's task is to show himself critical against all constructions, all fictions that sustain nationalist positions in particular, and thus against all the "counterfeiters of history." The task is to take position for the "facts," precisely, and against "fiction." It is in this context that Hobsbawm devotes himself to the following considerations on the very notion of fact.

> We have a general responsibility toward historical facts, and a critical responsibility toward the political and ideological abuses of history in particular. I do not need to elaborate on the first responsibility. . . . The other has to do with this intellectual, "postmodern" trend which holds sway over Western universities . . . and for which any "fact" that claims an objective existence is no more than a construction of the intellect; that claims, in short, that there is no clear difference between fact and fiction. But this difference exists.

The old-school historian thus blithely confuses the "construction of the intellect" and the meaning given to the event by the totality of narratives that constitute its reception and thereby its reality. I postpone to the next chapter an illustration of the argument that immediately follows: Hobsbawm suddenly introduces a mention of the Armenian "genocide" to explain the difference between fact and fiction! And then manages to say that it is not possible to decide. It is not possible to decide anything regarding the nature of the event. The latter is a brute fact. A brute fact is certainly not a fiction. But is it still a fact? Do facts have a historical reality when strictly nothing can be said of their context, of their meaning, or of their place in history? Hobsbawm enunciates the truth of negationist discourse: a brute fact is not really a fact. Enunciating this truth, declaring that facts are disqualified, such discourse even succeeds in evading legal proceedings or any judgment that could reproach it with a failure to prove the absence of proof. It manages this coup, which consist in the a priori dismissal of any judgment. Facts are disqualified—what then is there to prove? The judgment of the Paris high court could obviously not put a stop to this powerful, negationist discourse. It could do nothing but ratify it. Negationist discourse is even capable of asserting its own truth: in such a situation, there is no fact, no historical factuality, since validation did not operate. Or: there are only brute facts, beneath any possible qualification as to their nature, to which no *meaning* can ever be allocated and, consequently, no place in history either. A brute fact is a *contingent, uncertain* fact. This is the new category invented in 1994, during a campaign that will remain a model of the genre, conducted by a handful of historians, that no jurisdiction, no court, could ever deny.

2. BETWEEN AMPUTATION AND IMPUTATION

IN 1998–99, WHAT WILL HENCEFORTH BE CALLED THE
Veinstein affair shook our certainties more than any other. Gilles Veinstein, a distinguished French historian of the Ottoman Empire, had written a strange article in 1994, at the height of the Lewis affair, and obviously at the request of the interested party. In this article (published in
the journal *Histoire* in April 1995), he repeated, without precaution, but
also without originality, each and every negationist argument pertaining
to the extermination of the Armenians of the Ottoman Empire. In 1998,
Veinstein became a candidate to the Collège de France, and that article
conveniently surfaced again. Voices were raised to denounce the patent
immorality of the candidate. French humanism was therefore not dead.
One article in particular, written by Catherine Coquio ("Negationism at
the Collège de France" in *Libération*, 28 December 1998), caused quite a
stir, the memory of which will linger with us for a long time. The article

first occasioned uneven responses in the same newspaper: both Michel Cahen and Pierre Chuvin vehemently rejected the accusation it made of negationism. Writing in defense of Gilles Veinstein, they were in agreement on the following point: this eminent expert on Ottoman history had never denied the reality of the events, in brief, the amputation of an important part of the Armenian population of the Ottoman Empire. He would have done no more than doubt the imputation made against the Turkish state following this amputation and interrogated the ground for the qualifier "genocide" applied to this particular case of mass extermination. The two authors were also in agreement on the need to reserve the privilege of deciding this matter to professional history, to oppose any transfer of power from the "office of the historian" to that of the "judge." After these two contributions, the agitation increased. Pierre Vidal-Naquet put the full weight of his moral authority into the balance. Petitions circulated and were signed by the most eminent French scholars, all defending the integrity of Gilles Veinstein, expressing their indignation at the opprobrium hurled at him by a campaign of systematic denigration, a campaign orchestrated by Armenians who thought only of their particular interests and understood nothing about History. Where had humanism gone? Good taste was back in force.[1]

And yet, if I am not mistaken, the high court of Paris did earlier condemn Bernard Lewis for making similar allegations. That court did not judge itself incompetent. True, it did not have jurisdiction over a historical fact. It had the authority, however, to decide that supporting proof had not been provided and therefore that the state of affairs warranted the condemnation by law of the crime of genocide denial. The court condemned the irresponsibility of a man who put forward a thesis without sufficiently taking into account those "contrary elements" working against it. I quote again, briefly, the verdict of the court. "[Bernard Lewis] could not in any case conceal the converging elements of evaluation, upheld most notably by international organizations, which revealed that, contrary to the criticized statements, the thesis regarding the existence of a plan aiming at the extermination of the Armenian people is not only defended by this people."

What were the historians doing in 1999? What were those signing petitions doing, all those who were so ardently defending Gilles Veinstein? I have the ongoing impression that they were very close to challenging the judgment on a case closed. They were in any case putting up a front of resistance against the incursion of justice in a situation over which it did not have, in their opinion, jurisdiction. Were they refraining from asserting that it was not a genocide in order not to be summoned by it? Not even, as we will have occasion to note (and be surprised by). Pierre Chuvin was reiterating Veinstein's words, as they had been published in his journal: "Is there no room for the analysis of a 'historical catastrophe caused by multiple responsibilities'?" Did he by any chance mean that the Armenians would have to be considered responsible, coresponsible, for their own extermination? Were they to bear some responsibility, then the full burden of responsibility could not be allocated to the executioners, to the perpetrators, to the ruling authorities. In this way, one can equate victims and perpetrators, even eighty years after the facts. And how will the victims then prove that they were victims of a genocide? Pierre Chuvin wished for an analysis of the facts, but he had already announced with Veinstein (that is to say, before any analysis of the facts) that the responsibilities were shared and the versions contradictory. As a result, it could not have been a genocide. Between amputation and imputation there was a margin that needed to be respected. One letter changed and all became confused.

The paragraphs that follow were written in February 1999 as an immediate reaction to the articles written by Chuvin and Cahen, themselves circumstantial and very secondary actors in a drama that had been mine for decades. Yes, I was shaken to the deepest of my being by this "affair." Never before, I confess, had I been confronted with the idea that the memory of the events could one day be trampled upon at the feet of those who should have had as the task before them to defend it, to recognize and acknowledge it, French intellectuals, and among them my philosophy teachers, teachers of humanity first of all. Their unanimity served as proof. I was convinced. I do nothing here but translate this conviction, under the leitmotiv "It was not, therefore, a genocide."

This, of course, goes against their explicit declarations, read according to the letter. At the same time, it should be clear that I am summing up everything I had written and thought on the question over the course of the twenty preceding years.

It was not, therefore, a genocide. We had this suspicion for quite a while already.

Earlier, which is to say, over the course of the past sixty years, after all, whenever the reality of the facts was put into doubt, we were not paying too much attention to what was being said. When all is said and done, or so we thought, why would the executioner or the criminal confess his crimes when nothing compels him to do so? And then something shifted. It was no longer the reality of the events that was at stake, but rather their interpretation. At least this is what seemed to emerge from the multiple declarations made by all kinds of characters, well intentioned or not (how would one know?), declarations they felt obliged to pronounce over the course of many months, in 1994, in a manner at once repetitive, successive, and organized, the way one hammers a truth that cannot easily enter people's heads. I have, on occasion, referred to this shift as "the 1994 campaign." And so it was indeed. In France everything began with the Bernard Lewis affair.

But, at the international level, Bernard Lewis was hardly the first to enter the race. Before him, Sanford Shaw, a renowned professor of Ottoman history at the University of California, Los Angeles, had derisively dismissed the ridiculous Armenian claims to having suffered the first genocide of the century. Was he denying the reality of the facts or placing under interrogation their interpretation of genocide? There was a bit of both in his books, in his silences, in his mocking statements. He still did not quite know which way he should go. The conclusion of this particular chapter had not been decided yet. This was more than twenty years ago. Minds were searching for each other. The proper reaction to Armenian claims had not yet been defined. Besides, the case was similar to that of the honorable Professor Veinstein. Were one to dare argue in front of Professor Stanford Shaw that he was denying reality, the indubitable reality of the events, he would have defended himself vehemently. There had been many dead, of course. But where had there not been? Armenians had been deported for security reasons in the spring and autumn of 1915. Where does one *not* deport? In time of war, such things are unavoidable. In some places, deportation had taken a turn for the worse. But how could it have been otherwise in a country ravaged by war, in regions where the Kurdish *ashirets* were uncontrollable? (The deserts of Syria were outside the frame.) I know that these arguments do not belong entirely to the past. The very same arguments were, after all, reiterated in the French press in 1994, without any embarrassment or shame. They do not belong to the past, therefore, but they are dated. They form the old guard of arguments. They continue to discuss the facts. But one must discuss the facts, you will say! For if, in the final count, it is the genocidal interpretation that is in question, then this interpretation must be grounded on facts. And yet one would be wrong to think in this way. Indeed, what naïveté, what positivism! There has emerged a much better line of arguments, a fresh and rising guard that comes to renew the old, tired argumentation.

What does this new guard say? First of all, it accepts all the facts in their totality. Facts here are those that can be reconstructed by collecting all the testimonies, those of the deportees, the victims, but also of others, diplomats, consuls, German soldiers, physicians, American pastors, and random bystanders. The general extermination of Armenians from the High Plateau in the fall of 1915, the deportation in horrendous conditions of all the Armenians of the Ottoman Empire without sparing any city or the smallest village, except of course Constantinople and Smyrna. It may even be the case that the new guard accepts as fact the second wave of extermination, that of spring and summer 1916. And if it accepts the facts in their totality, what is left for it to accept? Quite precisely: everything. That is the subtlety of the entire affair. What is left to accept are the three essential elements that constitute any self-respecting genocide: the intent, the organization, and the execution. The precise intention, the centralized organization, the systematic execution. Were one to deploy different methods for administering proof, such as modern jurisdiction and jurisprudence have equipped themselves with—proof by behavioral pattern, proof by the materiality of the facts, proof by the chain of arguments—then the matter would have long been settled and there would be no one to revisit it. But the new guard has brought us to a new understanding of the juridical methods used in every prosecution: these have no role to play here. This is where the management of the proof fails for lack of ambition, something that Yves Ternon, the irreproachable historian of genocides, has underscored in a fairly recent volume.[2] History may be a tribunal, at least in the long term, but it does not use the vulgar methods of the courts. For the new guard of arguments—one must say this and know this—was the making of historians, sometimes great historians with prestigious names, our contemporaries, people whom we rub shoulders with in French or American universities.

History, then, does not wish to use the methods of the courts. It says so loud and clear. It claims and demands its prerogative. Here as well, I am aware that a certain hesitation is obvious. One could repeatedly read in the French press, in 1994 as well as in 1999, that the interpretation of a historical event was not a matter for the courts to adjudicate, but rather, precisely, for the historians. This unassailable assertion was, however, the product of a mixing of genres. The pending jurisdiction in France—still a state where the rule of law prevails after all—with the Gayssot law does show that the courts have something to say regarding the interpretation of an event.[3] This assertion, which I have deemed "unassailable" just a moment ago, must therefore mean, in reality, something else than what it seems to say. Minimally, it requires an explanation. The law has decided that, in France, there is no space for interpretation there where the facts are recognized and where the negation of these recognized facts was injurious for the victims and the survivors. In reality, the law does not forbid interpretation, nor does it intervene in any case in the interpretation of historical facts. It does something else, something entirely extraordinary. It admits, or better, it asserts that there are, after all, *recognized* facts in this world. For, without them, what would we do? There would be generalized insanity. No one noticed that this Gayssot law represents a veritable revolution in the evolution of human societies, as much as the affirmation of the equality of all human beings before the law, such as was presented by the philosophers before being inscribed in universal legislations only two centuries ago. There had to be a law to recognize something that no one had recognized until then, because no one had needed to recognize it, namely, that—in the extreme conditions of humanity, no doubt, but only extreme conditions can tell the truth of the human—*only the law can tell the fact* (*seul le droit peut dire le fait*). The sentence makes sense in French, even if it is paradoxical. I would be hard put, for example, to translate it into English—which partly explains why the present "debate" took place in France and not elsewhere. So, only the law can tell the fact. One knows that long ago, in a celebrated book, Jean-François Lyotard had underscored the aporias of reason in a situation of *différend*, that is, in a situation where the law has not yet spoken its fact or would be hard put to give it straight (*de dire son fait*) to the negation of the fact (Lyotard, of course, took as his generic example the genocidal fact). It would seem therefore that the matter is understood: the law should certainly not intervene in the interpretation of an event. Yet it has no choice but to intervene in order to posit a fact as such, there where the fluctuation of the very notion of fact could lead to generalized insanity.

Where, then, is the hesitation of the great historians of our century, our contemporaries? Once all the facts are accepted and recognized, history—speaking through their mouth—still has some reservations to express. It asks for further confirmation. It asks for archives. Why does it ask for archives when everybody knows that these are inaccessible or nonexistent, and when all the facts are recognized? I have said so earlier: the recognized facts are those that can be reconstructed after gathering the totality of testimonies. Should one conclude that the totality of testimonies does not constitute proof? Is that what they are repeating again and again? Yes, it is exactly that, although one has to engage in all kinds of subtleties in order to understand what this really means: the totality of testimonies does not constitute the proof of an interpretation. An interpretation cannot be proven. In sum, on the one hand, they demand proofs while, on the other, they affirm (and rightly so) the primacy of interpretation over the proof.

Is it already too complicated? Perhaps. But the stakes are so enormous that one should not be fearful of complication here. It is a matter of understanding, in the final count, why it was not a genocide, even though everybody—including French lawmakers in 1998—had thought that it was one. One also understands why the historians are hesitating on the final and decisive argument, which will put an end to the debate. Agreed, we are no longer debating the facts. We are now debating the totality of testimonies. For we must know what status we should grant it. For the totality of testimonies says nothing of the intention, except perhaps in an indirect way. It says nothing of it because it is not made for that. Testimonies can only testify to the facts, not to the intention.[4] This is the first segment of the historians' assertion: the totality of testimonies cannot by itself constitute proof of the intention to exterminate. It is a vulgar assertion, because it is tautological, and historians know this, of course. By definition, no witness could ever have proof, nor could therefore the totality of witnesses. Only the tribunal of history could decide here. Not for nothing did the phrase gain such currency. I have said earlier that history does not wish to use the methods of the courts. The tribunal of history is above the courts! The totality of testimonies does not constitute proof. This is what all the historians, in order of battle, who appeared successively in 1994 in the columns of *Le Monde* have said. And more or less what the very honorable Pierre Chuvin and Michel Cahen have said. These two know strictly nothing of the facts, but they are ready to admit their "magnitude" and their "reality." They know strictly nothing of the totality of testimonies, of which they have not read one line, but they are ready to admit them, as testimonies and in their entirety. On any other affair, they would never have dared speaking without having all the elements of the dossier in hand. In this case they do dare. There must be a reason for that. And the only plausible reason is that there is a question of principle, and it is sufficient to examine the matter a priori. They are right, of course. How could the totality of testimonies ever constitute proof?

Still, this is not enough. There is still a bit of naïveté in this principle. Every one can see that, and the last protagonists in this long trial also know it well. They know that what is at stake is not really, not entirely, a question of proof. They know it without having quite understood it. Hence their hesitation. One cannot negate the facts. One cannot bring proof of intention either, nor therefore of guilt. Why? Because there is no archive of intention and the totality of testimonies does not constitute an archive. Why is there no archive? This I have not yet said. It is an absolutely essential point, but I will not elaborate upon it here. I will only say it very quietly, in one sentence: there is no archive because the essence of genocide is the destruction of the archive (that is also to say, the archive *as* destruction—but I leave this for the next chapter). They know that as well. They are walking on absolutely safe ground. No mines on the horizon. They will not step or venture upon an archive that would suddenly emerge. Of course, they will never admit—or perhaps they will simply never understand—what I have just written here: that the essence of genocide is the destruction of the archive. But they are historians. One cannot ask them to understand a world grounded on the destruction of that which is their very essence, and not only their profession: the archive. Besides, this is precisely what enables them to reach, at their end of the journey, their most unassailable intuition: it is not a question of proof. It is rather a question of interpretation. No proof, no archive—is everything a matter of interpretation then? Some will say that it was a genocide. Others that it was not. But this is the most frivolous conception one may have of the word "interpretation." Sometimes, historians have recourse to it, but it would be insulting to think that they really believe in it. For, when they tell us, "Historians should decide, not the courts," they really think that historians can decide and that it is therefore up to them to say the truth on the truth, there where there is neither proof nor archive. How do they do it?

This is where there occurs the most extraordinary turn. For until now, even if it was formulated like a paradox, we thought we had understood that law posits the fact in the most extreme human situation, namely, the genocidal situation. So what is it that the historians would be deciding? And what is it that grants them more power even than law? What makes them the equals of Fate (which was, as everyone knows, above the gods themselves, while the latter were already sitting quite high)? Historians decide accessorily on the facts because they are the masters of the archive. They are the modern guardians of the Fact, of the very fact that there are facts, that there is, therefore, a habitable world and that we are not insane. But, I repeat, how do they do it when there is no archive? If they are, even here, perhaps here most of all, more powerful than the law, it must be because they must be endowed with another power, one different from their being the guardians of the facts and the masters of the archive. What power is this? It is simple. They are the guardians of sense and meaning (*ils sont les gardiens du sens*).

Not all of them have understood it. Not all of them know it yet. But it is well recognized. After the two campaigns of 1994 and 1999 and henceforth, we have known this: historians are the guardians of sense. I say so, believe me, with no irony or bitterness whatsoever, and certainly without resentment. I say so while deeply believing that it is so. I am, as one would say in English, dead serious. For not everyone has understood after all what took place in 1994. And the honorable citizens who found it necessary to respond to Catherine Coquio's article in *Libération* at the beginning of 1999 have not read well, I think, what was said over the course of that year. To begin with, they have not carefully read the article by Eric Hobsbawm, published in *Le Monde des Débats* of February 1994.[5] I have mentioned this article at the end of the previous chapter. I will not engage the context again but only cite the following, hallucinatory passage, allegedly intended to illustrate a point on the difference between fact and fiction.

> We cannot invent our facts. Either Elvis Presley is dead or he isn't. The question can be answered unambiguously on the basis of evidence, insofar as reliable evidence is available, which is sometimes the case. Either the present Turkish government, which denies the attempted genocide of the Armenians in 1915, is right or it is not. Most of us would dismiss any denial of this massacre from serious historical discourse, although there is no equally unambiguous way to choose between different ways of interpreting the phenomenon or fitting it into the wider context of history.[6]

More than four years have passed since I have tried for the last time, and vainly, to take the measure of these lines. I start over from the very beginning, therefore. The first question is: what is a fact? How does one know that Elvis Presley is dead? Who is the guarantor and the guardian of that fact? Accessorily, were someone to think of denying the death of Elvis Presley as a fact, would such a person be liable to juridical proceedings or to the scorn of historians? How does one know that a fact is a fact without ever having gone to verify it? (What would it take, by the way, to verify it? Should one open the grave of Elvis? Does the grave by itself suffice? Where is the proof and what is a grave? Does one need an archive, the death certificate, for example, signed and countersigned and duly preserved? And what if the certificate was counterfeited?) What if we were lied to regarding the death of Elvis? How would we know? Perhaps we do need historians here. The masters of the archives are the guarantors of the fact. And still, there appears to be a consensus on Elvis's death, and it does not come from the historians. It emerges rather out of a general rumor, a kind of universal narrative. Let us capitalize it, bravely: a narrative, a Plot (*Récit*) assures me that he is dead. But what is the Plot here, if not the totality of available testimonies? How strange! The totality of testimonies, sometimes, would suffice to constitute proof, without the intervention of historians and without their counterclaims. Is it not always the case? Of course it is. The Plot is the Grave. If my mother did not turn *completely* mad, it is because there was a story which assured her again and again, for all its worth, of the death of her father (whom she had not seen die, obviously, and on whose grave she could never grieve). Sometimes, though, the plot is not enough to constitute proof, to make a grave. One demands proof there where there is no grave. Those close to the tortured and the vanished know this well, from their specific point of view, which is certainly not that of the tormentors. It so happens that the tormentors and their representatives also have the gall to ask for proofs. And even when the totality of testimonies, for the entire world, says the truth about the truth, it so happens that there is still room for questioning, because there is room for interpretation.

Eric Hobsbawm, then, asks whether "the Turkish government" tells the truth or not. Is he seriously asking himself? It should not fall to the Turkish government to decide, it seems to me, but to Hobsbawm. And, as for him, well, he is all ready to do so. Let us see: will he decide on a fact or on an interpretation? He knows that there is no such thing as a fact unless it is universally validated. Does the totality of testimonies suffice to validate the fact as fact? In all the different cases, and whatever the figures and calculations, the answer is yes. In the case of the genocidal figure, the answer is no. But is the genocidal fact not a fact as well? On the one hand, Hobsbawm seems inclined to believe that yes, after all, it is a fact ("most of us would dismiss any denial of this massacre from serious historical discourse"). But here, even if he knows perfectly well what he is saying (serious historical discourse will dismiss the denial of the "massacre," he carefully says, not the denial of the genocide!), to my mind, he is still too timid. In reality, the genocidal fact is obviously not a fact. Were it one, serious historical discourse would not find itself in such a precarious position, and the totality of testimonies would amply suffice. How, then, does this fact manage to escape the web of facts, to escape validation by consensus? Is it because it is subject to many interpretations? This is what Hobsbawm seems at first to suggest. And, yet, did I not already point out that this is a frivolous use of the word "interpretation"? If there were diverse interpretations, after all, it would be the task of the historian to inform himself, to research and understand, to settle the matter, to look for "proofs."

I pause for an instant and recapitulate. Is the historian the guardian of the facts? He is—that is what Hobsbawm has always said and in this particular lecture even more than elsewhere. Are there no facts here? Are they not accepted in their entirety? There are and they are so accepted—otherwise historical discourse would lose its seriousness. Yet the facts are failing and interpretations are at war. There must be something, therefore, which prevents this fact from being one. Whether Hobsbawm, the positivist, likes it or not, we find ourselves in a situation in which the usual validation of the facts does not function. That is why all interpretations are here possible. Can one prove an interpretation on the basis of testimonies? Obviously not. Can one produce proof on the basis of the archive? One could, but the archive here does not exist, essentially and by definition. We are running in a circle. What then? Are we finding ourselves in a case of indecision and undecidability? Can we not know whether it is a genocide or not? In a sense, this is the way it goes. But this is what characterizes genocide as such. The decision about a genocide is essentially a decision against undecidability, and so in all cases, which means that it is also a decision against the historiographic perversion. Lyotard has demonstrated this sufficiently in his time. That is why, in all cases, and without any possible exception, there is no "genocide" without the intervention of the law. In the Armenian case, of course, no law has ever stated the fact. It is not, therefore, a genocide. Is the matter clear enough now?

But this recapitulation is still insufficient, even erroneous. I have summarized what Eric Hobsbawm said up until his provisional conclusion, according to which the case at hand is one of undecidability. No conclusion could be "unambiguous." The rest—genocide as decision and the necessary intervention of law—is my own contribution. Indeed, it is not at all what Hobsbawm says. For, even if every conclusion remains ambiguous, Hobsbawm does end up deciding. He resolves the ambiguity. He decides that it is not a genocide. And he makes this decision for a reason that no one has ever noted, not even he himself. Here is this reason: the event (in Hobsbawm's English, "the phenomenon") was never fitted "into the wider context of history." This, finally, is where Hobsbawm dispenses with the frivolous usage of the word "interpretation" (the different versions or interpretations of the event) and shifts to its powerful and—let us say—philosophical usage. There is indeed an undecidability of the fact, as they say, concerning the different versions. But there is another undecidability, more essential still, concerning the integration of the events and the historical context. This last undecidability is not at all of the same kind as the undecidability between the versions. According to the latter, one does not yet know whether it is a genocide or not. According to the former, it is not a genocide. Why? Because law has not adjudicated? Certainly not. For that would be a very vicious circle to entertain under the pen of an author asked to defend a colleague who finds himself in the middle of a trial, a colleague in trouble with the law, with justice and the law. Instead, Hobsbawm executes a superb maneuver against any decision by law, any present and future intervention of the law. In the final count, all things being otherwise said, it will still be history that will decide. Has it not done so already? Of course it has. That is what Hobsbawm says. History has already decided. The event has not found its place in the wider context of history. It is therefore not a genocide. But then, the second undecidability is not one. It is, on the contrary, a decision, there where history has not decided—by itself, as it were—that it was a genocidal fact. Supreme argument. The historiographic decision rests on the indecision of History.

How does an event find its place in this wider context of History? And besides, why should this context be "wider"? That is the last thing we have yet to understand. What is this History with a capital letter, so unusual a marker with this particular historian? All the facts are part of history. The death of Elvis Presley is also part of history. There is no need to capitalize that. At bottom, anything is part of history without capital, everything that has happened, everything that has emerged, every event, small or large. Yet, it is also the case that there are events that are determining while others are not. Can an event be determining by itself, as event and as event only? Certainly not. An event can only become determining because it carries a sense or meaning. Who gives it this meaning? This is the entire difficulty. Sometimes, the meaning is immediately recognized. Sometimes, some work is necessary in order to make meaning happen. In all cases, it is the historian who receives the meaning, even if he is not the one to bestow it upon the event. There is no history but there where there is sense. An event upon which no meaning has been bestowed, in which no sense was invested, revealed, received, or produced: this event is not really one. It does not really belong to history, this time to the wider context of history. Whether meaning is received or reconstructed, it is always a question of interpretation. The events, in order to be such, in order to find their place in the context of history, are in need of interpretation. They must be interpreted or interpretable. This is not a matter of conflicting interpretations, of different "versions" of the event. It is a matter of Interpretation as the promise of sense. In order to be such, events must carry, produce, or promise a sense. Must one have read Freud, his *Moses* and his theory of trauma in order to understand this? Must one have read Yosef Hayim Yerushalmi, Jan Assman, and the other inventors of mnemohistory? Perhaps the death of Elvis Presley carries the promise of a powerful interpretation that will overturn our understanding of the modern world. It is obvious, however, that such is not the case for the poor events that have occurred at the beginning of the twentieth century in this backward empire that was called Ottoman and did not yet have the pretension of integrally belonging to Europe. I am not joking. I have said it earlier: I am dead serious. What has no sense has no existence. This is the proof by sense. There has been no genocide.

Have the Armenians said or done anything at all to contradict such a conclusion? No, they have done nothing. They are still trying to prove that the event has occurred, producing an impoverished discourse that does nothing more than entangling itself, more and more, in the discourse of perpetrators and executioners. The logic of proof is the logic of the murderer. Armenians have never escaped it. How could one expect from them a work of interpretation! Such work would have to be a work of mourning as well, if it could only occur then. But Armenians continue to believe that the work of mourning cannot occur as long as the denial continues. In other words, they hold the executioner responsible for their own lack of interpretation, their lack of sense and hence of mourning. It must be said that such disaffection with meaning is quite rare. One could object: but what if all this made, precisely, no sense? Why should the absence of sense be explained by the frightening, the horrifying absence of interpretation, of any work of interpretation? What if the opposite were the case? I will not argue about this. In either case, my conclusion remains true. What makes no sense has no existence. There has been no genocide.

It has been a long time since this conclusion awaited the good will ready to receive and accept it at its just measure. What I have just called proof by sense requires yet more sharpening. One cannot really comprehend why this particular event is not making sense, why it does not find its place in the context of history. Would the production of a work of interpretation suffice to give it some "meaning" and some "place," both of which it lacks so much, a lack that robs it of deserving the label so ardently desired? Something prevents it, it seems, from claiming this label. Here again: a priori. And no consideration of the facts is relevant here. But this is already the character of two earlier levels of proof. There was, of course, at the beginning, the proof by silence, by the manipulation of facts, by propaganda. It was the proof of the murderer, of whom some historians have at times made themselves the accomplices. This belongs to a long-gone past. Since the campaign of 1994, and the claims made by Bernard Lewis, we have had the "proof by proof" (there is no proof, nor archive; the totality of testimonies does not constitute proof) and the "proof by sense" (there is no recognized sense, no meaning to reconstruct, and the proof lies in the fact that even the survivors have not managed to bestow meaning on the event). The Paris high court was wrong when it condemned Bernard Lewis in 1994. Indeed, it explicitly condemned him not for having denied the reality of a "genocide" (a court is not made for that) but for not having provided proof of the absence of proof. The Paris court was not capable of understanding that the totality of testimonies does not constitute proof and that there is no other evidence (of the absence of evidence) to present but for this a priori proposition. In the meantime, Eric Hobsbawm had done better still by managing to disable any potential intervention of the law and by repeating the fundamental proposition of the Western philosophy of Law: the only guarantor of reality is meaning. No reality (and thus no reality of the "genocide") there where there is no sense, no promise of Sense, no Interpretation. May I be forgiven the capital letters.

It seems, therefore, that everything has now been said. The dice are thrown and nothing more is to be done. But something does remain to be understood, and I repeat it now: why is it this event, this one among others, but also this one more than others, that cannot be fitted into the historical context widened by the production of sense? There must be a reason for that, a reason that neither Bernard Lewis nor Eric Hobsbawm could have known about and that they did not have to know in order to bring out their incontrovertible "proof by proof" and "proof by sense." Yes, there is indeed and a priori a third level of proof, and that is "proof by motive," to which I have already alluded.

I will explain, but my explanation requires that I leave aside the historians for now. In the second English edition of her book, *Eichmann in Jerusalem*, Hannah Arendt was already distinguishing the expulsion and annihilation of entire populations as "inhuman acts" from these same acts as "crimes against humanity."[7] Inhuman acts were those acts that could be explained by reasons still belonging to the human realm: colonization, homogenization, unification of a territory. Crimes against humanity were those acts "of which motive and aim are without precedent," something that means first of all that no existing human logic could explain them. These are completely unmotivated crimes. As a result, obviously, the extermination of the Armenians could not be fitted under the Arendtian category of "crimes against humanity." For the formidable paradox expressed by Hannah Arendt (but who had heretofore experienced and understood it as a formidable paradox?) was that, this time, it was *the absence of sense*, the absence of a recognized sense, under the name of intent, of reason or motive, that made *sense* of the event. All the collective crimes of the century, except for the median crime of the Nazis, have had a motive, a reason, or an intent. Such collective crimes are no doubt in need of an explanation (historiographic, ideological, sociological), but they do not need an interpretation. Every time the explanation is already given, it is contained in the crime itself. Every time one was killing for something. Something was at stake in the crime. One killed for an idea, for an identity, for the homogeneity of a territory. One killed in the name of something: Christendom, the divine right of the state, revolution, socialism. The victims, at least, knew what they were dying for, they knew to what Moloch they were sacrificed. Of course, the only example that Arendt gives is that of "colonialism." I have expanded her list by making use of complementary categories provided some time ago by Philippe Lacoue-Labarthe (I shall come back to this, of course).

Interpretation is only necessary where sense is absent from itself. What the renowned historians of the 1994 and 1999 campaigns had called genocide (rightly arguing at the time that the extermination of the Armenians was not one) is therefore precisely what Hannah Arendt had earlier designated as "crime against humanity." It is understood that these historians presuppose the existence of a motive in the Armenian case as well as in other similar cases. Here is Bernard Lewis's argument within this range of ideas: "These events must be seen in the context of a struggle, if unequal, with real stakes, and of an authentic Turkish concern—one no doubt greatly exaggerated but not totally unfounded." This is what he had said in his response to *Le Monde* of 2 February 1994. Let us grant to the historian the benefit of the doubt:

no, whatever one thinks and whatever this sentence might seem to say, he is not at all seeking to justify the extermination. He merely wants to explain why it was not a genocide, retracing his own steps on a road opened thirty years earlier by Arendt. There were real stakes and authentic concerns. Therefore there was a motive and an aim. In any case, the formidable paradox to which we are brought by the distinction made by Arendt depends on the following fact: for all human and worldly events, there is a coincidence of sense and existence or, perhaps it would be better to say, a coincidence between the sense and the reality of the event. There is reality only there where there is sense. On this point, Hegel was summing up the entirety of Western thought, which remains valid for us. But precisely the only event for which the Hegelian equation fails to function (although Hegel could not have predicted it) is the "crime against humanity" as defined by Arendt or "genocide" as defined henceforth by renowned modern historians. There is no reality of the genocidal event as such *but there where sense is absent*, where human reason fails, and therefore there were there is a demand for sense, a call for interpretation. The "sense" of the event is therefore the failing of sense and of reason. I should have known this already thirty years ago: there was no Armenian genocide.

It is according to the powerful logical matrix produced by Hannah Arendt in her reflections on the Eichmann trial that all the "similar events of the century" were going to be thought afterward. Historians do not know this. But here, again, one should no doubt refrain from asking too much of them. Moreover, it would be a mistake to believe that this "proof by motive" stands in contradiction to the "proof by sense." It is the same logical matrix, after all, that intervenes at the moment Philippe Lacoue-Labarthe locates all these "similar events" under the heading of a "systematic project governed by an ideology."[8] One can read this in his *The Fiction of the Political*, on that same page: "the extermination of the Jews . . . is a phenomenon which follows *essentially* no logic (political, economical, social, military, etc.) other than a spiritual one, degraded as it may be, and therefore a historial one." Of course, what is at stake here is an account of the historiality (*historialité*) of what was once called the Holocaust, but this cannot be achieved except by way of comparison. In every other case of collective murder, "the mas-sacre is linked to a situation of war or civil strife; there is a genuinely political, economical or military issue at stake; the means employed are those of armed struggle, police or judicial repression; and the operation is directed by some belief or rationality."[9] Again: one kills for some-thing, in the name of something, and not merely to kill, to eliminate. There are "real stakes," therefore, as Bernard Lewis would say, a famil-iar figure of repression and a "reason," a motive, an aim. In short, there is motivation. It is still the "proof by motive" we are dealing with. And one can see how Lacoue-Labarthe repeats almost word for word the dis-tinction projected by Hannah Arendt thirty years before him. Marthe Robert herself was doing nothing else in 1995 when she asserted that to speak of other genocides than the Jewish genocide was to demonstrate "a very subtle negationism." She was exaggerating a bit, of course, and perhaps getting ahead of her own thought. But she was also rehearsing the operations of the same logical matrix when she considered the Ar-menians to be "fighting a war [*belligérants*]." This is again more or less what Bernard Lewis said the previous year: two nations found them-selves in a dispute over the same territory; there was a threat, real or imagined, "greatly exaggerated but not unfounded," a reason governed the extermination; it had been triggered by an incitement. In the strict Arendtian sense of crime against humanity, it could not be a genocide therefore. One could not be any clearer.

I know. I promised an a priori argumentation, and suddenly it seems that we are back to the facts. Indeed, how would we know whether the "Ar-menian threat" was not entirely unfounded unless we consider the facts? How will we know if we do not enter into the complexity of the Ot-toman Empire, its history at the end of the nineteenth century and at the beginning of the twentieth? And who could do this better than the historians of the Ottoman Empire? There is no question here of hearing the victims and survivors. Obviously, they will all claim that they were innocent in order to gain rights to the genocidal label. And the kulaks were no less so. Victims will never understand that their "innocence" is all too relative. They will never understand that their very existence is a threat for the ideology that governs their "massacre." There is no collective massacre without real, ideological stakes, without means or reasons. And one might as well say it: in 1915, Armenians did represent "a homogenous political or religious force," if also a minor and diminished, a crushed and already disintegrated one, that had become a minority on its "own" territory. Still, they persisted in considering this territory their "historical" territory. What other stakes could one imagine as more real? They were, moreover, spread across the entire empire, across thousands of kilometers, and not one escaped, not one was forgotten. This does not make the stakes less real. In other words, it may be the case that the stakes were not phantasmatic. The Armenians' very existence was "belligerent." That is precisely why the event (if it is one, this time) of their extermination could not be fitted into a historical context by way of a production of sense, even if one were suddenly to invent a very powerful interpretation that would give a "sense" to the "event." Of course, the historical (or historial) context about which we speak is that of the West. In Arendtian language, the extermination of the Armenians was not a crime against humanity. In Heideggerian language, it was obviously not a historial event. Try as they might, Armenians will never enter into the only history that makes sense. That is why the proof by motive does not contradict the proof by sense (as one might otherwise think). On the contrary, it serves as its foundation.

———

One can also say this differently. It will only be a brief aside, following which I shall return to my main argument. This proof by motive is a "proof by sacrifice."

Here I am forced to be brief, as I have been earlier when I said without too much explanation that the essence of genocide is the destruction of the archive. Why is this a proof by sacrifice? Because all the collective events of the century, all the "similar" events, still had a sacrificial aspect. To put the matter simply: they all sacrificed a collective to a reason, an idea, or an ideology. This is true of all collective murders, except those of the Jews of Europe. I return one last time to what Lacoue-Labarthe says. "There was not the least 'sacrificial' aspect in this *operation*, in which what was calculated . . . was a pure and simple *elimi-*

nation. Without trace or residue."[10] And even if, on this question of sacrifice, the author confesses "a pure and simple embarrassment," I think that his remark is absolutely essential.[11] The only collective murder that was purely nonsacrificial is also the only one that was purely without motive, as well as the only one to have "a metaphysical significance," which means significance in the history of the West as the history of metaphysics. Yet the last thing that embarrasses me in this long series of "proofs," of which I have tried to reconstruct the logic, is perhaps that we have not quite understood in the West in what way the reality of an Eastern empire (but only Eastern? And only the Ottoman one?) was entirely founded on a practice of sacrifice—a matter that remains to be defined, since it is not "simply" of a religious nature. We have not quite understood therefore that the pure and simple elimination of an element of this empire, namely, of a *subject* people, was also the pure and simple end of this particular practice, that is to say, the end of Sacrifice. The Catastrophe would then be the end (or, rather, the achievement, the culmination, and the completion [*l'achèvement*]) of Sacrifice. And, if this is so, then the last proof, the proof by sacrifice, is no proof at all. A reflection on the Catastrophe would open a path of research on the nature and the functioning of the empire as such. I say this by proxy, for this is certainly not the place to go further in this direction. I am even willing to concede and withdraw what I have just said on the overturning of the "proof by sacrifice." The three other proofs are a priori amply sufficient: proof by proof, proof by sense, proof by motive. No, whatever Armenians think, the Catastrophe was not a genocide. And, in this parenthetical context, the interesting question is obviously the following: do subject peoples have anything to say about the sovereign people and about the political system in which the latter made them live, in what was after all a system of domination? Do they have anything to say of the system of *subjection* and of its catastrophic collapse? Of course, the catastrophic end of the empire must include, sealed within it, a measure of truth on the nature of the empire and therefore also on the nature of all the subjections in it. Those who have reaped the costs of this catastrophic end should have something to say. In any case, the Catastrophe as the completion of sacrifice would have to fascinate the experts on the Ottoman Empire (and, after them, the philosophers). But no one will venture there. Indeed, in order to do so, one would have to listen to the discourse of subjection, that is to say, one would have to listen to precisely that which was abruptly, but quite conveniently, eliminated from history. And everyone knows this: historians are the accomplices of history, of this great plot that is history (I shall return to the nature of this plot in the following chapter). One would have to listen to the postcatastrophic discourse of the Survivor, which is not of a historical or historiographical nature. One would have, in effect, to renounce history.

With the philosophical fallout of the distinction performed by Hannah Arendt, have we not just left the properly historical terrain? Was it the properly Arendtian sense of genocide as "crime against humanity" that historians had in mind, who intervened on the matter, whether pertinently or not? One will always be able to examine this further. I merely wanted to show how irreversible the "proof by sense" is, founded as it is on the logical matrix provided by Arendt and elaborated upon by Lacoue-Labarthe, that of the proof by motive. How had I not understood this earlier? Why did I not take the full measure of its consequences? I was not the only one. Even Jean-Luc Nancy was mistaken in his interview in *Le Monde*, again in 1994 (29 March), when he had the urge to speak of "similar" events of the century and of the "other genocides," in order to define and conceptualize the uniqueness of the Shoah. He was indeed speaking of the "Armenian genocide," whereas, in all due rigor, he should have dispensed with the term altogether. I have amply demonstrated it: it could not have been a matter of genocide.

———

At the conclusion of these two chapters dedicated to the "affairs" and to the perverse historians, I have no choice but to ask myself: Where are they leading us? Are all arguments equally acceptable? Why were we listening in France, in 1999, to a historian that was so obviously at the beck and call of the Faurissonian agencies of the Turkish state, who read their propaganda books, who spread their lies, and who proceeded to demand of the victims that they prove their own death? What game are they playing, precisely, they who say these things and all those who defend and protect them? And if there had been a planned murder, what are they, these perverse historians, if not the accomplices of this murder? The planned murder did not consist in mere killing. The planned murder consisted, however one understands this, in erasing the death of the victims, in eradicating all traces of death and (accessorily) of murder. It consisted in killing not life but in killing death. This last formulation is, alas, not at all rhetorical. The suppression of death by way of the suppression of the archive is the essence of genocide, as I have said earlier. It is the reason why no genocide is a fact as long as law has not made it so. Only law could silence the perverse historians. Perversion consists in adding to the suppression of death. It consists in repeating the act of the executioners, doing worse in a way than the executioners. The latter, those who did not rest until they killed the last of my kin, they must have had their reasons, indeed, some attenuating circumstances almost, some "real stakes" or imaginary ones—I do not know and I do not want to know. But what are the reasons, the motives, of the perverse historians? What are their stakes—real or imagined? Why do they want with so much force to rob me of my own death, to annihilate me in my death? I am at their mercy. They can do with my dead body, with the memory of my kin, what they please. They can trample them, tear them apart. They can make themselves into the relays and the spokespersons of the agencies of denegation, they can become the beloved buddies of the executioners. They are not paid for this. They gain no material advantage. I cannot believe that. They would not do this for a retirement fund, for a few trips to Turkey, to please their spouses, to preserve access to the Turkish archives, even if their entire careers were at stake. But then why do they do it? In solidarity? For the defense of history? Is the defense of history enough of a "stake"? Enough to agree to become an executioner to the power of two? Or is there a reason that I don't understand? I have put so much effort into understanding this. I have almost spent my entire life on it. I have produced levels of a priori proof in order to understand them. Yes, I know, there is the Arendtian scheme, the most powerful logical matrix, the philosophical matrix, which makes them act, think, deny. The perpetrators were murderers, even if they were exceedingly intelligent, exceedingly determined. In August 1916 the living were still too numerous; the dead not dead enough. Out of their demented intelligence, they have pulled the means to kill a hundred thousand persons in a few weeks. But the deniers, what are they? What are they who demand to see, who ask for a few more proofs, who produce alleged archives that I would have to refute again and again? I understand their logic. I have spent my life explaining this logic. But I cannot understand their motivation.

APPENDIX

In February 1999 I wrote a letter to Pierre Vidal-Naquet, who was kind enough to answer me. This letter has now been published by Yves Ternon in an appendix placed at the end of his book on the Veinstein affair.[12] I reproduce here two brief extracts.

I have read with infinite sadness your "Point of View" published in *Le Monde* of 3 February 1999 under the title "On the Imaginary Negationism of Gilles Veinstein." No other voice than yours could have had, in France, more resonance. Your books, *Jews: History, Memory, and the Present* (1981) and *Assassins of Memory* (1987), have defined, at least for me and for my generation, what had to be an exemplary attitude, made of militant fervor and of moral height, against the distortions of history.[13] No one was more prepared than you against the different, hideous and insidious, forms that "negationism" can take in this century. Moreover, no one was more informed than you on the question of the Armenian "genocide." Some time ago, you had written the foreword to a book by the Permanent Peoples' Tribunal on the "crime of silence." You had summarized the theses you advanced there in a gripping page (I will cite it later on) of your 1987 book on "state historiography." You know much more, therefore, on the events themselves, and on the process of denegation, than you suggest when you modestly write: "as far as I am informed after having read a certain number of books . . . " Today, then, you have just maintained that the accusation of "negationism" launched at Gilles Veinstein was "inadmissible," that it belonged to the domain of "insults" and "slander" rather than to just critique. That is what I would like to examine with you for a moment.

. . .

I conclude this examination of the arguments (the absence of proof, belligerence, political trials, condemnations in martial courts) with a declaration that I would wish solemn. No one, before Gilles Veinstein, and, I repeat, no one, not Stanford Shaw in the United States, not Bernard Lewis, nor Eric Hobsbawm, of course, no one then had dared to do what Gilles Veinstein has dared and done: to cite without hesitation as sources and as critical resources the publications of the Turkish state and its accomplices, without asking for an instant what the status of these publications had been. We all know their provenance. Need I go into details? I will do no more than cite you, Mr. Vidal-Naquet, if at some length, and I hope you will forgive me. "The worst of all historiographies is plainly state historiography, and governments rarely confess to having been criminal. Perhaps the most painful case of this sort is that of Turkish historiography concerning the Armenian genocide of 1915. Nothing could be more normal than for the Turks to insist on the wartime situation, on the support many Armenians voiced for the Russian offensive, on the local conflicts between Armenians and their neighbors, in which the Armenians did not always behave like the lamb in La Fontaine's fable. But the Turks do not stop here: they offer the very exemplar of a historiography of denial. Let us put ourselves in the position of Armenian minorities throughout the world. Imagine now Faurisson as a minister, Faurisson as a general, an ambassador, or an influential member of the United Nations; imagine Faurisson responding in the press each time it is a question of the genocide of the Jews, in brief, a state-sponsored Faurisson combined with an international Faurisson, and along with it, Talaat-Himmler having his solemn mausoleum in the capital." This passage is on page 120–121 of your book, *The Assassins of Memory*. Now, I beg of you, Mr. Vidal-Naquet, do open Gilles Veinstein's article: the entirety of Turkish historiography is cited there in the notes, with no critical commentary and in rather a laudatory manner. Frankly, what more can I say to convince you?

3. REFUTATION

A CONFERENCE AND A CRISIS

IN 1991, UNDER THE DIRECTION OF SAUL FRIEDLANDER, A conference was held at the University of California, Los Angeles (the proceedings were published soon thereafter under the title *Probing the Limits of Representation*).[1] As a project, but also by way of its historical importance and its synthetic intention, the conference was similar to one held in Paris ten years earlier that is also available in book form as *L'Allemagne nazie et le genocide juif* (Nazi Germany and the Jewish genocide). The resemblance of the projects and of the intentions hides, however, a very important difference. The 1981 conference was almost entirely dedicated to developing historical and sociological (as well as philosophical) premises toward a possible comprehension of the event. At the 1991 conference it was the question of "historical truth," of the status of truth in history, that occupied center stage—this in an un-expected manner and to the extent of occluding everything else. One could think that this shift of perspective and this obsession with truth as such, this defense of the historical discipline, in short, was due to a sudden resurgence of revisionism regarding the reality and the modali-ties of the extermination of the Jews of Europe. And yet such was not at all the case. Were revisionism to have been obsessing the historians, it would have done so much more in the 1980s in France than ten years later in the United States. In a more general manner, were revisionism to have served as a negative engine, a painful thorn, likely to shake the his-torians' certainties concerning truth in history, those holding on to the discipline could have, they would long have had to confront the extreme forms taken by the rewriting of history in the twentieth century and, in particular, the form of different state negationisms. But this too failed to be the case, as scandalous as it may seem. One of the rare and sustained historical reflections on this general question of state negationism is that of Pierre Vidal-Naquet in France, even if he did not remain true to him-self to the end. The obsession of the 1991 conference on the question of "truth in history" was rather due to a crisis internal to the discipline it-self, a crisis of which historians have not known how to correctly master the reasons and consequences. In the United States, this crisis coalesced absurdly under the intellectual configuration named postmodernism and the individual figure of Hayden White. It is true that American post-modernism wished itself, God knows why, "relativist" with regard to truth in history. The extreme irony of the matter (but it is not a fortui-tous irony) being that the 1991 historians gave themselves a representa-tion of their own crisis in a conference on the historiography of exter-mination, while painting (and refiguring) their own internal dissension under the traits of revisionism and choosing a consenting scapegoat.

What was this all about, then? Quite simply, it was a concerted attack on Hayden White, one orchestrated from beginning to end by the mas-ter of ceremonies and to which the critic-rhetorician of historical litera-ture was obliged to lend his presence if only by way of his participation in the conference. The entire first part of the proceedings is dedicated to a critical examination of White's theses and positions, the master blow being delivered by Carlo Ginzburg in a ferocious article entitled "Just One Witness." I will mostly focus on this article here, if at a later stage. At stake is, of course, the issue of testimony. It is around an indestructible idea of testimony, as clearly suggested by Ginzburg's title, that the devastating critique of White's position is conducted. On testimony itself, there is in truth nothing new to report from the historians' corner. That is the entire problem. But one will only notice this slowly, over the course of pages and pages, reading and rereading them. The problem is not immediately visible, in other words. As we will see, however, the issue of the "nothing new" is also at the center of Ginzburg's demonstration, which is why it must be closely scrutinized. But let us first say a few words about the general introduction written by Saul Friedlander. Friedlander was, after all, the organizer of this painful debate, whose stakes he identifies with much precision. Two limpid citations will provide a necessary frame for the question at hand.

> Postmodern thought's rejection of the possibility of identifying some stable reality or truth beyond the constant polysemy and self-referentiality of linguistic constructs challenges the need to establish the realities and the truths of the Holocaust; conversely, the very openness of postmodernism to what cannot yet be formulated in decisive statements . . . directly relates to whoever considers that even the most precise historical renditions of the Shoah contain an opaqueness at the core which confronts traditional historical narrative.[2]
>
> White's by now familiar position aims at systematizing a theory of historical interpretation based on a fundamental redefinition of traditional historical understanding: Language as such imposes on the historical narrative a limited choice of rhetorical forms, implying specific emplotments, explicative models, and ideological stances. These unavoidable choices determine the specificity of various interpretations of historical events. There is no "objective," outside criterion to establish that one particular interpretation is more true than another. In that sense White is close to what could be termed a postmodern approach to history. (6)

This summary of White's positions, quite brief and generally devoid of animosity, could be usefully completed by the pages which Paul Ricoeur devoted to White just a few years ago. There, he revisits what is known of White's theses on the generalized rhetoricity of historical *and* literary discourse in order to conclude, however, that, in spite of his originality, White was ultimately mistaken "in dealing with the operations of emplotment as explanatory models."[3] While paying homage to the systematicity of the author's views, Ricoeur announces that "it becomes urgent to specify the referential moment that distinguishes history from fiction. . . . We shall never find in the narrative form per se the reason for this quest for referentiality. The work of reconstructing historical discourse taken in terms of the complexity of its operative phases is totally absent from Hayden White's preoccupations."[4] But the real difficulty is not to be found at this very general level, concerning the nature of historical discourse and the distinction or conjunction between its three moments such as the epistemology of historical science can reconstruct, namely, that of the choice of documents and the constitution of the facts, that of the setting into form or the rhetorical representation, and finally that of interpretation. By broaching the subject of the 1991 conference and Saul Friedlander's introduction, Ricoeur does after all note that "the Shoah . . . proposes for reflection both the singularity of a phenomenon at the limit of experience and discourse, and the exemplarity of a situation where not only the limits of representation in its narrative and rhetorical forms, but the whole enterprise of writing history, are open to discovery" (254). In order to understand this, we must engage the precise reasons that have brought White in front of the tribunal of historians. He would never have been summoned in this way had he refrained from going beyond his work on the generalized rhetoricity of discourse. It is indeed the specter of revisionism that occasioned the debate on "truth in history."

THE CIRCLE OF INTERPRETATION AND OF OCCURRENCE

The one article in which Hayden White had gone, it seems, too far beyond the critique of historical and historiographical truth was entitled

"The Politics of Historical Interpretation."[5] In the first part of this article, White pleads for the need to reconsider the category of the "sublime" in historical writing. At the very least, he denounces one of the essential aspects that have governed, according to him, the formation of a properly historical writing and historical discipline in the nineteenth century. This peculiar aspect is precisely that of "desublimation." It is not only part of the inaugural program of history as a science of facts; it also allows historical facts to be "politically domesticated."[6] This domestication transforms history into a "a comprehensible process, the various parts, stages, epochs, and even individual events of which are transparent to a consciousness endowed with the means to make sense of it in one way or another" (73). The condition of possibility of history as a discipline, whatever its mode and matter, would then be the presupposition of sense, a desublimating assumption in its nature and a constitutive one in its function.

Having reached this point (and almost at the end of his article), White suddenly suggests that "fascist politics is in part the price paid for the very domestication of historical consciousness that is supposed to stand against it." Must one understand that the formation of history as a science presumes to open the way for an understanding of twentieth-century fascisms without considering its own role and function in preparing their advent? White obviously goes down this dangerous path in order to examine the "social responsibility" of the historians' history in the face of fascism "in its Nazi incarnation and especially in its aspect as a politics of genocide." At this time, in 1982, he had already been taken to task by the corporation of historians because, it was said, his relativistic positions were providing a hold for a negation of "the reality of the referent" and thus for an always possible negationism. White violently defends himself against this accusation and, in a characteristic manner, he does so by way of a counterattack. I cite at length the passage that makes the transition to the very last section of the article.

It is often alleged that "formalists" such as myself, who hold that any historical object can sustain a number of equally plausible descriptions or narratives of its processes, effectively deny the reality of the referent, promote a debilitating relativism which permits any manipulation of the evidence as long as the account produced is structurally coherent, and thereby allow the kind of perspectivism that permits even a Nazi version of Nazism's history to claim a certain minimal credibility. Such formalists are typically confronted with questions like these: Do you mean to say that the occurrence and nature of the Holocaust is only a matter of opinion and that one can write its history however one pleases? Do you imply that any account of that event is as valid as any other account, so long as it meets certain formal requirements of discursive practices, and that one has no responsibility to the victims to tell the truth about the indignities and cruelties they suffered? . . . In such questions we come to the bottom line of the politics of interpretation which informs not only historical studies but the human and social sciences in general. (76)

It is therefore quite clear that White wishes to defend the "formalist" position (a label he accepts without wincing) against the obscene accusation of revisionism or of potential negationism. How does he go about it? By suddenly taking to task a French historian, Pierre Vidal-Naquet, and an article of his that had been recently published: "A Paper Eichmann." Why target a historian whose passionate positions have always been marked by moderation? For a simple reason, which does not, however, explain the vehemence of the tone: because Vidal-Naquet believes in the existence of a "historical method," in scientific rigor, and in an asceticism of objectivity and because the scandal, for White, resides in the fact that revisionist "historians" claim to uphold precisely the same values of objectivity and of scientificity, the same rigorous methods of historical research, the same reference to documents, and the same coherent use of archives. White is puzzled by the scandal of the historian. It may very well be that he is not wrong. At the time of the Veinstein affair in France in 1999, Pierre Vidal-Naquet did not show a particularly great sensibility toward another negationism (which made itself the relay and spokesperson of a state negationism under the cover of objective history), even though he himself had fustigated earlier its state sources and variants.[7] One cannot under any circumstance suspect him of having abandoned his principles or changed his opinions on the matter. One should rather consider that, behind the denunciation of state negationism in its intentional character, there lies an even more complex, secret, and active phenomenon, which remains invisible or did not lend itself to denunciation of any sort. It seems that, in 1982, Hayden White was aiming quite precisely at this phenomenon in what he was calling "the politics of historical interpretation." The position of the great moralist Vidal-Naquet did not enable, it seems, a similar perception of that phenomenon. It is crucial to understand what this is about.

A DOMINANT REPRESENTATION

White's perplexity is provoked by the confidence that Vidal-Naquet shows in the historical method, by the assurance with which the French historian claims that "on the terrain of positive history . . . true opposes false quite simply, independent of any kind of interpretation;" by his certainty that the historian's position is the touchstone that makes possible the distinction between historical truth and ideological distortion or negationist lies. In order to give support to his perplexity, to show that things are not so simple, to prove that historical truth cannot be so easily and so naturally distinguished from distortion and lies, White says that he would have to rely on events "less amply documented than the Holocaust" (77). But, instead of following the path of less-documented events (to which I shall return), White lingers instead on another distinction made by Pierre Vidal-Naquet: the distinction between the Israeli interpretation of the Holocaust, which certainly does not deny the reality of the event, and the revisionist interpretation, which is a pure lie. He then pauses on a profound reflection of the historian, according to which "the war is over" (by which he meant the "war of memory") and following which history must take up the task. For White, war is never over, even in the case of the Holocaust. Any interpretation can transform itself into an ideological lie. Any well-seated certainty can suddenly feel the ground give under its feet. Any truth can cease being universally accepted and become the particular thesis of a party in a conflict over truths and interpretations. And, indeed, the truth of the Zionist interpretation of the Holocaust is worth no more than its value as historical interpretation, which is to say that it consists in its efficacy or "effectiveness." Finally, this is true of all interpretations and consequently of all truths. In sum, there would be no objectivity in history. History would be a reconstruction, a work always in progress, an uninterrupted reappropriation of the past. It must be said that we have come quite far from the formalist considerations on the generalized rhetoricity of discourse. We are rather on the side of the will to power. Or are we supposed to think that White is carried away by his "relativist" critique of historical (or historiographical) discourse and that he arrives therefore to a position in which the "reality" of the event is contingent on the power of its interpretations? In this case, the truth or the reality of the event would become purely and simply an issue of power. The question is, therefore: how far can one push such an argument?

Actually, I have pushed White's argument one notch beyond the point he takes it himself. To be sure, from the moment he considers that the validity of historical knowledge stands in a direct relation to its political instrumentalization, he no longer says a word about the referentiality of discourse and the "reality" of the event. From the moment he recalls that history—presenting itself as an objective science and claiming that "war is over"—plays the game of established power, he no longer says a word about negationism. What is certain is that history is always an essential stake. Cleansed of the narrative aftermath of the historian's history, it should recover, says White, "the historical sublime which bourgeois historiography repressed in the process of its disciplinization" (81). And yet, one should ask Hayden White: What is the history that functions as such a stake? Is it history as guardian of the facts? Is it history as producer and guarantor of interpretations? Is there no difference between one and the other? And, in the final count, is not Hayden White a bit too fainthearted? In fact, the perplexity with which he was countering Pierre Vidal-Naquet earlier was indeed concerned with the nature of historical knowledge, which weighs between memory and objectivity, between the establishment of facts and instrumental truth. But this perplexity was formulated around the subject of the genocidal event. White's article, however, ends on a reference to certain kind of events less documented than the Holocaust, the kind of event in which "subordinant, emergent, or resisting social groups" (in other words, subaltern groups) would be in need of conquering anew their history and establishing their own truth (81). In the case of the genocidal event, to my knowledge, there is no such subaltern group. And, in fact, it is really an enormity to place on the same level the established truth of the Holocaust as event and the truth of the colonizer against which the subaltern is trying to wrestle out his own truth.[8] Let me quote the text itself, for fear that I might omit an additional subtlety on the parallel made between the two types of established truth. These are almost the last lines of the article.

> It seems obvious to me that such instruction [i.e., "the war is over"] is the kind that always emanates from centers of established political power and social authority and that this kind of tolerance is a luxury only devotees of dominant groups can afford. For subordinant, emergent, or resisting social groups, this recommendation . . . can only appear as another aspect of the ideology they are indentured to oppose. (81)

Why, then, is "truth" at stake? And for whom would it be so? Once the thesis on truth as effectiveness has been enunciated, White offers no consideration whatsoever on the particularity of the genocidal event among all historical events, the truth of which would be at stake for an ideology or for the groups involved. In particular, at no moment does he state that the genocidal event, among all possible and imaginable events, is that which inherently constitutes its own negation and that this genocidal event is not, *as such*, an event. Thus, White offers no means to understand why the crisis of historical consciousness occurred precisely around the historiography of genocide and why it concerns in reality the status of witnessing.

In his own violent reaction, Carlo Ginzburg goes straight to the end goal. He does not bother with niceties on the conquest of the past and the reconquest of history by subordinate or subaltern groups. He behaves as if White had really said what I have made him say in the preceding paragraphs. He understands that the true stake of the 1982 article and of White's formalist and postmodernist positions, or of his rhetorical conception of historical discourse, was the very status of reality, of the reality here put into question and with which, he nonetheless thinks, no historian, no historiography can dispense. He understands White's philosophy, therefore, as essentially negationist. He thus returns to the original accusation, against which White was already defending himself in 1982. His defense was, we have seen, exceedingly ambiguous, and even awkward, since it was avoiding the question of referentiality, preferring instead to place itself on the terrain of interpretation. White was avoiding the assertion that the thesis of truth as effectivity could also be understood as applying to the reality of the genocidal event. And yet such was precisely his point of departure, since he was voicing his perplexity in the face of the quiet certainties of Pierre Vidal-Naquet concerning historical truth, opposed not only to ideological distortion but also, and essentially, to negationist lies. Would the truth of the event, of any event, be a question of power, of dominant representation? I was asking earlier: how far can one push this argument? Ginzburg's severe treatment makes it appear as if White had really taken the argument to the point at which the *truth* of the genocidal event (its interpretation and its *occurrence*, its reality) is dependent on a *dominant representation*.

There is a confusion here, which must be dispelled. And it is indisputably Hayden White's confusion. That is why, even before attending to the hallucinating treatment that Ginzburg inflicts on the argument, to the point of demonstrating that any "relativist" position is essentially a fascist one, it remains for me to summarize what we have—if negatively—learned from Hayden White. It remains for me to dispel the confusion, because upon it the Italian historian hangs his own demolition enterprise. The real problem is that Hayden White defends himself very poorly against this attack mounted against him by an ad hoc tribunal of historians. But why, at bottom, does he defend himself so poorly? I think there are three distinct reasons for this.

First, he visibly lacks a concept that would allow him to designate and describe the moment in which the nonsensical is seized by sense, in which it makes sense and even makes historical sense. Instead of such a concept X, White introduces two things. On the one hand, a conceptualization of a genealogical kind, one that is therefore also historical, in part, and that provides an account of the institutionalization of history as a discipline by way of the expulsion, the occlusion, and the repression of the sublime. On the other hand, White introduces the very idea of a setting-to-intrigue, a setting-to-narrativity, or *emplotment*,[9] which enables him to describe how everything—everything that is fact, everything that is reality, everything that is event, and everything that is world, even (and each of these words should be suspended in quotation marks in order to be cleansed, by way of a kind of phenomenological *epokhe* without return, of all realist dimension)—reaches us and constitutes itself as fact, event, reality, and world, but through an operation White describes as linguistic but that is really the very operation through which there is language for us *at the same time as* there is a world and a history.

Second, White lacks the capacity to free himself from the very category of relativism, this absurd notion so typically Anglo-Saxon, since it is the sheer reverse, without mediation or discussion, of the notion of realism. It is entirely dependent on this last notion and does no more than counter it. After all, it is well known that, in the struggle he has conducted without reprieve for most of his life against the historians, Hayden White has been entirely dependent on them, which is to say, entirely dependent on their realism, precisely, regarding facts, their ignorance of rhetoricity, their ill will in considering truth in history through the conflict (and the politics) of interpretations. In spite of all his efforts to find allies among the French thinkers of structuralism, White has been depending on the historians for his problematic and his conceptual apparatus.

Finally, White lacks an event. He lacks the kind of event of which we spoke earlier, one that would be "less amply documented than the Holocaust," of a genocidal character, and could demonstrate and prove that historical objectivity regarding facts, the quiet assurance of established history, is no more than a luxury of those who can enjoy truth without conflict, who can afford to believe in truth; he lacks something that could provide an understanding of the genocidal event as inherently endowed with an attribute that goes well beyond the debates on the constitution of history as a discipline, well beyond the discussions on various revisionisms.

HISTORY IS A PLOT

In sum, Hayden White does not know enough about the varied history of twentieth-century genocides and about their historiography. At the same time, he knows nothing of the genocidal will and its challenge to law and history. History needs facts, still and in spite of everything. It needs them like anyone else, for reasons of transcendental necessity. The fact constitutes itself as such at the very moment of the giving (*donation*) of sense, of historical sense. The fact is the transcendental ideal of history. What Hayden White could not have said is that the genocidal will does not want to kill, exterminate, destroy lives and communities, societies, and even the social bond. The genocidal will wants to destroy the fact, the factuality of the fact. It is this will to destruction of the factuality of the fact that operates—always invisible—in the background of "state negationism." And it is always invisible because it is found at the very heart of the event that is named "genocidal." It is invisible as well because no one can imagine a society in which the fact as such would be abolished. For one would have to imagine the genocidal will as a philosophical will. One would have to be able to understand that it wants to abolish not this or that fact but the fact as transcendental ideal. And it gives itself the means to do so! What Hayden White has been missing, therefore, is an event in which he could have exhibited the destruction of the fact. In order to do this, we have to admit that he would have had to be endowed with a prodigious imagination and, thereby, one properly philosophical. Indeed, such an event in which the destruction of the fact is nonetheless exhibited, in its very definition, cannot be visible as event. It cannot be present and available in its historical guise, in historical books, narrated and analyzed as one would narrate the other events of the century. Only stable historical realities (of which there is simultaneously memory and interpretation, without contestation regarding occurrence) enter the history books. And yet it is precisely what White was pointing toward when he spoke of a "less documented event." Could he have known that an event can be infinitely documented and yet still contested in its very *occurrence*? He would have been in need of an imagination worthy of the genocidal will. But such an imagination of the genocidal will was also lacking for Pierre Vidal-Naquet. He was lacking it too in 1999 during the Veinstein affair (but he was therefore also lacking it in 1987, while writing *Assassins of Memory* and mentioning there a negationism at the level of the state), since he did not know then how to discern a discourse overtly negationist that arrogated to itself the freedom of research of the scholar in relation to existing sources and interpretations.

A concept was wanting, then, that would enable one to speak at once of the giving of sense and of the reality of facts, of the sense of sense and of the fact of fact; a capacity was wanting to free oneself from the unfortunate category of "relativism"; an event was wanting that would be its own negation as fact. This triple absence explains why Hayden White constantly wavered between the level of the constitution of facts and the level of the politics of interpretation when he set to work his idea of historical truth as dominant representation. And yet his concept of *emplotment* could have solved all insufficiencies. Well read, it could also have prevented any misunderstanding. Indeed, until now, I have followed the usage of French readers of White and have rendered the word "emplotment" as equivalent to "setting-to-intrigue" or "setting-to-narrativity." Instead, and in truth, one would have to render it with the term "plot" (*complot*), without forcing its meaning.[10] The giving of sense as history and the constitution of the historical fact are made possible through a narrative, an intrigue, and a conspiracy, a common *plot*. They imply a linguist fabric, a social understanding, paths of communication. It is not only the tale of the historian that intervenes here. It is also the institution of the discipline, the mediatic circulation (at all levels) of the news that will become fact. It is also the work done on the document, the setting into form of an interpretation. All this, as a whole and in details, makes a plot. All this obviously partakes of the great plot that ensures that there is, for us, history, there are facts, there is historical sense, there is what we call a historical truth, in sum, a world. For Hayden White, *history partakes of a plot*. Or, better yet, history *is* a plot, of which historians are no more than servants, mere derivative schemers. The plot is an existential category, in the Heideggerian sense deployed in *Being and Time*. It is by way of a plot—and well before the intervention of the historians—that the nonsensical acquires sense, that it is seized and coaxed by it, that it enables the tracing of lines of reference of historical sense. It is a plot that facts impose themselves, that they are located in space and call for an interpretation. It is a plot that truth imposes itself. It is a plot, finally, that the genocidal event, although destined to annihilate itself as fact by the very will of the perpetrator, can nonetheless be retrieved and extricated from this will and exist in a world of stable realities. The essence of this affair is thus the following: it is not the case that there are many plots, for example, a plot of colonizers opposed to a plot of subalterns, a plot of dominant truth against another, vanquished, and crushed plot of dominated truth. No, there is only one plot, and it is history. History is this intrigue and this conspiracy, this fabric woven in common, well before any perverse refutation of the facts and any counterrefutation of the nonreality of these very same facts.

That is why the historian's truth and the negationist lie both make reference to the same history and why the war of interpretations is never over. Hence Hayden White's perplexity when confronted with the scandal of Pierre Vidal-Naquet. But then will one say that there is no difference whatsoever between historical truth and negationist lie in the futile or vital exercise of refutation? One must respond brutally. Of course there is a difference. It is only that this difference *is not of a historical or historiographical nature*. And that is precisely what Hayden White was saying. It is also what Jean-François Lyotard said after him, particularly in a short sentence of *The Differend* about Nazism: "It has not been refuted."[11] It is not the historian's objectivity that enables a resolution between refutations, between the truth (the refutation of nonreality) that would belong to facts and the lie (the refutation of reality) that would belong to ideology. What is the nature of the difference? It has to do simply with the fact that the negationist lie is on the side of the "perpetrator" and therefore on the side of the genocidal will. It does nothing but prolong and repeat and perpetuate this will. That is part of the response, which I would have liked to read from the pen of Hayden White in the two pages of his 1982 article, where he goes so far astray on the issue of genocidal historiography. He could not write this, I have said. And it is because he could not that he came so absurdly to locate the historical truth of the Holocaust on the same plane as the historical truth of the colonizer, in the name of dominant representation. Why could he not? I have suggested an answer, I think. The lack of a concept, a relativist position, a lack of historical imagination. Indeed. But all this ultimately comes down to the structural ignorance of the genocidal will. On this point, in spite of all his perspicacity, in spite of his constant altercations with the historians, White does not distinguish himself. It is Western consciousness as a whole that has decided thus. Really, how could he ever have said that what the genocidal will wants is an event that would be its own destruction as fact and therefore the destruction of fact as the transcendental ideal of history? By way of the incredible philosophical power of the genocidal will (in fact, no one will believe it, no one has ever believed it), an event has occurred that thus denies in itself and by itself its belonging to history, that negates and denies its own factuality. This has taken place in the twentieth century. And even Hayden White, so preoccupied with the circumvolutions of the generalized rhetoricity of discourse and with those of truth as effectivity or as dominant representation, even Hayden White, who has contributed so vigilantly in revealing the crisis of modern historiography, no doubt believes that this was an event that still obeys the norms of history, such as they have always been in force, of history such as it traverses the filter of intrigue, the giving of sense, the original constitution of fact, the *plot* and conspiracy. Even he believes that this is an event that does not put into question the existential category of the plot as the category that accounts for the originary hatching of a historical world. White goes so far as to use this category in order to explain the strange peculiarities of this event, which does not let itself be described as all the others, in the neighborhood of which there occur all kinds of aberrant perturbations of the human magnetic field, as if there existed a black hole of historical knowledge. He pauses at relativism with regard to interpretation, to the war of refutations, to the politics of dominant truth. And this, I say it again, even if, for him, the difference (with or without differend) between historical truth (that of facts) and the negationist lie, the difference between these two kinds of refutation that are truth and lie, is not of a historical or historiographical nature. It is the fact that is at stake. We are before and beneath history.

TWO WITNESSES, TWO INTERPRETATIONS

In his very quick description of Carlo Ginzburg's reaction, Paul Ricoeur expresses a doubt regarding the title of the intervention, "Just One Witness," and its meaning. "The title," he writes, "sounds a despairing note, as though the accumulated documents remain below the threshold of double testimony, unless by antiphrasis we point to the excess of such testimonies in regard to the capacity of plots [*intrigues*] to produce a coherent and acceptable discourse."[12] If this were true, it would be as if all testimonies were speaking in one voice, as if altogether they constituted one immense testimony with no probative value and no indication as to the possibility of producing a narrative that would not be exposed to refutation. The two hypotheses proposed by Ricoeur would be equally plausible and, finally, equivalent. I am therefore not certain they are correct. Ginzburg's article is dedicated to Primo Levi. It offers a reflection on testimony in general and on its particular place in the catastrophic event. It is this reflection I would now like to examine.

The central section of the article is devoted to the fascist inspiration of Hayden White, first to his fascination with Benedetto Croce, then with Giovanni Gentile (even if the latter is almost never mentioned in White's work). Thus, White's assertion that "tropics is the process by which all discourse constitutes the objects which it pretends only to describe realistically and to analyze objectively" would be an echo or a combination of, on the one hand, Croce's constant preoccupation with language and history as artistic creation and, on the other hand, the "extreme subjectivism" of Gentile. Relativism or skeptical ideology on the matter of history would thus be fascist in their essence and in their origin. White's efforts to pull both of them toward the principle of social tolerance are properly mistaken and, in any case, bound to fail. Moreover, White is vulnerable to this critique of his sources of inspiration, since he writes in his 1982 article that his conception of history partakes of "the kind of perspective on history . . . conventionally associated with the ideologies of fascist regimes," the political practices of which he nonetheless rejects with horror.[13] The subsequent analysis made by Ginzburg of the thesis on history as dominant representation and effectivity brings him to conclude that "if Faurisson's narrative were ever to prove *effective*, it would be regarded by White as true as well."[14] This is where he most clearly locates White's critique of history in the general frame of negationist discourses, as I was announcing earlier. All this constitutes a brief summary of the treatment inflicted by Ginzburg upon White's thought. Yet what is more interesting from my perspective is the reflection he proposes on the question of historical "reality" in the last two pages of his article. There Ginzburg turns his attention to a 1912 essay written by Renato Serra, in which the latter goes as far as possible in questioning the relation between fact and testimony, to the point of contradicting Croce, who deemed absurd Tolstoy's demand according to which one would need an infinity of testimonies in order to account for any collective event, failing which one can only have an impoverished, flattened, and no doubt biased idea of history (for Croce, "at every moment, we know all the history we need," and there is therefore no need to concern ourselves with the kernel of reality that would be waiting for us beyond the available testimonies and historical narratives). This questioning insinuates itself between the relation of trust (or mistrust) usually established between the event and the document ("a document can express only itself," writes Serra). And yet, in spite of all reservations, in spite of this strenuously critical attitude toward any historical positivism and any peremptory discourse on the reality of the facts, it nonetheless remains the case that, for Ginzburg, "reality . . . exists."[15] It is thus once again an antirelativist position that is taken by the historian.

(I open a parenthesis here in order to consider the Croce-Serra file gathered by Ginzburg on the subject of truth in history. The elements of the file are the following. a. Croce's essay, "Storia, cronaca e false storia," published in 1912 and republished in *Teoria e storia della stori-ografica.*[16] b. Renato Serra's essay, "Partenza di un gruppo di soldati per la Libia," written in reaction to the former, but remaining unpublished in its integral version until 1927.[17] c. a letter dated November 1912 from Serra to Croce, in which the writer expresses directly, if discreetly, his disagreement with the philosopher.[18] Let us begin by saying that to sum-marize (as Ginzburg does) Serra's "agnostic" position on the matter of historical truth, as well as his subtle disagreement with Croce, under the formula "reality exists" is somehow peremptory. Serra's startling mo-dernity has to do with his insistence on the proliferation of testimony and, finally, with its total independence vis-à-vis the historical "fact." With Serra, and perhaps for the first time in the twentieth century, tes-timony ceased to be a document for history and acquired the value of fact for itself. It is clear that Serra was, in this manner, repeating on the one hand the critique addressed by Croce to "philological," "poetical," or "rhetorical" history, but he was also putting under radical interroga-tion the history identified with philosophy (on the Hegelian mode, dear to Croce, of the becoming of spirit). Moreover, Serra was not doing so as a philosopher but as a writer, in an essay that was at once narrative and reflective, testifying to a collective moment that was destined to be-come historical, all the while asking himself: "Who is it, then, that tells history?" He was thus interrogating in a radical manner the entirety of procedures through which the historical event is constituted. This es-sentially modern operation was conducted in a short piece that was go-ing in the precisely opposite direction than the one Ginzburg attempts to impress upon it. But we have been used to such things. Testimony, along with the multiplicity of writing that, according to Serra, was putting the entirety of the historiographical project under interrogation, has been largely recuperated for decades now by microhistory, oral history, and the idolatry of memory as historical matter. History has thus miracu-lously escaped its own crisis. But Ginzburg goes after the evil, as it were, at its root. He erases the disruptive character of proliferating testimony, which Serra turns *against history*, that is to say, in reality, already against the historiographic perversion. Renato Serra did rehabilitate, it is true, this "ghost of the thing in itself," which Croce wanted to exclude from the domain of history and from much else. Ginzburg interprets Serra, however, as if the latter sought to affirm once again, and against all odds, the "reality" of the historical fact behind all discourses, all fractal proliferations of testimonies. Here is one of the decisive passages at the end of Serra's essay:

All the critiques that we launch at history imply a concept of true history, of absolute reality. One must confront the question of memory, not insofar as it is a forgetting but insofar as it is *memory*. The existence of things as such. The sensation of losing, of being unable to remember, unable to tell and understand the whole, the sensation of things that escape a consciousness arrested at some point, that of things lost, that come back less, that we will not be able to revive—all this finds its origins *in a world where nothing is lost*: in eternity which, while penetrating our time and becoming ephemeral, remains in spite of everything, pure, in itself, eternal.[19]

This passage, like the rest of Serra's text, does call for a commentary that would be worthy of its measure. But to deploy the "true history" and the "absolute reality" of Serra in an argument *for* the historians' history and its "realism" when these are so obviously directed *against* it, and this merely to beat down Hayden White and his "relativism"—this is something that will not fail to surprise. In any case, I will be forced to return elsewhere to the content of this parenthesis, which concerned the modern status of testimony and historical truth.)

The antirelativist position of the historian, such as Ginzburg defines it, is a position that claims some nuance. It rejects the complicity it discerns between "positivism and relativism." On the one hand, a literal reading of the documents, on the other, a narration that would allow itself to interpret the event without suffering contradiction or refutation. This is the aim pursued by Ginzburg in his use of narratives implicating only one witness, examples of which he gave at the beginning of his essay, narratives that are properly unverifiable and that validate themselves by way of a mythical and legal mention of two witnesses to the event, whereby the latter becomes a fact. "In fact, the narratives based on one witness that are discussed earlier in this chapter can be regarded as experimental cases which deny such a clear-cut distinction: a different reading of the available evidence immediately affects the resulting narrative. A similar although usually less visible relationship can be assumed on a general level. An unlimited skeptical attitude toward historical narratives is therefore groundless."[20]

After this provisional conclusion, Ginzburg will take an additional step, to which we shall turn in a moment. But it is necessary to pause here. For, until now, the historian's reflection has been conducted simultaneously on three planes. It dealt with the status of the witness and the validity of historical narrative; it has concluded its demolition of Hayden White's positions, inspired by fascism and explicitly leading down the path of negationism; finally, it has advanced a series of nuanced propositions on historical "reality." The "generalized skepticism" here denounced is that of relativist positions that draw their authority from the rhetoricity of discourse and a concept of truth as dominant representation. The moderate skepticism of the historian toward dubious documents, the testimonies that contradict each other along with peremptory interpretations give no reason to conclude that thereby is put in doubt the whole of reality as such, the reality of facts, in general, that "exists," Ginzburg says, independently of any discourse, any representation, and any interpretation. *It is not discourse that creates the facts.* That is what Carlo Ginzburg does not cease to repeat. That is what (the destitution of the fact in the works and theories that carry the *institution of the fact*) he reads or invites us to read in White's critique of historical discourse. One can see how realism and relativism are playing the same game, in a double and painful, mirroring refutation—and this without adding to a debate that is hardly illuminating for the reader. Hardly, because there is no reflection here on the common plot (*com-plot*), which makes history possible, in which there originates the fact understood as real. Inversely, there is no reflection whatsoever on the *possible* destruction of the fact and thus on the will to destitution and destruction, a very real will, this one, entirely efficacious, with no possible refutation, that one must see in operation in order to believe. And it has been at work throughout the century by the doings of the genocidal will in action. The historian's eye is apparently insufficiently trained for such "seeing." It would have to turn toward the archive, its "own" archive, since historiography cannot remain indifferent to the destitution of the fact by the destruction of the archive, its own archive, and it would have to be concerned first of all with this destitution. Perhaps then, will the historian's eye understand "why there is archivization and why anarchiving destruction belongs to the process of archivization and produces the very thing it reduces, on occasion, to ashes, and beyond."[21]

In the meantime, a few words on Tolstoy's aporia may prove useful. What precisely does it say, this aporia to which Croce opposed the idea of an adequate knowledge? That one will never know anything of the event in its totality or in its details, for example, of such historical battle? It so happens that Hagop Oshagan, the only Armenian writer who has ever conducted a sustained reflection on the representation of the Catastrophe, has used the very same argument, referring as well to *War and Peace*. Testimony will never be but fragmentary. In reality, even if one had all the testimonies of both dead and living at one's disposition, the collected testimonies would still not encompass the Catastrophe. For the Catastrophe is nothing if not the totality of murders and sufferings. But the totality of atrocities committed and the indignations endured cannot be presented as such. One can see that the argument acquires a completely different dimension once it is applied to the catastrophic event and to its impossible representation. Yet representation and referentiality are two different things. It is the same Oshagan who said in another context that history is a plot (in fact, he said, in his own words, that it is "a series of denegations" or perhaps "a series of refutations"), but he was clearly distinguishing between the plot of refutations (if a plot can make history, than the same plot can undo it) and the limit of novelistic language (or of language as such) confronted with the catastrophic dimension. At least he did not discuss them in the same context. That is what seems to me essential, which I will have to explain (this is the object of the next chapter). Are testimonies imperfect, distorted, insufficient, fragmentary? No doubt. Or are they, on the contrary, too numerous, too individual to be brought down to a common denominator? Indeed. But from all this there is nothing to infer regarding "reality," its existence or its inexistence. Here again, as in the strange but decisive debate in which White expressed his perplexity vis-à-vis the scandal felt by Vidal-Naquet, the difference between the unpresentable truth of the event and its refuted or refutable reality is not of a historical or historiographical nature.

To sum up: Carlo Ginzburg is more than ready to accept the difficulty of establishing a relation between testimony and reality. This does not mean, he however says, that the latter can or should be placed under interrogation in its concept. The reality (of a fact? of an event?) would depend in no way on what can be said of it, of what can be known of it, and therefore of the available archive. But is this not precisely what is commonly understood by reality? Is not this thing assumed to be there, beneath the archive? A perfectly useless concept, and yet still operative! It eludes and thwarts all the twists and turns of the archive. It renders superfluous all the questions on the possible or impossible memory of the event, all the interminable interrogations on its inscription in human time. It serves, moreover, as the authority claimed by the historian, that which founds him, the "thing itself" from which he makes his daily bread. One would have thought that the historian is preoccupied with the archives and their deciphering. And he is, of course. But he owes his power of speech elsewhere, beyond the archive. Let us say it with Derrida again, who says it like Freud the archaeologist, who speaks of the moment of discovery, of the statement "but reality . . . exists" with (and in view of) the authority of the origin.

> A moment and not a process, this instant does not belong to the laborious deciphering of the archive. It is the nearly ecstatic instant Freud dreams of, when the very success of the dig must sign the effacement of the archivist: *the origin then speaks by itself.* The *arkhe* appears in the nude, without archive. It presents itself and comments on itself by itself. "Stones talk!" In the present. *Anamnesis* without *hypomnesis*! The archaeologist has succeeded in making the archive no longer serve any function. *It comes to efface itself*, it becomes transparent or unessential.[22]

The last step taken by Carlo Ginzburg engages Jean-François Lyotard, without transition and almost without commentary. It cites some passages from the extraordinary moment of *The Differend*, which I have quoted earlier as a kind of preprogram in the form of an announcement for the task to come. It is the passage in which Lyotard speaks of the "meta-reality that is the destruction of reality" in paragraph 93 of that book, where we are first asked to imagine an earthquake that would not only destroy lives but also "the instruments used to measure earthquakes directly and indirectly."[23] We are in the midst of the debate on the extent of "the cognitive rules for the establishment of historical reality and for the validation of its sense," these rules invoked with so much insistence by revisionist historians of all allegiances, followed by them with rigor and competence, the very same rules that Pierre Vidal-Naquet was scandalized to see claimed by these perverted historians. These, says Lyotard, "plead for the negative, they reject proofs, and that is certainly their right as the defense." Again, and as we have not ceased repeating since the beginning, it is quite clear that history, as objective science, cannot resolve nor decide on this situation. The difference, we were saying, between truth and lie, between the refutation of nonreality and the refutation of reality, is not of a historiographic nature. In Lyotard's words: "If justice consisted solely in respecting these rules, and if history gave rise only to historical inquiry, [the revisionist historians] could not be accused of a denial of justice" (57). It is, after all, the revisionist historians who say: Establish the facts. Prove them, go on and prove them! They demand the facts. They are true historians (something that does not prevent them from being provocateurs, since they repeat the sentence of the executioner, a sentence that is addressed to me, to me personally, and this for so many years now: "Prove it, go on and prove it if you can!" And I, for so many years, numb with shame, I stand up and I prove it, I do not cease to prove it). Yet, in the situation already evoked of the earthquake, we are not dealing with facts, but with signs. That is the central statement, cited in its integrality by Carlo Ginzburg: "But, with Auschwitz, something new has happened in history (which can only be a sign and not a fact" (57). Deploying a Kantian vocabulary, and referring us back to ulterior notices on Kant (notices that come much later in the book), Lyotard had already said the following about the sign. "Signs are not referents to which are attached significations validatable under the cognitive regimen" (56). Signs do nothing but indicate. In the admitted idioms, those of justice, law, history, objectivity, acceptable testimonies, there is nothing to receive that which they indicate, that toward which they point (*ce vers quoi ils font signe*). One does not prove, one does not validate the reality of this referent, which is not one. It is even indecent to think that one could prove and validate it in this way, with the discourse of proof and the coherence of testimonies. It is in this sense that we were evoking shame. Maurice Blanchot had already said it, and I have repeated it here with him, from moment to moment: "We will bring no proofs." Historians are reduced to silence. And this silence signifies: it makes a sign (*fait signe*), it does not make a fact (*il ne fait pas fait*). Lyotard continues then and Ginzburg with him (since he still cites him without expressing any disagreement on everything we have just said).

> The facts, the testimonies which bore the traces of *here*'s and *now*'s, the documents which indicated the sense or senses of the facts, and the names, finally the possibility of various kinds of phrases whose conjunction makes reality, all this has been destroyed as much as possible. Is it up to the historian to take into account not only the damages, but also the wrong? Not only the reality, but also the meta-reality that is the destruction of reality? Not only the testimony, but also what is left of the testimony when it is destroyed . . . ? (57)

Carlo Ginzburg interrupts the citation at this point and therefore does not read (nor does he let his reader read) the answer that Lyotard gives to his own question, an answer that concerns historians, the task and the deepest responsibility of historians, which therefore concerns him who cites and refrains from citing.

> Yes, of course, if it is true that there would be no history without a differend. . . . But then, the historian must break with the monop-

oly over history granted to the cognitive regimen of phrases, and he must venture forth by lending his ear to what is not presentable under the rules of knowledge. (57)

Yes, it is up to the historian to take into account not only the damage (something that can be articulated in a court by speaking in an audible and refutable language, in exchange for which one can receive damages and interests, as we say in French) but also the wrong (for which no audible language exists, no language that could enter into the game of historical and juridical refutations); not reality (that which "exists" in spite of everything, in the phantasmatic universe of things in themselves), but this metareality, says Lyotard beautifully, which is the destruction of reality; not testimony (that which is conjured in Tolstoy's parodic aporia in order to corroborate other testimonies and contribute to a historical knowledge of the event), but that which remains when testimony has been destroyed (in its validity, if not in its archive). Yes, it is up to the historian. . . . It is part of his historical and metaphysical responsibility. And yet, if he could do so, if only one of them could do so, he would already have broken with what makes the historians' history. That is why Ginzburg skips over the entire passage, considering it as if it were mere rhetoric, and immediately reaches for the following: "Its name [the name Auschwitz; the English text of Ginzburg's citation, badly cut, does not permit understanding what is spoken about] marks the confines wherein historical knowledge sees its competence impugned" (58).

This is where Ginzburg finally intervenes—and in order to say this: "Is this last remark true? I am not fully convinced. Memory and the destruction of memory are recurrent elements in history."[24] The destruction of memory? There is nothing new in that. It is just as much a part of history as memory itself. Conquerors have always destroyed the archives of conquered peoples. Colonizers have always managed so that the archives would reflect their perspective on history rather than the perspective of the colonized. One has always converted, massacred, annihilated, while also annihilating the very memory of the conversion and the annihilation, erasing the monuments, the tombs, the funerary stones, the traces of the sacred, the sites of life and the sites of death, of mourning. Not only has one erased lives but one has always acted in order that, just about anywhere in the world, these lives would never have been. In the final analysis, so often throughout history one has destroyed the archives that would have enabled the validation of the fact, of the annihilation. There is nothing new under the sun with Auschwitz, then, or with the genocides of the twentieth century, if one may also speak of the latter for a moment at least. Consequently, there is nothing new in the status of the survivor and of the witness after Auschwitz. Already for the Romans, one of the words for "witness" was *superstes*, "survivor." Today, as yesterday, the rules of testimonial narrative are the same, the strategies for the validation of narrative are the same, the doubts of the historian confronted with this narrative (just one witness? several witnesses? do they corroborate each other?) are the same. There is, *for the historians*, nothing new under the sun of Auschwitz.

Carlo Ginzburg wants to preserve at any price the old sense of the word *witness*, even if he understands better than anyone the stakes of the metareality defined by Lyotard (unpresentable event in the sphere of the archive and no longer fact in the sphere of reality) in the aftermath of the most terrible achievement of the genocidal will in the twentieth century. Is this because to concede on the status of the witness would be tantamount to accepting that historical knowledge sees its competence impugned on the confines of our experience and our knowledge? Understanding everything of the problematic of the witness and the archive, of the genocidal will and the catastrophe, Ginzburg nonetheless wants to save history from its referential crisis in the age of genocides, and for that he is ready to reiterate the historians' positions against the archive. One could agree with his defense of historical refutation and with his plea for an unchanged status of the witness. But, in his request for corroboration, in his exclusive confidence in the cognitive regime, and in his comprehensive, if forced, indifference toward "metareality"—with whom is the historian working? Besides, from the historian's position, how could he account for this un-named and un-nameable thing that is the destruction of the fact? Is that, in its turn, a fact? How would the historian be able to account for the destruction of the archive as event, an event whose condition of possibility is given by that which, at the same time, enables destruction? How could he do it if he fails to lend "his ear to what is not presentable under the rules of knowledge," that is to say, if he does not turn his attention to the rule and to the power of the self-devouring archive and, consequently, to the radical change that has occurred in the status of the witness in the postcatastrophic time?

This radical change has been the occasion of the most beautiful pages written by two philosophers, Jean-François Lyotard and Giorgio Agamben, twenty years apart. Both of them have confronted squarely the stakes of referentiality (and thus, in a certain manner, negationism) and debated with history as a discipline. Immediately after his injunction (already cited above) to break with the monopole of the cognitive regime of assertions on history, Lyotard adds the following words: "Every reality entails this exigency . . . Auschwitz is the most real of realities in this respect."[25] A reality that can only be a sign and not a fact. But, of course, the question of referentiality is not exhausted by the charms of the historicizing sphere and of its critique. It merely takes its flight from it. Similarly, Agamben writes about the paradox of Primo Levi (according to whom the witness who speaks is not the complete witness; he is the one who testifies to the impossibility of testifying): "Levi's paradox contains the only possible refutation of every denial of the existence of the extermination camp. . . . If the survivor bears witness not to the gas chambers or to Auschwitz but to the *Muselmann*, if he speaks only on the basis of an impossibility of speaking, then his testimony cannot be denied. Auschwitz—that to which it is not possible to bear witness—is absolutely and irrefutably proven."[26] Here, in an explicit manner, it is testimony that is in question, and one therefore finds the project of liberating testimony from any historical usage, from any reduction to a "probative value" of any kind, any attempt to read it as if it were destined to provide proof or to establish facts.[27] But, in spite of all, it is nevertheless a question of proof and of an irrefutability beyond the historicizing usage of testimonies, that is to say, beyond their archival value. One will recognize here Agamben's general project in his treatment of the archive and of testimony. If one holds together, for no more than an instant, the characteristic traits of the two approaches, so close in their spirit and in their object, one obtains the following, without amalgam, in the respect of differences, but in a simple formula, the simplest possible: *It is not to the event as fact, but to the event as sign, that testimony testifies.* Let us grant the validity of this formula for now. There is still something troubling (for me, it is exceedingly troubling) in seeing the vocabulary of *proof,* of *reality,* and of *refutation* used in the context of the significance and vocation of testimony, well beyond their function in the establishment of the fact.

It is not possible to conclude this section other than with new questions. The preceding analyses had only one purpose: to extricate ourselves from the unhappy state of a debate with no outlet on the writing of history and truth in history; to dispel some confusions on relativism; to interrogate the realist position of the historian; to underscore the necessity of thinking the category of testimony from entirely different premises than those of objective history. But, of course, behind this modest project, there are formidable questions having to do with the redistribution among the disciplines and the centers of decision. These centers intervene, in the final analysis, to define the modes and models of validation of facts and of the existence of "stable" realities for a humanity racked by the diasporeity of knowledge and by the extreme violence of interpretations. At stake is, it seems, referentiality each time. How is the fact constituted for you as fact? Who posits the fact? Who is the guardian of the fact? History and the historian? Law and the judge? These are not abstract or arbitrary questions of the kind that uselessly provoke the wisdom of well-intentioned intellectuals. One could see to what extent such questions have poisoned the debates that took place around the Veinstein affair in France in 1999. And yet this French debate on negationism (not quite well known in its premises and conclusions, but that nonetheless mobilized the signatures of a large part of the intelligentsia), different from the American debate, has contributed to publicly impose a problematic to which all will have to expose themselves. The historian or the judge? What is this strange, henceforth unknown, alternative? History, law: each time it is a question of archive.

THE FACT AND THE SIGN

It is not over yet. I have another note left, a supplement, the subject of which is too important to be avoided, even if it demands a much deeper treatment. So I place this note here as a kind of waiting stone, to mark and voice my concerns, at the end of a trajectory in which were summoned the dead and the living, the philosophers and the historians, on truth in history. "Auschwitz" would then be the name of a sign and not (or not only) that of a fact. Are we so certain that we have well understood what Lyotard was saying thereby?

The passage in which this assertion occurs refers us, as I have said, to two historical notices on Kant. The notices come much later in the book. By the time the reader broaches these notices, the decision has long been carried over on what Lyotard makes of the fact and what he says of the sign. That is why I too only bring this up now, at the end of my trajectory. I have not sought to define precisely what a "sign" is for Lyotard and why the sign ("Auschwitz" as the name of a sign) would suddenly cut the knot of an irreducible differend over reality itself, also irreducible, but the status of which is, as reality, problematic, as we know, and with the consequence (or perhaps it is the cause) that follows: we do not know to what genre the discourse that is habilitated to establish this reality belongs. We are examining the requests for habilitation. The historians' history has imposed itself as the main candidate; hence the debate with the historians, entirely explicit, conducted by Lyotard as much as by White. Besides, by the end of a first trajectory on the referent and the name, thus of a first debate on the *quid* and the *quod* of the guardians of referentiality, there where the "new" that has occurred in history is given as a sign, Lyotard does refer to Hayden White's decisive article, which unleashed the whole debate, the 1982 article to which Carlo Ginzburg referred as well ten years later. Another candidate, the legitimacy of which is much less obvious, has manifested itself for sixty years now (let us say it clearly, since the invention of the word "genocide" by Lemkin and the exhausting struggle he conducted to impose it in the frame of international law and not simply since the adoption of the Gayssot law

in France) and with increasing insistence as the guardian of referentiality or the last railing of factuality: law—it is a controversial candidate,
however. We should return to this. Confusion is at its apex.

It is not that the sign is not a referent. For we find that both the sign
and the fact function as referents but do not belong to the same genre of
phrases or, as others would say, to the same genre of discourse. In a first
stage, all we know of the sign is that it is not possible to attach to it "significations that are validatable under the cognitive regime." The historians' history has not a word to say on this point, unless it mends its ways.
It is a question of limits therefore. We are tracing the limits within which
the discourse of history remains valid in order to liberate the space where
it is no longer so. All this is beginning to look very familiar. And there is
nothing surprising in this familiarity. Lyotard had announced it from the
beginning. The two thoughts that signal (*qui font signe*) to the author, he
wrote, while referring to himself, are those of Wittgenstein (for the linguistic turn in Western thought, as he formulates it) and of Kant in the
fourth *Critique* (that is to say, the texts that engage history and politics).[28]
Lyotard borrows the term and the concept of "sign" from Kant. It is
the *Geschichtszeichen*, the "sign of history," introduced in paragraph 5
of the "Conflict of the Philosophy Faculty with the Faculty of Law,"
dated 1795. The first moment in this reasoning is in a paragraph on "historical science" and the critique of revolutionary politics: this politics
(let us say of a moral nature) "confuses what is presentable as an object
for a cognitive phrase with what is presentable as an object for a speculative and/or ethical phrase; that is, it confuses schemata or exempla with
analoga."[29] The sign is an *analogon*. As such, it is the very object of the
historico-political. Paradoxically, historical science does not have much
to say about the historico-political in this sense. Of course. It deals with
facts and not with signs. On the one hand, then, with Kant as redeployed
by Lyotard, one encounters the chaos of a history that is, in the end, insane and nonsensical (*insensée*); on the other, freedom is at work, alone
capable of making sense. That is how we have "families of heterogene-
ous phrases" that deal with history (or that make history). And yet they
are compatible phrases. "A single referent—say a phenomenon grasped
in the field of human history—can be used qua example, to present the

object of the discourse of despair [when confronted with the chaos of history], but also qua bit of guiding thread [the guiding thread of which the *Critique of Judgment* speaks], to present analogically the object of the discourse of emancipation."[30] The same referent, Auschwitz perhaps, can be, of course, at once a fact and a sign. The sign would be an event (Kant sometimes uses the term *Ereignis*), a nonintuitive given (*Begeben-heit* and not *Gegebene*), the causality of which does not belong to the sphere of temporal schematism. This nonintuitive given, this event without temporal causality, is what brings closer the two rims of the abyss (this is Lyotard's vocabulary) between the two orders of reality, while maintaining between them an infinitesimal gap. Event or given, it is sufficient "to fix the status (inconsistent and indeterminate perhaps but sayable and even 'probative') of the historical-political."[31] It is according to this status, therefore, that one can say of Auschwitz that it is "the most real of realities" (even if Lyotard does not recall this again in his chapter on "the sign of history"). Why "probative" in this context—why the incredible use of this term? Because the event provides the test and the proof of a moral sphere, of a moral sentiment, of the existence of a moral order (Kant would say of a moral disposition), much as inversely it is proved and experienced as event in the context of this sphere. Circular proof. It is true that Lyotard never returns to the index Auschwitz in this last chapter of his book, but still, it was to the Kant notices (I have summarized a section of the second notice) that he was referring us on page 56 in order to establish the *status* of this reality and, therefore, to provide for it a circular proof and probation. Kant "proves" the moral disposition by way of the event (for Kant, as we know, this event is not the French revolution but the enthusiasm of the participants or of the spectators witnessing the revolution). Lyotard proves the event by way of the status ("probative") of this moral disposition. We are well within the frame of a refutation. On one point, at least, the style of the refutation is very similar to that of Hayden White. This is not the occasion to show here how this comes about, but this refutation does mobilize—as did White himself, if indirectly—the category of the sublime. But, in the twentieth century, who is the spectator-participant confronted with the sublime of the aesthetic analogy? It is the witness, of course. There is only one step left to make in order to establish an aesthetics or a writing of the sublime, as the proper *instance* for this "something new [that] has happened in history and which can only be a sign and not a fact," an aesthetics, writing, or instance of the sublime White was already calling for in 1982 and that would provide an account of the radical novelty of postcatastrophic testimony. In conclusion, then: we have the witness according to the fact and the witness according to the sign. It is the very same witness. And yet he is radically different from himself, depending on whether one considers him in the optics of one or the other among the two instances. The confusion between the two orders of reality and thus the two genres of testimony would be damning, even if practically unavoidable.

Should one then think *according to Kant*, according to Kant at any cost? Should one distinguish, in the last instance, between orders of reality, instances, in order first of all to circumscribe or clear out the terrain of factuality, then liberate testimony from the grasp of historicizing reductionism and from the rule of the archive, and finally open the unheard of dimension in which the modern, postcatastrophic witness expresses himself? I cannot believe it. (But what else does Giorgio Agamben do, what else if not distinguish among instances when he announces the staging of a "new ethical element" with modern testimony and when he articulates, on the same occasion, a "radical refutation of negationism" and therefore a reality more real than reality?) Hayden White would still have much to be perplexed with, not only with the historians' certainties regarding the realism of the fact, and the decisive objectivity of historical science with regard to the fact, but also with these philosophical *refutations* of nonreality.

4. TESTIMONY

FROM DOCUMENT TO MONUMENT

1

WE HAVE SEEN THE HISTORICAL SENSITIVITY CARLO GINZBURG demonstrated vis-à-vis the transformation that has occurred in the status of testimony over the course of the twentieth century. Of course, his denegating position does not motivate him to name it or to seek after its characteristics. There is, after all, a largely public aspect to this transformation. The recent book written by Annette Wieviorka, *The Era of the Witness*, traces the different stages through which the testimonies of Nazi camps survivors have had to go before being largely received and transformed into an object of reflection and a subject of study: first, the narrative compulsion was confronted with incredulity, with the emergencies of reconstruction, with the discourse of revenge, with the imperatives of the cold war. Then, in the 1960s, there was the globalization of television and, simultaneously, the historical contextualization of the Shoah. This was followed by successive campaigns for the gathering of testimonies, in particular at Yale University, with the nexus provided by the book written by Dori Laub and Shoshana Felman on the crisis of testimony (I shall come back to it in a moment). Finally, at the end of this trajectory, there was the unbelievable acceleration of the movement for the gathering of testimonies initiated by the Spielberg Foundation. The importance of Wieviorka's book goes beyond its historical dimension: it shows the extent to which we are in need, because of these very public phenomena, of an interrogation on testimony. Wieviorka knows well that the "truth" of testimony does not coincide with historical truth, with that of the fact. Pressed to say what then would be the value of testimony if it were not made to serve establishing factual truth, she proposes that its value resides in the fact that it testifies to the *experience*, in this case, the experience of the survivor. One had to find a category in order to inscribe and signify the modern revaluation of testimony at the hands of the historian, that is, by way of that which enables its recuperation in historiography. At the same time, testimony increasingly becomes a source of discomfort for the historian and marks the limits of historiography confronted with the genocidal event. The most extreme moment of confession in this direction on Wieviorka's part comes when she reiterates the words of Anne-Lise Stern, according to whom testifying is the fourth among the impossible professions of which Freud spoke at the end of his life: governing, educating, and psychoanalyzing.[1] Wieviorka even seems to endorse these words, although they put into question recuperations of all sorts. Testifying would be an impossible profession because "the teaching of horror always threatens to become itself a source of pleasure." It is the entirety of the phenomenon of "memory," the gathering of memories from those who were deported as much as their presentation in the public sphere, that is here interrogated in its premises. "Interviewers who may or may not be trained to listen, historians, sociologists, filmmakers, philosophers or other intellectuals—they take up this task or seize hold of it, by necessity and often with noble intentions . . . It could be that all sides, psychoanalysts among them, in fact dispossess the survivors and the dead."[2]

All this (which would require a more detailed treatment) is not without relation to what I said at the beginning of this book on the realist shame, the despair of refutation, and the historiographic stranglehold, that is to say, also with the inaugural transformation of testimony into a document and a piece of archive. Testimony is from the start, from the moment it is uttered, destined to become archive, to be thrown back into the limitless domain of the archive, the latter also being secondarily at the service of historical truth, that of facts or an experience. It is the illness of the archive, the "archive fever" of which Derrida speaks and of which the Spielberg Foundation is only the latest avatar, in its mad compulsion to archive testimonies. Among Armenian survivors of the Catastrophe, archive fever has raged for eight or nine decades, without fault, dominating the entire landscape, forbidding any reflection on the very status of testimony. One would have to "save" testimony from the archive, even if we know that there is no difference between testimony and archive. But, then, how can we "save" testimony? In spite of the immense efforts deployed by Agamben, who follows Lyotard and White, to make testimony into something other than an archival document, to register its changed status, to let it echo on the side of wrong and not of damage, of the emblematic name and not of the generic name, on the side of the sign and not on the side of the fact, to ensure that it would be heard as the speech testifying for those who cannot testify—yes, in spite of all this, *we have no concept of testimony*. We are still in a situation where we have nothing to oppose to testimony as "document." Let us after all recall that "the authority of the witness consists in his capacity to speak solely in the name of an incapacity to speak. . . . Testimony thus guarantees not the factual truth of the statement safeguarded in the archive, but rather its un-archivability, its exteriority with respect to the archive—that is, the necessity by which, as the existence of language, it escapes both memory and forgetting."[3] It is true that Agamben here gives almost definitive form to the change that has occurred in the status of testimony. For a historian like Ginzburg, the resistance to acknowledge the crisis of a discipline faced with the *inhuman* nature of genocidal events is reinforced by a similar resistance to acknowledge testimony as a concept (if not as a practice) that has undergone a radical change in significance over the course of the last decades. With this change, we can recognize the nature of the genocidal will because, for the first time perhaps, it enables us to overcome the shame of the executioner's injunction, addressed to the survivor beyond the generations, an injunction that hurls "Prove it. Just prove it if you can."

Has this change really taken place? Is what is at stake no more than to transform it into a concept and to find it a name? Or, are we working here toward its occurrence by searching for its name? Everything leads us to believe that testimony—which used to be *document*—is now demanding to be read as *monument*. As long as testimonies were merely documents, they were read (if they were read) as the silent vestiges of memory that would help us to reconstruct the facts or that would bear each time the traces of a tragic experience, as the instruments of a universal memory, current or to come. A document is always instrumentalized, it serves something else than itself. A monument, on the other hand, exists only for itself. To put it differently, with Lyotard's Kantian vocabulary: testimony as document belongs to the witness according to the fact; testimony as monument belongs to the witness according to the sign.[4] And yet, the difference between the two is infinitesimal. In the last analysis, it is perhaps also untenable. True, testimony as monument has no "probative" value in the sense given to that word by historiography or even by law (but such was already the case for testimony as document, as we have amply showed in chapter 2). Here, it is its appearance in the public sphere, in the space of general visibility, that creates a problem. As we were saying at the beginning, testimony remains divided between the realist option and the emblematic option.

2

In the remainder of this chapter, we are going to preoccupy ourselves with two things at once: testimony as document/monument and the space of visibility. We are going to do so by examining the moment when testimony, in order to free itself from the realist option, tends toward that which is called art. Let us say it clearly: testimony is not only the narrative gathered and preserved in the libraries of oral history in European or American universities. Testimony is that which, at first, wants to render the event visible, that which wants to make the event manifest in the orb of the civilized world. Testimony is nothing without this will, and that is why, in the final analysis, it is a filmmaker who decided to create the largest library in the world of survivors' testimonies. That is also why it is a film, *Shoah*, that has done the most, and in the most convincing manner, to take into account testimony as monument and no longer as document, with the immense ambiguity inherent to that endeavor. It is a filmmaker, finally, Atom Egoyan, who, with his film *Ararat*, has wanted to do the work of testimony in order to introduce (for the first time, according to him) the extermination of the Armenians of the Ottoman Empire into the space of public visibility. Why have I said "civilized world"? Because it is the expression used by Hagop Oshagan in his monograph on Andonian, whom I have had the occasion to mention. But, most of all, because neither the survivors nor the executioners of the genocidal act can be part of the civilized world; and this because of the very fact of their mortal face to face (or because of their mutual ignorance), which has lasted, for the Armenians, for nine decades. Try as they might to evolve in it and to bring their own contribution as individuals, try as they might to participate in the concert of nations as political entities: there remains the structural necessity whereby the civilized world is beyond their respective horizons, and this from the moment survivors and executioners intervene as such. Survivors call on the civilized world to witness (*les survivants prennent le monde civilisé à témoin*; as one says so well in French); they are condemned to do so. The executioners (and with them, the crust of the historiographic perversion), equally spontaneously and with no ulterior motives of any sort, cry out in indignation, offended, swearing by all the gods that never, never ever, have they committed such acts, which insult national memory (and secondarily, international morality). There is no escape, not even today.

Out of this demented, if also logical in its coherence and persistence, historical situation, it follows that any reference to the catastrophic event within the civilized world today is under the obligation to abide by the logic of the executioner. It cannot content itself with an appeal, once more, to a "third party" in order to call on him to witness or render possible a transmission of the event, such as never transcribed by historiography, an event around which there is simply no consensus and that is therefore not a fact. Genocide is not a fact. Any reference to the event must interrogate itself, at the very heart of its appeal, on the historical significance of such an appeal. Minimally, it must engage itself in a reflection on the need and the necessity for a "call to witness." Is this what Egoyan has done with *Ararat*? Was he calling on someone to witness? Did he want to reflect, in an artistic manner, on the necessity of calling to witness and the significance (or, let us say, the paradoxical structure) of the call to witness? In the *paraphernalia* of the film (interviews, statements, articles, DVD), at any rate, Egoyan does insist on this aspect. It is clear that he wanted to bring to term a task that the Armenian postgenocidal tradition has always (again, to his mind) tried to accomplish, until now without much success. He wanted to call on "the world" to witness. Of course, this will is also represented (and thus already partakes of a *mise-en-abyme*) in the film through the confrontation with a representative of the civilized world.[5]

The idea and the project to "call on the (civilized) world to witness" constitute in every case (and for all the testimonies of postgenocidal survivors) a strange—in truth, unbearable—paradox. "Look what was done to us . . . " says the survivor. He appeals to sight and to vision. The civilized world is supposed to have seen that which has occurred. The problem being that it has not seen anything or that it has forgotten, which comes down to more or less the same thing. That is why the "monstration" is always, and at the same time, a "demonstration." This formulation comes to me indirectly from François Niney, who makes explicit the challenge issued by the genocidal will to the "categories of the showable [*montrable*]." Niney writes that "genocide appears first of all as in-de-monstrable."[6] This statement is related to our "genocide is not a fact," and it is equally paradoxical, since it speaks of an "appearance" of that which cannot appear. It says two very distinct things. First it says that the genocidal "in-de-monstrable" (and therefore the historiographic perversion that operates in its background) is always calling onto that which cannot be showed (*l'in-montrable*; but this we knew, of course, since our "proof by proof" discussed in chapter 2). It also says, inversely and in an even more significant manner, that behind any surviving monstration, behind any desire to show, there is the *specter of a demonstration*. In a powerful shortcut, the statement thus invites us to a reflection on the complex relations that are established between the sphere of the visible and the twists and turns of the archive, between the irrefutable and the unpresentable, between history and image, historicity and representation, between the destitution of the fact and the tear of the gaze, which must always (this too is part of the statement) be *distinguished* in order for something, anything, to appear on the screen. And, consequently, the statement invites us simply to a reflection on the status of testimony. The "taking as witness" is also "an appeal to witness," and this appeal is perfectly desperate. For the Armenians, this comedy has lasted nine decades. Today, it rages on more than ever. The survivor is forced to replay for the eyes of the civilized world the scenes that the latter was supposed to have witnessed, for which it should henceforth testify, in order to render justice to the victim (to render justice by way of memory, if not by way of law). The survivor is thus under the obligation to fabricate, all by himself, the scene, the gaze, and the event. Following which, and following that only, the civilized world will be able to testify that it has indeed "seen," that it has witnessed what was supposed to be seen. Of course, all that will have been seen will be no more than a representation. But is it ever possible to see (to really see, to see otherwise than a representation) when what is supposed to be seen is an irruption of the real under the name of Catastrophe?

One could no doubt say that what is in question here is merely a matter of making a fact known to the international public. But this manner of stating the issue, aside from its lack of rapport with an artistic project, has two major shortcomings. The first, one understands, is that a "fact" is never constituted as such, precisely, except to the extent that it is already part of a public memory, of a knowledge or an acknowledgment operative in the space of the civilized world, to the extent that it has a place in the orb of the visible. The second shortcoming is that, in reality, we are not dealing here with a war of images, as is too often believed.

(There are not enough images, we will produce images. We will compensate for the lack of images with a multiplication of images). It is not a war of images. It is a war of gazes. This war of gazes cannot be "won" (and before being won, cannot be fought) except under the conditions that would enable the staging of a scene, the production of imagery within the civilized world itself. What imagery? That of destruction and of atrocity. You haven't seen anything? Well, I will force you to see the destruction and the atrocity, I will put them in front of your eyes, I will force them open for as long as necessary, as if on the operating table. The films of Yervant Gianikian, another filmmaker of Armenian origin, are representative in this context.[7] In the last segment of his trilogy on destruction and atrocity, there is a long sequence of enucleation, shown in real time. It is a central scene, and it explains why the entire enterprise could only be made out of archival footage. Gianikian could not, after all, enucleate an actor and provide the representation of an enucleation. The archival image nonetheless enables him to reach the same result. It is indeed a war of gazes, a war for the gaze of the Other, who is forced to look at the very tear of the gaze. But it is equally clear that we are here at the limit of cinema. We are at the limit of cinema as "art," as one kind of art among others, and of the filmic work as a "work of art." The limit of cinema is enucleation. Through an operation on the eye, cinema shows its own limit, it lets it be seen. The limit is the irruption of the real in the image.

In *Ararat* such a limit is reached (and avoided) by entirely different means. This occurs in a scene where one of the characters (a modern Electra) tries to slash the Arshile Gorky painting (*The Mother*) at the Whitney Museum of New York. In the published version of the screenplay, the laceration actually occurs.[8] The scene was supposed to be recorded by a cameraman. Which means that the initial screenplay did foresee *a representation of the tear of representation*. As if it were possible. In the film, such as it was shown publicly, the real laceration does not take place obviously. No doubt, Egoyan knew that it was necessary and at the same time impossible. A torn painting can no more be replaced than an enucleated eye. He therefore imagines the laceration (and, through it, the enucleation) and he avoids it. The real tear could not come to representation. It nonetheless endures through its effacement. It is missing. The tear of the visible cannot be made visible. But then how to make one understand that the executioner has already settled in advance, at home, as it were, in the domain of the visible in order to bar access not to the visibility of the "genocide" but to the invisibility of the Catastrophe, that is, of the event as such?

In the preceding chapters, what was at stake was not the tear of the gaze but the destitution of the fact. It was not the representation of the Catastrophe, but the historicity of the "genocide." We studied there the disruptions that occur around the historiography of genocides, in which the self-destruction of the archive and the destitution of the fact are at the heart of the executioners' will. That is what gives the manifestations of the genocidal will in the twentieth century their air of kinship on the background of unavoidable differences. They constitute in themselves their own negation and, as such, they are thus not historical events. That is what explains the crisis of historical consciousness, which is tied to the historiography of genocides. That is what explains the change in the status of "testimony."

Moreover, if one understands the extent to which this is, *in every case*, a purely Western phenomenon (even if the extermination occurred in the depths of Anatolia, in the deserts of Syria, the forests of Cambodia, the thousand hills of Rwanda, or in other distant and famously inaccessible places), one will then appreciate the true value of the following lines written by Claude Lanzmann in 1979, sarcastically enough, and in reaction to the "banalization" of the Holocaust.

What has happened to the Jews is, in sum, very ordinary. . . . History is only a series of massacres and one mixes and cites the Saint-Barthélémy, the Armenian genocide in 1915, the gulags, or the segregationist violence of the United States. As for the Turkey of Sultan Abdul Hamid it was, as everyone knows, one of the most developed and modern nations of the Western world . . . and the Sultan had obviously—a precursor in this of Adolf Hitler—constructed a coherent doctrine of universal reach in order to justify the annihilation of the Armenians![9]

It is with some sadness that I quote these lines, because with his film *Shoah*, Claude Lanzmann is also someone who has known how to erect the most extraordinary monument to the memory of the extermination of the Jews of Europe, who alone has known how to raise "art as testimony" to the full dimension of a genre, to impress upon it a value it never had before in history, to impose it in the face of the world as a major turning point of a crisis of testimony, and to definitely disrupt the peaceful relations that art had had with testimony until then, since art and testimony belonged to two different worlds.

3

In one of the most beautiful texts written on Lanzmann's movie (a text that is also one of the founding documents of the modern reflection on testimony), "In an Era of Testimony: Claude Lanzmann's *Shoah*," Shoshana Felman—already in 1989—writes the following.

> *Shoah* is a film about the *relation between art and witnessing*, about film as a medium which *expands* the capacity for witnessing. . . . *Shoah* embodies the capacity of art not simply to witness, but to *take the witness's stand:* the film takes responsibility for its times by enacting the significance of our era as an *age of testimony*, an age in which witnessing itself has undergone a major trauma. *Shoah* gives us to witness a *historical crisis of witnessing*, and shows us how, out of this crisis, witnessing becomes, in all the senses of the word, a *critical* activity.[10]

It was no doubt the first time that the transformation undergone by the term *testimony* in the last twenty years was so clearly thematized. Shoshana Felman was here broaching, from the first pages of the essay, a reflection on the relation between "art" and "testimony." The essential thesis developed throughout this reflection was that the Holocaust represents "a radical crisis of testimony," to the extent that the Holocaust appears as "the unprecedented, inconceivable historical advent of *an event without a witness,* an event which historically consists in the scheme of the literal *erasure of its witnesses.*"[11]

All this has an air of strange familiarity with what we have said earlier on the tear of the eye and the destitution of the fact. If it is true that the nature of the historical event, here, is to be a "nonhistorical" event, one must immediately ask (all other questions relative to the historicity of such an event notwithstanding), what then is the place of art in the face of it? I repeat: historically, this event is obviously not one, unless one considers the erasure of testimony as the event itself (whereas it seems that the entire Western tradition has, without saying so explicitly, made the possibility of the event contingent on the possibility of testimony). If one formulates it simply, the place and the function of art would have to be such so as to counter this erasure of collective vision (of the "community of seeing"), tacitly considered here as constitutive of the historical fact.[12] But what visibility, precisely, what images are themselves possible when the event that demands visibility consists in the destruction of the visible as the sharing of world? This question is itself divided into two distinct parts: 1. Can the event here in question be the object of a historiography? Is it still a "fact" (for which one could still provide an account among all the other facts that make up history and on similar grounds)? Did it have its own witnesses or can one produce, construct, a posteriori witnesses? 2. Does art (any art or an art that needs vision and visibility) still make any sense in this context? One knows Claude Lanzmann's response to this kind of interrogation. It consists in a radical refusal of anything that could recall a "second degree" representation and theatrical or discursive distancing (counterfeited imagery, historicizing reconstruction, archival images). To what end? To gain the absolute presence of the past in the filmic moment, of course. It is not merely a matter of giving undeniable priority to testimony. It is a matter of questioning the very limit, which had heretofore been respected throughout the history of Western humanity, between art and testimony. Here is another formulation in this direction offered, again, by Shoshana Felman: "It is the silence of the witness's death which Lanzmann must historically challenge here, in order to revive the Holocaust and to rewrite the *event-without-a-witness* into witnessing, and into history."[13] These are arresting, stupefying, and challengingly beautiful declarations, written and published seven or eight years after Hayden White's article and Lyotard's book, but only a couple of years before the witch trial conducted against White by the historians. What should one think of it? What is this kind of event, which occurs only by means of an art that has become testimony? What should one understand when Felman writes that "*Shoah* is the story of . . . the decanonization of the Holocaust for the sake of its previously impossible historicization"?[14] Is this said about the invisible event, the Catastrophe, the event as the erasure of the witness? Or is it said about the visible event, the historians' object, genocide, the fact constituted by a universal memory (in which case, strangely, the fact would have managed to constitute itself only now, to seize substance and receive historical stability, to historicize itself a posteriori, only thanks to Lanzmann's film, that is to say, thanks to the representation of the crisis of testimony)? So, is it one or is it the other? Or is it both at once, in a puzzling mixing of genres? I cannot say and I ask the reader to suspend judgment for now.

In a proximate configuration, one may also recall the striking formulation proposed by Jean-Luc Nancy: "To show the most terrible images is always possible, but to show who or what kills every possibility of the image is impossible, except by recreating the gesture of the murderer. What forbids representation in this sense is the camp itself."[15] This formulation is in reality very close to Felman's. For her, there was no event at first, which would have then been followed by the forbidding of representation. In fact, the event inheres in the erasure of the witness as much as it inheres in the forbidding of representation. These two analyses of the event, as different as they are from each other, are to my mind exemplary and for identical reasons. In both cases, the event is something that occurs *to* the image. It is a disappearance in and of the image. And yet, in both cases, this has nothing to do with the *destitution of the fact* and the genocidal interrogation of history. Mixing of genres in the first case (art replaces the event in history by way of a staging of testimony!). Indifference in the second (it is representation that is at stake, not history, the tear and not the destitution!).

It is impossible to ignore the models I have just described. And yet it is impossible fully to accept their formulations and their conceptuality as they stand. Perhaps the difficulty is simply that we are dealing with an event that is, as White would say, "less amply documented." But I do not believe for an instant that it is a matter of documentation. History is a war in which the factuality of the fact is at stake. But if historical consciousness is "impugned" by the genocides of the twentieth century, the work on testimony cannot serve the function of history. The Armenian "survival" from one end of the century to the other and the reflection conducted on the Catastrophe by all the great writers in the Armenian language in the diaspora have not ceased to show that one must avoid the mixing of genres to understand anything about the event. One had to know how to distinguish the visible from the invisible, genocide from Catastrophe, the space of recognition from the internal tradition of testimony, historicity from representation, the destitution of the fact from the tear of the image. One had to know how to distinguish them and treat them separately in order to problematize their encounter. Most particularly, there is an Armenian "history" of the reception (and thus of testimony and representation) of the Catastrophe, in fact, an immense history, which extends over the entire century and includes different genres. To ignore this history is a choice. But to say that the Catastrophe has been underrepresented, as is sometimes heard—that is to make such ignorance into a criterion for truth. Survivors have never stopped telling. Writers have not ceased to expose their art to the impossibility of representation. Here the opinions and the philosophical positions taken are of no use. One has to visit the immense building site of Armenian literature and testimony, a building site that has remained open and received an uninterrupted supply over the course of the century. That is how, tomorrow perhaps, it will be possible for some images to be *seen* for what they are and not as fragments of shipwrecks thrown about the ocean of the visible or as elements to be reconstructed according to some redeeming finality. The texts of the survivors will then be *read and commented upon* and not used for pseudo-historical ends. The narrative of survival will then escape the gravitational field of the historical gaze; it will be offered to the public as a monument. No one has been reading the narratives of the survivors, we know that well. They are, in fact, unreadable. They do not cease to interpellate, after the fashion of ghosts tormenting their descendants. They do not cease to cry out: "Read me!" They do not cease to place themselves at the site of the tear, wanting to try to present it, to *replace it*. Testimonies as monuments will have, perhaps, a chance to be read. With no spectral presence. Finally rid of the fact and of the historians' history! Finally rid of the reality principle! They will end up achieving the suture between irreconcilables: the lack of the tear in representation and the destitution of the fact in historicity. Is this a dream?

4

And now, to conclude this chapter, and as I have announced earlier, I will make a very brief incursion into the domain of Armenian testimony or, rather, into the discussion of testimony in the Armenian language.

This discussion is not easy to follow, first because of its ramifications, but also—and mostly—because it is often implicit and must be drawn out of the narratives themselves. The authors of the first generation of educated survivors who have given an account of their experience in the form of memoirs, longer or shorter reports, or narratives written almost immediately upon return to Istanbul, have also made residual remarks on the necessity of testifying, conserving the memory of the events, tell the story of their ordeal, or pay homage to the dead. Sometimes (as is the case of Zabel Essayan, already in 1917) they have pronounced, in a few sentences, their condemnation of literature and have opened an abyss of questions on the capacity and the dignity of art faced with the atrocities collectively suffered and the immensity of the loss. Sometimes as well (as is the case of Aram Andonian in 1919), they have deemed literature indispensable in confronting the reality of suffering and abjection. It goes without saying that there is also found a series of testimonies that belong to neither of these categories and that do not engage in any way the dilemma of art/testimony. Among the latter are a few of the rare authors who returned from the two deportation centers where intellectuals had been rounded up in the early stages (Tchangere and Ayash), but most of these testimonies come from people who had practically never held a pen beforehand. Their only concern then is to tell their own way of the cross. And then there are those who, from the beginning, have wanted to do the work of historians, I would almost have to say the work of collectors. Already, very early on, they began to gather testimonies of all kinds, transforming themselves into librarians and documenters of the testimonial narrative. Essayan began her work as a documenter of the Catastrophe in the Caucasus. Andonian dedicated to it close to the totality of his energy, first in Aleppo in 1918 and later in Paris.

These two endeavors, that of the personal narrative and that of the gathering, even if they both began very early and simultaneously, may not have answered to the same imperatives. The fact remains, though, that this incredible memorial fervor has had a collective dimension until 1922. After that date (which marks, for some time, the end of Armenian cultural life in Istanbul, when most of the educated survivors had to flee before the advance of the Kemalist troops), testimony became a purely individual affair. I have just alluded to the testimonies written by the educated. To delve into the other categories of testimonies, which are by no means less important, would take too long. The most poignant, to my mind, are those written in Turkish. They are hardly studied, and all are unpublished, but their authors must have had some sense that they were only writing for themselves.[16] There are also contributions made by intellectuals from the provinces, those of orphans who learned Armenian after being taken in to the sheltering centers of the Middle East and who wrote down their atrocious memories much later. Finally, there are many contributions written in the different European languages other than Armenian, mainly English, from the 1920s onward. In the "educated" testimonies (which I consider here to the exclusion of others), one of the striking attitudes is the astonishment at having nonetheless returned from the ends of night and terror. Linked to this astonishment, one can see the very small distance that they all establish between "having been a witness" and "bearing witness," which is also the infinitesimal distance between the document and the monument. They want to act as if they could have been "only" witnesses and, consequently, to render an account of the facts and the experience in a manner that would be as "truthful [*véridique*]" as possible. There is an obsession with truthfulness (*véridicité*). Here is, for example, what the writer Yervant Odian says on the last page of his voluminous narrative of survival, *Anitseal Tariner* (Cursed years), published in serialized form in an Armenian newspaper of Constantinople:

> Here then is the story of my three and a half years of deportation. Of course, the readers will have noted that I have written this story in the most simple manner possible, sometimes even in an uncultivated style. More than anything else, I wanted to be truthful [*chshmartapatum*] and tell everything precisely as it happened, without falsifying any fact, without exaggerating any event.
>
> And yet the reality was so atrocious that many readers have thought I was exaggerating. Those who have gone through the suffering of deportation and have managed to survive, those will testify that I have not distorted reality.
>
> . . . My three years of deportation have taken the place of my thirty years of literary activity.[17]

These are the last lines, at once clear and mysterious, of the narrative of survival. He will have been as sober as possible, he says. He will have told only what he has seen, as if he had been a witness external to the atrocities and consequently external to himself. It is the convention of the genre, without which there would be no truthful narrative and thus no narrative of survival. What Odian says in the very last line of his story, "my three years of deportation have taken the place of my thirty years of literary activity," is, however, stranger. Here, he seems to escape the convention. Does he mean to say that he has learned more over the course of these three years than during the thirty years in which he was writing novels in the Armenian press? Or that he has survived precisely because of these thirty years, which have made him a figure of renown, whom the other deportees have almost always helped wherever he went, at the expense of their own lives, knowing that he would speak for them one day, that he would bring their sufferings to the world's eyes, which would otherwise remain unwritten as facts in the memory of humanity? Or does he mean to say that one had to *abandon literature* in order to be faithful to the experience of the deported? The three hypotheses are plausible and constitute, in fact, a constellation. Odian here formulates an ethics of representation. Such ethics, enunciated eighty-six years ago, was buried in the pages of a newspaper and only brought to the public attention a few months ago, posthumously, thanks to the labor of Grigor Hakopyan, to whom my own book is dedicated.[18] And yet, once again, this is a sign: the sign that something has changed in the reception of testimony. In his preface, Hakopyan uses, without even paying attention to it, the Armenian word *vkayagrut'iun* for "testimony." It is a new word. It designates, I think, testimony as monument and no longer testimony as document. For a long time, though, this status and this fate of testimony have been ignored by the writers themselves, for structural reasons, of course, having to do with the very nature of testimony, its originary belonging to the archive and thus, in the final analysis, to the historiographic perversion. It is this ignorance that, in any case, explains what I would want to call the failure of the Armenian intellectuals of the twentieth century, their failure when confronted with the task of *speaking* the Catastrophe.

In 1943, as he was writing his history of Armenian literature in the form of a "General Survey," a writer like Levon Shant did happen to stumble upon the names of the writers of atrocity (Siamanto, Bartevian, Andonian). Each time he felt the need to express a disavowal and disapproval toward this type of literature. The atrocious, according to him, should have remained the prerogative of collections of testimonies and of survivor narratives.

> The description of the bestial and savage treatment to which the Armenians have been subjected provides no help to anybody. Inversely, these descriptions are in no need of the benefits of art. Reality is sufficiently atrocious and powerful. It is better to leave it to the care of white, blue and yellow collections of government documents, gathered from the very lips of the witnesses.[19]

We have here the formulation of a kind of moral imperative against the "artistic" representation of the bestial, the inhuman, and the atrocious. It is again an ethics of representation, but in terms that are quite different from those of Yervant Odian, which we have read above. For Shant, testimony must remain a pure and truthful exposition of atrocity. It deserves no other approach. The collections of different colors he mentions here are the blue, yellow, and white books published by the different European ministries of foreign affairs between 1890 and 1918 and do, in fact, contain thousands of pages of atrocities, conscientiously reported by the French, English, and German consuls of the Ottoman Empire. For Shant, the category of testimony would therefore have to be confined to the domain of the document, to which the domain of art is opposed. An artistic treatment, of whatever kind, would run the risk of diminishing the reality effect that these descriptions must forcefully exercise. One must tear the gaze of the Other. I cite again, while abridging.

> These stories of suffering, mourning and torture that relate to our cruel reality must be carefully told, in all their details, perfectly bare, with no embellishment whatsoever, without fictional complements, with no exaggeration, exactly as they were gathered from the lips of the witnesses and from the official documents, while avoiding all aesthetic twists. It is the only way for these crude descriptions to reach their highest levels, as exact representations of a bestial reality.[20]

Any "embellishment" would deprive the testimony of its value as lived experience and as objective account of the facts. One could admit as much. But, in reality, what Shant says is simply revolting. The memories and narratives of the survivors only have value as documents in order to prove the facts, in order to elicit pity or revenge or whatever! There would be no other path either than artistic or political. Shant chooses the "political" definition of testimony. It will be understood by now that these antithetical choices are purely symmetric. Testimony as document inherently excludes any recourse to art, any transfusion or transformation of its nature. Inversely, those who favor a literary treatment have nothing to oppose to the documentary conception of testimony and to the omnipotence of the archive. There is a manifest impasse, from which none of the participants in the debate, conducted at a distance, across oceans and generations, have been able to extricate themselves.

5

I have already mentioned in my introduction that Zabel Essayan, who in 1917 was the first to transcribe and publish the testimony of a survivor, also found herself under the obligation to place literature out of bounds. In 1911 Essayan wrote an unforgettable book, *Among the Ruins*, a book of pain and mourning, after the massacres of Cilicia in April 1909. A modern Antigone could rise against the interdiction to mourn and erect a monument in the form of a testimony. This was on the eve of the Catastrophe. After 1915 the same Zabel Essayan, who miraculously escaped the roundups of intellectuals and found shelter in Bulgaria, later in the Caucasus, wrote at least once the narrative of her joining the underground and her flight. But she was perfectly incapable of writing a new monument of mourning comparable to that of 1911. Instead, she devoted three years of her life to gathering testimonies, transcribing them, translating them into French, one more time, in order to place them obviously in front of the eyes of civilized humanity.

The very first testimony ever published in its entirety is that of a survivor, Hayg Toroyan, which Essayan fully transcribed and rewrote in her own hands. Hayg Toroyan went down the Euphrates in the company of a German officer for whom he served as interpreter from October to December 1915. He therefore saw, one after the other, all the concentration camps of Mesopotamia. He and the officer had written notes and taken pictures. Upon their arrival in Iran, the German soldier committed suicide. Toroyan was able to cross into the Caucasus and recount his journey to Essayan, who published under her own name, with a two-page preface in which she says, among other things, the following: "Painfully imbued by the task that has fallen to my lot, I considered that it would have been a sacrilege to transform into a literary subject the sufferings in which a whole people agonized."[21]

The greatest writer of her time was thus becoming the substitute of a witness, a pen at the service of the true witness, *the secretary of the archive*. She was writing under dictation, submitting to the rule of the archive, to the originary belonging of testimony to the archive. She was exposing herself to shame and exposing it as well. The impossibility, henceforth verified, to confront and avoid the interdiction to mourn was marked with the intimate will to archive the words of the witness. Archivization was cutting short the memory of the victim and the impossible mourning.

The case of Andonian, whose name has appeared a number of times in the previous pages, is also fascinating. Andonian was deported first to Tchangere, then to the deserts of Syria. He miraculously survived a first time (in 1915) and a second time (in 1916) because, like Odian, he was a figure of renown and was therefore aided and hidden by his companions of misfortune. He is the one who initiated the immense labor of collecting testimonies in Aleppo in 1918. Here is what he says about it in his *Mets Vochirë* (The great crime) two years later.

When the British entered Aleppo, I profited from the situation in order to save history and I began to interrogate those among the survivors who were capable of recalling the unspeakable terror and atrocities of the past five years. Thousands of women, young girls, and men came to see me. They spoke and they wrote. Each one of them had their own story to tell and not one of the tortures they had to endure were similar to the others. Often, I have thought that for each one of them, an entire volume would be necessary in order to give an idea of their sufferings, at least in general terms. And they were more than a hundred thousand who had a volume of things to tell. Even if this were done, we would still be missing the story of those who have disappeared, carrying with them the loss of a million volumes.[22]

"To save history"—what a strange expression when one knows that this history can never be written. But, in reality, Andonian did publish two books. In 1919, *Ayn Sev Orerun* (In these dark days); in 1921, *Mets Vochirë*, of which I have just spoken.[23] The 1919 book is a collection of narratives written on the spot, each more atrocious than the other. It is a book of obscene literature on the abjection of the victim, and it is bad literature simply because it is literature. The second volume was published in French translation already in 1920 (thus before the original Armenian), under the title *Documents Concerning the Armenian Massacres*. It inaugurated the historiography of the event and was addressed to civilized humanity. Here the naked eye can see the vertiginous paradox of testimony and an illustration of the impasse in which all these writers have found themselves trapped. From the beginning, Andonian knew, with a knowledge that imposed itself on him independent of all reflection, that he had to make literature in order to escape the shame of testimony (I shall come back at some length to the question of shame in the conclusion to this volume), that is to say, in order to escape its becoming-archive. He could obviously not escape the dichotomy of literature (art) and testimony (history), which is itself conjured and regulated by the archive.

Eleven years later, in 1931, Hagop Oshagan was deep into the writing of his novel *Mnatsortats*, which, after two parts devoted to the pre-catastrophic world, was meant to approach the Catastrophe in a third part, entitled "Hell." We know this precisely because of the 1931 interview already mentioned. This third part was never written. In 1934, after writing the two thousand pages of the first parts, Oshagan stopped. He stopped on the threshold of the Catastrophe. After this sudden death sentence, he still wrote tens of thousands of pages, but he never came back to the survivors. Somewhere in these pages, in volume 9 of his *Panorama of Western Armenian Literature*, there is a monograph devoted to Andonian in which Oshagan reflects again on the Catastrophe, this time on the basis of Andonian's two volumes, the books published in 1919 and 1921, one of literature, the other of testimony for proof and for history. On the latter, Oshagan writes (speaking of the secret telegrams, which contained extermination orders that Andonian extracted from a Turkish administrator from the Deportation Bureau): "I wonder what he was thinking while exhibiting these telegrams, when, deep in his heart . . . he knew very well who the authors of this drama were and what aims they were pursuing."[24] The work of memory, if this is how we ought to call it, will therefore have to guard itself from administering a proof and, in any case, from any documentary use of testimony. That is where Oshagan voices a decisive objection to his own statement: "But civilized humanity?" and he immediately answers: "History can prove nothing; it is a fabric of denegations."[25] Here are announced and denounced, long before their literal advent, both history as "plot" and the historiographic perversion. Moreover, Oshagan dismisses, in one phrase, once and for all, the entire debate on the referentiality of the event, the very debate that has occupied us, nonetheless, throughout this book. *The question of representation is not the question of referentiality*. Oshagan will never come back to this radical and essential distinction. Indeed, but where is the alternative? Had Andonian not collected testimonies as proof, had he not answered the injunction of the executioner, he would have written literature. It is the originary phenomenon of the reversal of testimony into the rule of the archive, consistent with the very will of the murderer. This reversal is endowed with a double turn of the screw. It seizes testimony. It produces literature. Yet this phenomenon, which I call *originary*, for lack of a better word, does not freely walk around. It cannot be apprehended as experience.

It so happens that only those writers have apprehended it who have been subjected to it in their very project as writers—as well as because of it. They were subjected to it and they have subjected themselves to it without understanding what was happening to them. By way of this subjection, they enable us today to speak the phenomenon, the heart of shame, the primary transformation of testimony into a discourse of proof and its engulfing into the archive, through which the survivor is literally deprived of his own memory. The catastrophe in this sense is a catastrophe of memory. That is why it is so ridiculous (have I said it already?) to speak of a "duty of memory [*devoir de mémoire*]." The only event worthy of being kept in memory is the very event of which no memory is possible: the destruction of memory by the becoming-archive of testimony. Is it even an event? The archive is coextensive with the Catastrophe.

We are in 1931 then. Hagop Oshagan is in Cyprus, and his novel has begun to appear in the newspaper *Houssaper* in Cairo. Journalists from *Houssaper* come to pay him a visit in August to conduct an interview with him on his work. The interview is published the following year in Boston. It is the only place (before the 1944 monograph he devotes to himself, as the last volume of the *Panorama*) where Oshagan speaks at length about *Mnatsortats* and his project to approach the Catastrophe. It is here—I repeat this now—that, speaking of the last part of the novel, he says: "A topographical study will minimally be needed, the reading of thousands of narratives and hundreds of volumes, testimonies, before I could be able to begin and write [the last part]."[26] These lines strongly recall Andonian's declaration ten years earlier that "they were more than one hundred thousand who each had a volume of things to tell." Obviously, the archives that Oshagan wanted to have at hand were not available, neither to him nor to anyone, ever. This is said about phantas-matic archives (or else these are the archives neatly assembled today on the shelves or the electronic sites of American universities). But, equally obvious, it is the archive (in the singular, this time), the logic of the ar-chive, that makes him utter this phantasm. It is the archive that makes him say that he is forced to *limit himself* to the novel: "I must content myself with what I have. Hence the necessity of the novel form." The novel becomes *the last resort of history*.

In volume 8 of *Panorama*, the same Oshagan devoted a monograph to Yervant Odian. It is here, I think, that, for the very first time, he had taken into consideration the testimonies of his contemporaries: *Armenian Golgotha* by Father Grigoris Balakian, *Tales of the Yeghern* by Garabed Kapiguian, *Our Cross* by Doctor Salpi, *Memories of an Armenian Deportee* by Ms. Captanian, but also *Cursed Years* by Odian, *Tribute to Armenian Intellectuality* by Mikaël Shamdanjian, and Andonian's two books—the entirety of the testimonial production of the educated writers in the Ar-menian language.[27] This production does not satisfy him. Here is what he says about it:

They have not risen to the height of literature and consequently they remain outside the sphere of our interest. In the daily and monthly *Haïrenik* [of Boston], the stories that have been published these past twenty years have not had the good fortune of being written by the pen of a writer. And the terrible event has remained inaccessible.[28]

What then did he expect from these testimonies? What did he want that they could obviously not provide? Did he want literary testimonies? Did he want more than testimony? What could he hope, in fact, from a testimony written without "embellishment" and without "exaggeration," that is to say, without literature? He wanted an overcoming of the realist convention of the witness under the name of literature. He wanted to "sublimate" testimony. What he wanted, he expected, of course, from himself. Yet, and simultaneously, this literature was entirely determined by the engulfment of testimony in the archive and by its definition as document, which de facto prohibited any literature. Thus the event will have remained inaccessible. The time had not come for testimony as monument and for the emblematic name of the event.

———

In all the cases I have mentioned, it is the status of testimony and that of the witness that is at stake, even if literature itself was undergoing an ordeal. In this ordeal what is revealed is the originary phenomenon of archivization, in all points equivalent to the impassable interdiction of mourning. It is revealed simply because these writers (Essayan, Andonian, Oshagan) have encountered it on their way. There was nothing they could do about it. And they did nothing to counter it. The three of them were perfectly powerless, unable to liberate testimony from the archive. Here only the fate of testimony was at stake. Nothing else.

It is now known, at least, that *the event-without-a-witness* of which Shoshana Felman writes (or the interdiction of representation pronounced in the camps of which Jean-Luc Nancy speaks), that is to say, the nonhistorical event par excellence will not become *suddenly historical* by the grace of a "representation," by the "monumentalization" of testimony, or by a "monstration," that is, by a public visibility extended to the genocidal "fact," by an amplification of the testimonial project of an "artistic" nature. The event-without-witness will not be suddenly transmuted into History. There will be no possible representation of the tear of representation. The historiographic perversion still has many beautiful days ahead of it. Do not doubt it for an instant. Genocide is not a fact. No refutation can contradict this, not even the refutation of the witness according to the sign. "To establish oneself . . . outside the archive," said Agamben.[29] He wanted to think testimony *against and counter to the archive*. We have illustrated this "against and counter to" in the experience of a quite involuntary encounter with the archive, by following *in fine* some of the avatars of postcatastrophic Armenian writing. For all that, we still do not know what the archive is and whether it is possible to establish oneself outside it. We have not dwelled enough with the shame, not confronted testimony enough in its illegibility as a piece of archive. The archive is still to come. It is to come in the anterior future. Like the Catastrophe.[30]

CONCLUSION

SHAME AND TESTIMONY

AND NOW, IN THE GUISE OF A CONCLUSION, IT REMAINS FOR me to do what is most difficult. It remains for me to speak of shame, the logic of shame, and to do so not in an allusive manner and in passing, as I have done so far, but by taking shame as a theme, by really speaking of it and from it, by confronting it face to face.[1]

As long as I remember myself, in fact, I have felt shame. The confession of shame has in itself something irrefutable. You can refute my arguments. You could cast doubt on any expression of my "emotions." Shame, my shame, in the moment I confess it to you, cannot be refuted, nor put in doubt. It is truly a strange emotion and a strange argument, this shame. It is, first of all, and precisely, that which one should not be able to confess. Never, neither in public, nor in private, have I spoken of the shame I have always felt within me (even if this "never" can only be said once; once it has been said, it is no longer a "never"). I did not even speak of it with myself. Of what have I always been ashamed? I will tell it in a moment. I will say it with some precautions because I am not sure that shame has any object, a "reason," a cause. One can try to say of what one is ashamed, but shame itself, how could one say it, communicate it verbally? It can come to the surface in the form of a blushing, a terror. It can invade me, seize me, no longer leave me. It can act in such a way that I will want to bury myself under the earth. It can turn me inside out like a glove at the moment I am exposed to you without speech. If I feel shame, it is always and again of myself that I do. If I am shamed by what others might be, do, or have done, it is as if I were that myself, as if I were doing so, had done so, myself. I cannot detach myself from it. Shame links me to them. Should I say that it links me to "my own," my kin (*aux miens*), thereby marking a strange collective, a reverse identification? I do not know, I did not even know that they were "my own" before shame came. No, it is me, it is always of me and for me that I feel shame. I am a glove turned inside out; I have no inside. I am "them," all those who shame me, by whom shame thrusts itself upon me.

There is no testimony of shame. It might even be the only thing for which there cannot be testimony. Shame itself is its own testimony. In the same way, there is no shame of shame. One can feel shame for being beautiful, for being ugly; one can feel shame for one's parents; one can feel shame for having committed such and such innocent misdeed in order to survive. One can feel shame, in a manner at once abyssal and absolutely unspeakable, for having been touched at the very core of one's identity (and those who torture or rape in genocidal times know very well that shame is totally destructive). Yes, one can feel shame for all this. But it seems to me that one cannot feel shame for feeling (or having felt) shame. Why this radical absence of reflexivity of shame as well as of testimony? Obviously because testimony is shame. It is shame itself. Which makes two propositions. "Shame itself is its own testimony" and "Testimony is shame." If these two propositions are true, then all discourses on testimony that know nothing and say nothing of shame, that are not moved by shame, are no more than empty chatter.

But is it so obvious that testimony is shame itself? The obviousness of which I speak would thus not be the most commonly held thing in the world. Why? Is it because this is the intimate experience of the survivor? It is with the experience of the survivor that Giorgio Agamben begins his great development, which concludes with the assertion I would summarize as follows. "The subject is the witness, he who testifies to the impossibility of testifying." One could put this in a more abbreviated form. The subject is the subject of shame. That is Agamben's theorem. But, in reality, the analysis that arrives at this assertion does not start out from the shame of the survivor, the shame of having survived. No, it starts off with this terrible scene that Agamben reads in Robert Antelme, where the latter tells how, during the absurd march of the prisoners under the advance of the Allies, one SS suddenly hails a young Italian student. The student looks around him, understands that it is he himself who is hailed and . . . blushes. He turns red in the face. Antelme does not say that he blushes out of shame. Yet that is how Agamben understands it. At that precise moment, at the instant his death is announced, the student blushes out of shame. Why is this shame, this flush, at the moment where no escape is possible any longer? Agamben says: "In any case, the student is not ashamed for having survived. On the contrary, what survives him is shame."[2] Thus he seals the road to all complacencies on the feelings of guilt attributed to the survivor. It is a terribly polemical text. And Agamben repeats the question: Why would the student feel shame? He does not know any way to answer but this:

> It is as if the flush on his cheeks momentarily betrayed a limit that was reached, as if something like a new ethical material were touched upon in the living being. Naturally it is not a matter of a fact to which he could bear witness otherwise, which he might also have expressed through words. But in any case that flush is like a mute apostrophe flying through time to reach us, to bear witness to him.[3]

It is shame that survives. It is shame that testifies. One finds here the two propositions folded into one discrete and dreadful flush (Shame itself is its own testimony. Testimony is shame). I feel shame. That is a pleonasm; you have felt this since I have begun to say that I feel shame.

There is no I but that of shame. Strange structure than this I, which does not coincide with itself except in the moment in which it testifies of its non-coincidence, of its total dereliction.

(It is strange, indeed, that in the thousands upon thousands testimonies left by Armenian survivors, it is never a question of shame, for example of the shame of having survived "in the place of another," or of the shame of having sold a daughter, a sister, for the sole aim of surviving. And yet, my own—that is how they have survived, in fact. Yet all the cases of shame that are found in the Armenian literature of testimony, of which there is an infinite number, obviously, are always linked to suicides. He who survives never expresses his shame. There is here a radical impossibility. There is no survival with shame. Only shame survives, would say Agamben. And it can testify to nothing, except to itself).

This was then Agamben's theorem. In its most abbreviated form: I feel shame. One must inhabit shame, one must come back to it, dwell in it, in order to succeed in saying something, anything, of testimony. On this, I will now be more specific, and we will have to change register. I have always felt shame, I said, as far back as I can remember. I have grown up with shame. I have felt shame every time we spoke of ourselves. For, each time we spoke of ourselves, we did not speak to ourselves. Each time, an appeal was made to a third party, to the West, to the observer, to what Hagop Oshagan called "civilized humanity." And, thus, I have felt shame continuously. As survivors, we have never ceased, in fact, to appeal to the external gaze. In the moment of this appeal, it is testimony that was constituting me. It was constituting me by the shame I was feeling, by my belonging to this "we" I have just uttered, under the gaze of the civilized other, by this gaze itself. All my life, then, I have not ceased feeling shame. Was it because we were exhibiting our wound in public? Was it a matter of modesty? But why an "us," at this particular moment, and what wound after all? But no. It was always because we did not speak to ourselves. Again, and always, we wanted to produce proofs. I have felt shame, therefore, each time testimony was exhibited, presented, offered as proof. Each time, we were, we had to be so many living proofs of our own death. Living proof of one's own death—that is also the Italian student. That is the moment of shame. Testimony is shame.

Testimony obligingly offered as proof, as I have said. But let us see. Is there a moment in which testimony does not exhibit itself as proof? There are even books written today to validate the probative value of testimony and construct a social model, a model of social life as communication and thus of truth as consensus from which one could, it would seem, receive testimony as proof. In *Remnants of Auschwitz* one can read the ferocious passage (but the entire book is ferocious) where Agamben calls on one of these philosophers of communication, of truth as consensus, Karl-Otto Apel. He invites him to go back in time, to repeat his philosophy for a moment in front of the *Muselmann*, he who no longer communicates, who would not know how to utter one word of testimony, who could not testify for himself. Agamben asks: since he has no words, since he no longer communicates, are we going to exclude him from the human and from truth? "Only if language is not always already communication, only if language bears witness to something to which it is impossible to bear witness, can a speaking being experience something like a necessity to speak."[4] And, already here, Agamben presents his fabulous argument on refutation. "The *Muselmann* is the radical refutation of every possible refutation" (66). I return therefore to what I was already saying in the introduction, regarding the genocidal will and testimony. It is certainly not for testimony to refute, to serve as proof. The only thing that, if need be, could serve as proof is the impossibility of testifying and of proving, the silence of he who will never speak, never again, of his own destruction. "We will bring no proofs." But, after all, it is perhaps not *if need be* that the constitutive paradox of testimony refutes all denegations and even provides "the only possible refutation to all negationist arguments." Stating so, in fact, Agamben frees testimony from the high functions it has been made to serve as probative value regarding the fact. At the same time, he does engage in a refutation of the archive. That will be the price to pay to save testimony from all probative usage.

Shame, specified—this is when one forces testimony to function as proof. Even though, we know it well: not only will we bring no proofs, but testimony can never constitute a proof, never, in no case whatsoever.

Testimony does not constitute a proof of the fact. If one must prove the facts, testimony has no probative value at all. And I would even say that, not only does testimony not constitute proof, but it does not even constitute memory. Testimony has nothing to do with memory. And it is a shame, a shame all too current, permanent, and renewed to make it play, in any way, the role of proof or support for the memory of events. Shame, in sum, is to make testimony play the role of the archive for proof or for memory. Shame is transforming testimony into archive. Yet, and here again we know this all too well, we are doing nothing else: in the United States, in four of five different locations, there are archives of Armenian testimonies, gathered through long campaigns of forced interviews with aged survivors, for whom the dubious pleasure of testifying coincided necessarily with the approach of their physical death. Moreover, for twenty years and more, these archives have slept quietly on the shelves of institutes and universities that have sponsored said campaigns of testimonial collection. Never does anyone look at them, never does anyone listen to them, read them, study them. Testimonies are not made to be read, heard, and consulted. Besides, they are literally inaudible, illegible, these testimonies. Never has anyone opened them, taken them into account, written a line out of them, integrated them in an interpretation, a reflection. They exist only to be placed on a shelf. They have no more than a potential, never real, existence. That is their very essence. And that is specified shame: the archivization of testimony. But every time one speaks of recognition, of the recognition of the "genocide," as they say, the same thing occurs. Every time, one appeals to the power of the archive, since one asks that the event be recognized as a fact in the world of mortals. Any discourse of recognition thus fundamentally wagers on the archivization of testimony and thereby renews the shame, without ceasing. Each time one utters the word "genocide," even by stating the truth of its occurrence as if it were a fact (since that is what one does when one utters this ignoble word "genocide"), every single time it is a shame.[5] I am numb with shame. For there is no fact without archive and thus without archivization, the becoming-archive of testimony and the functioning of testimony as proof. Each time, the young Italian goes toward the SS. Each time, the Armenian child makes one step forward in the direction of his murderer, entirely abandoned to him. Aram Andonian describes such a scene in his 1919 book, *In These Dark Days*, in which the executioners, simple soldiers accompanying a convoy of deportees in 1915, notice a child hiding behind a mound of sand, no doubt in a corner of the Mesopotamian deserts. And they play with his terror until the child dies of it. Each time, the child is here, abandoned entirely. And each time, the child blushes. He blushes for shame.

In reality, we have seen this abundantly in the last chapter. We are not the ones who make testimony function as proof, we survivors, we jurists or university professors, we candidates for proof. Testimony has always already functioned as proof. It has always already reverted into the archive. The monument has always already been corrupted by the document. The shame (from which I would like to extricate myself so much) is only the sign of this inaugural and irremediable corruption. In the very moment when the first survivor has uttered a word of testimony, at the very instant the first sound came out of his mouth to tell his calvary or his observations, the archive has already seized his speech. That is the catastrophe of the survivor. From the beginning, before the beginning even, the murderer is here, facing me, and he tells me: Prove it! Prove it then if you can! And I, for ninety years, I have stood up and proven it. For ninety years, the fact is amply proven, proven beyond necessity and yet, I stand up always; always I prove, by myself, by my testimony. Everything takes place the way it does when God calls Abraham, in Kafka's rendering.[6] Am I the one called? I answer to the injunction of the executioner. For ninety years, by proving, by making testimony function as proof, I answer to the call and injunction of the executioner. For that is what he wanted from the beginning, is it not? To kill, to eliminate, to exterminate? Of course, he wanted that too. But, above all, he wanted me to prove—and to prove again. And yet . . . why do I stand up? Why me? Did he know in advance that I would rise? Inversely, does Abraham not feel shame? Should he feel shame? One can imagine that divine logic is not so different from the logic of the executioner. One will also understand, for the same reasons, that the paternal sacrifice of the son is not absent from the postcatastrophic Armenian literatures. But that is the object of another work.

AGAINST HISTORY

GIL ANIDJAR

These islands of baobab, shea butter, locust bean, and fig trees preserved the history of the stateless; they were the archive of the defeated.

SAIDIYA HARTMAN

It is necessary, and it is perhaps time to come back to the ahistorical in a sense radically opposed to that of classical philosophy: not to misconstrue negativity, but this time to affirm it—silently. It is negativity and not positive truth that is the nonhistorical capital of history.

JACQUES DERRIDA

History can prove nothing; it is a fabric of denegations.

HAGOP OSHAGAN

TO WRITE HISTORY AFTER AUSCHWITZ IS BARBARIC.
Thus the inescapable conclusion toward which Marc Nichanian leads us.[1] At the provisional limit of the singular trajectory traced by his extended work (of which *The Historiographic Perversion* constitutes a small, if remarkable, part), this formulation is hardly forced, nor does it appear to articulate a substantial departure from Theodor Adorno's famous assertion ("to write poetry after Auschwitz is barbaric"), only an intensification of its claim, indeed, a version or translation of it.[2] Yet, the formulation practically engages with *historical difference*—"our historical differences actually make a difference"—in its claim to bridge the unbridgeable (whence already the importance, or lack thereof, of translation, across time, place, and language) by way of rupture or continuity, given and constructed, particular and universal, included and excluded, contingency and development, pedagogy and progress.[3] It thus partakes

of an attempt, desperate as it may be, to displace the enduring and increasing privilege of *this* difference, the imperialism of historical difference and "the transcendence of its dignity" over others—beginning with the emblematic name of the event, which, Nichanian explains and underscores, makes a difference as well, functioning, as it does here, as another instance of a "difference [that] *is not of a historical or historiographical nature*" (*HP* 54); to contend with its role in the unbearable permanence of the conditions of the event.[4] If, as Michel de Certeau claimed, "the past is first of all the means of *representing a difference*,"[5] what differences are occluded by its privilege? How to conceive of the nature of *historical* difference in the larger field of differentials? What is it that "has put history in the place of the other intellectual powers . . . establishing it as the sole sovereign"?[6] What of the "scientific signature" of history and of its claim to primacy or dominance?[7] How is it, in other words, that "Meaning becomes History"?[8]

The enduring prominence of history at a moment in which "an unnecessary restriction of the battleground for historical power" is perhaps less pertinent than the question of how the matter of power has come to be seen as irrevocably linked to history, as if history were power and, more important, as if power were history.[9] And perhaps it is—yet, assuming it maintains itself, power "works effectively through institutionalized differences," through the institution and management of numerous differences.[10] It is formatted and regulated by them as well. How is it then that, over and against its manifestations, everything still appears as if "power works together with history," associating more strenuously (or subverted and fragilized more dangerously), so we should believe, with this singular, at times even odd, difference?[11] History itself has long become "the power of a discourse that is always susceptible of allowing entry into its community of those excluded when its circle is drawn."[12] These are the politics of historical meaning as well (the relation "between life and history," as Nietzsche puts it), whereby history has been made into "the measure of all social things" (and the quasi-exclusive route toward a demonstration of their resilience, contingency, or finitude), explicitly and implicitly identified as foremost among "cultural technologies of rule," part and whole of "a cultural project of control."[13] After Auschwitz, after the Catastrophe, "history is still a disguised theology;"[14] it is still "the primary discipline of all human sciences."[15].

By what means does it become so? How does history function and operate? How does it *manage*? Nichanian's empirico-transcendental answer—the archive—is deceptively simple.[16] Yet, understanding it requires that we first consider how history extricates itself from "among the discourses even after the process of disaggregation has codified their differences."[17] History limits itself "to one rationality" (one might say: to one theory of meaning) and thus "respects the outcome of that long (and uneven) process of disciplinary disaggregation." And, indeed, respecting this outcome without understanding not only "the historical process" but also the other, numerous differential operations that fashion and structure its path and aftermath, "tends to obscure the traces of likeness that linger in modern discourses," of which history is but one.[18] Thus history spreads and grows across an increasingly large discursive field. But it does so out of the source of its legitimacy, its ground and legitimation, at times quite literally a legal and juridical one: the archive.[19] History—which is to say, the discipline of history, as well as, beyond historicism, "the overlapping sites where history is produced, notably outside of academia,"[20] and finally the general discourse of proof, evidence, and testimony *whereby facts are understood and validated as contingent on the archive*—is the condition of possibility of mass murder in the age of technological reproduction.[21] As Nichanian cuttingly puts it: "The power of the archive is what has made possible the genocidal will as such" (*HP* 16).

As for poetry (as Adorno calls it) and, more generally, literature—history's paradigmatic other—whether it relinquishes the discourse of proof and evidence (confining itself to nonarchivization, as if it were possible) or seeks to create another measure of evidence (claiming a more inclusive or subtle archive), it may turn out to be less complicit with history than coconstituted with and by it.[22] Literature, in other words, may be less of a threat, less even of an alternative, to history than we think. Instead, it validates the archive that history fashions (a popularized Vichian artifactuality—the omnipresent rhetoric of making and production—has, after all, long united history and literature, fact and fiction).[23] And the validation of the archive, the repetition of its legitimacy—"the archive is first the law of what can be said"—as that which guards and ensures preservation and the endurance of memory, is the crucial mechanism whereby a fact is defined as leaving a *documented*, archivable, and archived remainder.[24] The alleged silence, the muteness of witnesses, among others, is thereby explained, revealing the essential relation of the archive to silence. For that which is neither in, nor of, the archive, nor admissible by its guardians, remains mute (that is to say, it is marked and produced *as* mute).[25] Even if it can be uttered, it does not register as having been said, much less heard. Worse: once archived, *if* archived, that is to say, once it has surrendered to archivization, testimony *becomes* inaudible, illegible, merely that which *awaits* those who will "make it talk"—if at all.[26]

THE DESTRUCTION OF THE ARCHIVE

At stake is something more, something else, than the growing attention to knowledge *production*, to the way in which "any document presents itself and . . . contributes to constructing the 'reality' of the past."[27] For this is where the destruction *of* the archive (double genitive) begins.[28] This is how the archive "constitutes the condition of possibility [and impossibility] for any destruction to become a historical fact in the eyes of civilized humanity" (*HP* 12). Equipped with such facts and with its historical consciousness, "civilized humanity" (and not only the historians) ignores one alternative fact—albeit one that is bereft of factuality—that the archive is not only, or even necessarily, predicated upon production and exclusion, even destruction and loss (of life, of individuals, communities, and cities, of books and libraries), but that it is itself an instrument and a technology of mass destruction.[29] Surely, we have learned that the archive "defines the mode of occurrence of the statement-thing"; it is that "which gives to what we can say—and to itself, the object of our discourse—its modes of appearance, its forms of existence and coexistence."[30] But it constitutes therefore the conditions of the object's appearance *and* disappearance, existence and nonexistence; the fact, as it were, of its nonoccurrence. Beyond "the rarity of the documents,"[31] then, the archive raises an issue that also goes beyond "the possibility of access to the documentation" or the ability "to learn to read the evidence against the grain, against the intentions of those who had produced it."[32] It grounds a capacity whereby, contemporary with, yet in excess of, recent technological developments, the possibility is "offered to part of humankind to make reality appear and disappear with a simple gesture."[33] The archive is this very capacity and the site of its erasure, for, without it, facts—the only reality there would be for "apologists of the factual"—disappear.[34] And what "civilized humanity" ignores is precisely the silent way in which this occurs (as another event of dubious factuality), what, following Jacques Derrida, Nichanian designates as "the violence of the archive itself, *as archive, as archival violence.*"[35]

The archive, in other words, is hardly remedial, or even a palliative to the ills of loss—and the dream of a better, all-inclusive, or more plural archive, which is the very dream of history as total history (and histories), only denies this further.[36] Instead, the archive ensures once and for all that what is and what is not preserved in it *becomes*, as it were, twice over, lost and, indeed, destroyed.[37] This is how history "speaks of the past only in order to bury it."[38] And that which the archive guards and preserves, in other (silent) words, it *guards to death.*[39] Institutionalized by historical discourse (which may or may not master it—"I am not capable of taking part in the production of the sources I analyze," says the historian—but finds in them his ground), sealed and confirmed by jurists and by the law, the archive regulates disciplinary divisions and guarantees that the perfect murder—a crime without a trace—will never achieve the status of fact.[40] For, had there been a murder, "it would have been remembered and recorded." And, since this was not so, since no document is found, the historical conclusion is inevitable: there was no murder.[41] Better yet, the persistence of traces enables its erasure and, ultimately, its destruction. As Eduardo Cadava puts it in a proximate context, "we could even say that truth means the making of ashes."[42] Surely, it is difficult to erase all the traces of a murder, but such erasure is the precise challenge to which the "genocidal will" (*la volonté génocidaire*) decides resolutely to rise.[43] Along with the historian, and together with him, the genocidal will acknowledges, nay, relishes that only the archive counts. It recognizes as well that some traces may remain, but that these may never make it into the archive, that they may never become *documents*, much less qualify as *evidence*. Such traces need not be erased therefore. They have already been destroyed, that is to say, invalidated by history—the growing discourse of the archive.[44] "The functions of memory and storage on which the law is based dominate the phantasm of a 'recollection,' which in spite of its name was evoked to make the truth forgettable."[45] This is how one can accumulate, in a manner that is at once practical and utterly impractical, thousands and thousands of pages on the shelves of libraries, thousands and thousands of images and video recordings, all of which go unread, unwatched ("This was probably the first time that people in a writing culture were reduced to the recognition of signs," writes Friedrich Kittler about the onset of this practice).[46] This is also how one can register and even admit that massacres did take place, while insisting that genocide did not occur. Thus, there is no silence to reclaim, for the work of the archive ensures that some traces will never amount to evidence (the archive, as we will see again, regulates disciplinary divisions, between history and literature, for example). In this context and others, as Nichanian shows, no testimony ever suffices to *prove* genocide, nor could it do so without participating in the validation of the archive—and of the historian.[47] No evidence, at any rate, could resist the particular contribution made by the genocidal will by means of the archive, namely, the planned destruction of the notion of fact by way of the archive ("The genocidal-denegating machine is dedicated to destroy *the very notion of fact*," *HP* 27). No archive, no fact. This is why it must be said that "genocide is not a fact." For genocide—singularly defined by Nichanian as the bringing about, following the strictest rules of history and law, of a nonevent "which thus denies in itself and by itself its belonging to history, which negates and denies its own factuality" (*HP* 73)—is the perverse achievement of a will that has learned everything it needs to know from historians and from their definition of the fact. It has learned everything it needs to know from the exponential growth of the archive—and its destruction.

This is why, finally, to write history—that "Handbook of Inward Culti-vation for Outward Barbarians," as Nietzsche called it—after the Catas-trophe is barbaric.[48]

IN PRAISE OF HISTORY

Nichanian's conclusion, and the demonstration leading to it such as it occurs in *The Historiographic Perversion*, may well be irreceivable. And not only by historians, who are hardly its only target (as if poets were Adorno's addressees!). For what would it mean not so much to do away with (much less to improve or reform) as to *indict* history? It is a pecu-liar feature of our age that, in a manner that appears to be at odds with the general culture (what Christopher Lasch diagnosed as "our culture's indifference to the past"), historical difference continues to dominate at once consciousness and understanding of "our time" as "historical time."[49] Whatever meaning one grants these phrases—indeed, what-ever meaning we may find in history—the wish to "make history" and the multiplication of histories and "historical breakthroughs," along with the rush to an irremediably redemptive future; the fact that we are unable "to conceive of a politics without a fantasy of the future" or to relinquish the figure of the survivor at the center of our political imagination; the generalized imperatives of memory (what the French called *le devoir de mémoire*); not to mention the drive, indeed, the com-mand to protect and back up our private and collective hard drives on "time-machines" (assuming, that is, we could do otherwise and actually manage to *erase* those ever so important bits and gigs of data along with the fantasy of plenitudinous conservation), all testify to the enduring force—rather than to the poverty—of history.[50] Indeed, in the face of repeated calls (not to mention pedagogical, cultural, and political prac-tices) consigning it to its own dustbin ("History is more or less bunk," as Henry Ford famously put it) or announcing its end (Fukuyama style), history has managed to preserve and even accrue a surprising measure of symbolic and cultural capital, doing so in a way that few discourses, not to mention disciplines, have, whether in the public sphere or in the human and social sciences.[51] And so it is that "in the last generation or so the universe of historians has been expanding at a dizzying rate,"[52] while "the scope of historical writing has expanded enormously in the past thirty years."[53] Sublime in that it is marked at once by utter fascination and total disdain for history, ours remains a historical time nonetheless, dominated by "the still existing belief in secular progress" and enduring notions of "meaning in history";[54] pervaded by the Vichian notion that history is made by men, "that men have themselves made this world of nations";[55] perversely preoccupied with history and histories, new historians and new historicisms and ever newer histories, made and re-made; as well as simultaneously obsessed with "the end of history" and other eschatologies, that is to say, still, with history.[56] And, although there are distinctions to be made between these signs of a historical drive and the unprecedented intensification of technologies and processes of archivization, the rule of the archive cannot fail to have strengthened micro- and macropractices of history and historicization.[57] And so, like the desert, the archive grows.

It might be worth lingering on this. History, "mother of all the sciences of man," as Foucault called it, is hardly standing out among the *embattled* disciplines. Instead, it has successfully managed to remain in fashion. In this country, history programs and departments are among the largest in faculties of arts and sciences, their size having for the most part remained stable over the past few decades, while in some cases they have even grown bigger, expanding to other departments by way of joint programs or others.[58] In publishing trends (assuming these do grant access to meaning of any sort), historical books and historical biographies are significantly represented at the top of best-seller lists. The presence of history, and of historical experts, in specialized television channels and programs as well as in film production, in museums and memorials, and in public debates, as well as, finally (or perhaps first of all), in courts of law—all this cannot be considered negligible. Nor can one ignore the endless, and necessarily historical, discussions of "modernity" (or better yet, "modernities") or the fact that, along with it, "historical time" too has received renewed attention. Our historical age, its historical sense, and its numerous sources of support have been scrutinized, hyperbolized, and, again, historicized. As well, there have been highly public disputes among historians, disputes that have increased rather than diminished the importance of their claims and the public investment, however managed, in the work of history. It is most likely along these lines as well that one should consider the dwindling opposition or at least the resistance to history. For there *are* numerous critiques of historicism if not of history (Friedrich Nietzsche articulating the most famous among them) and of some aspect or other of the discipline of history (more recently Michel de Certeau, Hayden White, Robert Young, Michel-Rolph Trouillot, Ranajit Guha, and Dipesh Chakrabarty). Yet, had history been rendered vulnerable by these "attacks" and internal dissensions, one would expect historians to be on the defensive *as historians* and understandably so. Professional feuds and laments about irrelevance notwithstanding, one looks in vain for the "unhappy consciousness" of historians—or their institutional fragility. Instead, everybody is a historian, as one utters or hears ever more calls for historicization, articulating "a reaffirmation of historicism almost as if nothing had happened."[59] New kinds of histories are made and remade (microhistory, the new cultural history, among others), new methods as well, and novel objects (from the family to masturbation and from the book to the footnote) pass with great speed under the steady gaze of the historical disciplines. Compared to literary critics, whose very object and function have rarely been more uncertain and fragile (unless they become literary historians or biographers), even vanishing, and who can, with good reason, write of "the death of a discipline";[60] compared with anthropologists, whose collusion with colonial powers was singularly criticized (but they are making a strong comeback now, courtesy of the U.S. military);[61] and compared to Orientalists, whose legitimacy was brought under spectacular interrogation,[62] historians seem simply to have failed to perceive themselves as humbled or marginalized, as being in any significant way under duress. This is why one can hardly imagine, with any degree of seriousness, an *apologia pro vita historia* being written today, one that would argue that history is *not* bunk, that it *is* in fact important. Who, after all, would doubt it? Who would consciously oppose the claims of history? One may, of course, remain indifferent to history, or ignorant of it, but one would hardly go so far today as to *oppose* history (thus resistance to history more often than not translates in proposing a new and improved history—or better yet, histories). What need could there be to defend it? to attack it? There are, to be sure, those who resist history (or more precisely, historicism), those who do not engage with history, and those who refrain from deploying historical thinking. But these are easily deemed ahistorical or worse: essentialists, who rarely make an explicit case against history. Then, there are obviously those—entire disciplines, in fact—who can afford to ignore history. Set in their ways (which, it must be said, they do not fail carefully to archive), they hardly dent the extraordinary and resilient faith in the efficacy of history's lessons, or the current debates over creation and evolution, not to mention the genetic longings that favor communities of ancestors over exploded solidarities (no doubt, the search for origins and/or beginnings is *almost* over, and genealogy sites are about to go out of business too). What's more, there are still many who uphold history and aggrandize it, seeking to question its ethnocentrism in order to claim it for themselves and a larger dominion for it; those who dread the possibility of studying (or worse, of ever having been among) "peoples without history" (or, God forbid, without historians). Entire collectives celebrate—and are celebrated for—their "return to history" or for discovering that they too were blessedly endowed with historical consciousness. There are yet others who see in history—or again, histories—our inescapable condition, who exhibit a melancholic sense that we have lost an otherwise mediated access to tradition, and that for better or for worse we live in historical time. Simultaneously shrinking and expanding, the "world domain of history" lacks clear contours, no doubt, and yet it seems to determine ever more of *our* time, which must thus rightfully be called, still, the historical age. Henry Ford himself would testify to this dominance of historical difference, with his own impatient insistence on "the history we make today" and his devoted investment, ultimately, in the future. It is in paradoxical ways then that history prevails. The call to "historicize" is thus still heard loudly, along with the obligatory lament that our historical sense is disappearing. Memory, at least, must be defended. But history? The answer, implicitly and explicitly running through growing archives, libraries of scholarly inquiries and historical novels, appears to be resolutely negative. And if history needs no defense, what then of its critique? Must history be assaulted? Must the archive? The specificity of our time, the manner in which we identify in this historical concern (or lack thereof) the ground of our singularity (our modernity) and the incessant drive toward progress and the new—such would be the expanding sum of history's presence, the difference history makes, and, perhaps, its rule over us.

FOUCAULT'S HISTORY

"The age of history," as Michel Foucault in fact called it, is the age in which historical difference reigns.[63] In *The Order of Things* Foucault describes a constant oscillation and redistribution between conditions and elements or moments, differentially and strategically isolated.[64] Signifying a historical break, "man" is an apt, and related, illustration here, since Foucault obviously never claimed that there were no human beings before the modern period. Rather, whereas in the classical *episteme* "nature, human nature, and their relations, are definite and predictable functional moments" (*OT* 310), whereas in it human beings were allotted "a privileged position in the order of the world" (*OT* 318), modernity would bring about a new man, man "as a primary reality with his own density, as the difficult object and sovereign subject of all possible knowledge" (*OT* 310). Man, in other words, is now "designated—more required" by the novel distribution of things (labor, life, language) (*OT* 313), transcending while partaking of them. As subject and object, man belongs to two distinct levels (he is the "empirico-transcendental doublet"), at once element and condition. In the general distributive field of the episteme, one recognizes that history is also affected by this division. History is an empirical science; even "the first and as it were the mother of all the sciences of man" (*OT* 367). Yet, if history has "a special position," it is "because the object of the human sciences—man—is a historical being."[65] History is thus much more than a particular science. In fact, it is "the fundamental mode of being of empiricities, upon the basis of which they are affirmed, posited, arranged, and distributed in the space of knowledge for the use of such disciplines or sciences as may arise" (*OT* 219). Singled out and isolated and, more important, generalized and universalized, history "defines the birthplace of the empirical, that from which, prior to all established chronology, it derives its own being. It is no doubt because of this that History becomes so soon divided, in accordance with an ambiguity that it is probably impossible to control, into an empirical science of events and that radical mode of being that prescribes their destiny to all empirical beings, to those particular beings that we are" (*OT* 219). Like man, history appears as an empirico-transcendental doublet.

It is not surprising that Foucault would assert about it that "History has become the unavoidable element in our thought" (*OT* 219), just like Order was for the classical age.[66] And nowhere is this unavoidability more ironically apparent perhaps than in Gary Gutting's assertion that the value of Foucault's own work in *The Order of Things* is contingent on the *historical* work it should have generated. Gutting underscores the (somehow dubious) fact that the book "has not yet provided a major stimulus to further *historical* work. It therefore remains to be seen whether it will be justified by its refutations."[67] As a fundamental, and unavoidable, mode of being and knowing, history comes to occupy a transcendental position. It obviously belongs to the conditions of possibility of the modern episteme. And its novelty must therefore be contended with, but to declare this novelty *historical* is paradoxically to erase its contingent emergence ("the harshness of its historical irruption," as Foucault writes [*OT* 250]) across a wider epistemic and doxological field, as well as the possibility of its demise.[68] As one element among others (but the great expanse of the word *element* has now grown and become divided at once), as one discipline among others, history still belongs to an ephemeral arrangement, to a field of distribution, a set of *dispositions* that testifies to its own limits. Can we not say about history that which Foucault said about man? The question then would not be "does man really exist?" but "does history really exist?" (*OT* 322). And for how long? Indeed, if a disappearance of man was conceivable (is it still?), what of a disappearance of history? What would thinking be without a history of thought? Without history? And who would be thinking then? ("Who is speaking? [*Qui parle?*]" is a central question of modernity [*OT* 305]. Thinking otherwise than history would perhaps not answer to, nor answer for, such inquisitive requests or means for identification.) Would we, *could* we, we humans, be without history? At stake is less "the end of history" (as the familiar slogan now has it), but a giving up (Foucault uses the verb *renoncer*, as does Nichanian) of historical thinking—a cutting of history and of historians down to size. Foucault is pointing toward this finitude of history when he suggests that space was the inescapable dimension of the classical age, whereas, after Hegel at least, "it is just as absurd to fancy that a philosophy can transcend its contemporary world, as it is to fancy that an individual can overleap his own age, jump over Rhodes."[69] If space could become the figure of contingence (who, after all, has not "jumped," if not over, certainly out of her "own" space today? Who has not embarked on Hannah Arendt's Sputnik?), then what of history?[70] Indeed, what if history had been no more than "a figure occurring between two modes of language"? What if history too were to "return to that serene nonexistence in which [it] was formerly maintained by the imperious unity of Discourse?" What "if those arrangements were to disappear as they appeared"? What "if some event of which we can at the moment do no more than sense the possibility— without knowing either what its form will be or what it promises—were to cause them to crumble"? What if one were to wager that history will be erased, along with man, "like a face drawn in the sand at the edge of the sea"? (*OT* 386–387). Foucault signaled toward the promise (or the threat) of this very erasure and disappearance in the "countersciences" of ethnology, psychoanalysis, and linguistics. He pursued it in setting for himself the task of revealing "a *positive unconscious* of knowledge" (*OT* xi). More visibly, he inscribed it in the very titles of his works. Placing less emphasis on "the diachronic progress of knowledge but much more on its synchronic depth,"[71] Foucault underscored the difference history makes and, more important, the difference it makes *among* differences (resemblance or identity, structure or function, words and things). It is a new kind of difference and, to be sure, "an invention of recent date." Foucault thus insisted on what would seem like a paradox only to an all-too sedimented *doxa*, namely, the historicity of history. Yet, were it possible, a history of history (or of "resisting history") would hardly constitute a "counterscience" ("it is always possible to make human sciences of human sciences—the psychology of psychology, the sociology of sociology, etc." [*OT* 354–355]). Quite the contrary. It would be the confirmation that finitude is not an attribute of history, much less of the historian who finds historical meaning even where it escapes him. Indeed, "when historians historicize history, which itself is rare, they do so according to the strict rules of historiography."[72] Foucault, for his part, pursued "a background interrogation of the nature of history as *historia*"— he had to contend with those who perceived his work as denying "the very possibility of change" (*OT* xii). But instead of looking to another history, or asking for one, Foucault defended a "comparative method" (*OT* x) that he called "archaeology" and "genealogy"—not history ("Such an enterprise is not so much a history, in the traditional meaning of the word, as an 'archaeology'" [*OT* xxii]). It is only later on that he explicitly "returned" to an affirmation of history (a return that resonates no doubt with his "return to the subject").[73] After him, many were those who followed, seeking their own "return to history," and so history expanded and increased its hegemonic rule over intellectual labor in the humanities and social sciences.[74] And who—and in the name of whom—would want to *criticize* history and claim to tread at its *limits* or at its *ends*?

This, then, is the historical age—otherwise as implausible a moniker as "the secular age"—providing the background upon which two seemingly distinct conceptions coexist awkwardly, if ultimately with little conflict. One is grounded in the imperative to "always historicize" (increasingly translated perhaps as "always archive"—and, certainly, always back up your hard drive) and in the faith that its implementation will bring about redemption and improvement (indeed, that it has brought precisely such improvement, if not redemption, about and will continue to ensure and protect it).[75] The other is the conviction that the progress so far achieved is of such magnitude that no lesson from the past could possibly benefit us. In geopolitical terms, one could roughly call the first conception Europe, and the second the United States of

America. At any rate, in both cases, one singular difference—historical difference—functions as the primary determination that, trumping race, class, gender, and religion, grounds self-perception and self-presentation and the imperious drives of self-expansion. In both conceptions, one finds, as Reinhart Koselleck did, "that the more a particular time is experienced as a new temporality, as 'modernity,' the more that demands made of the future increase."[76] But—and here is where Nichanian's contribution lies—it is not the rule of development that defines history (read: historicism). It is the rule of the archive. Nichanian's assault on history, or, more precisely, his devastating recognition that history—the discourse of the archive—is the condition of, not simply the prelude to, barbarism, implies a hyperbolic, and impossible, call for total rejection ("One would have, in effect, to renounce history," *HP* 54). Impossible, if only because barbarism may be inevitable (to invoke a different, but related, sphere of practice, those who believe that "once an alcoholic, always an alcoholic"—the rule of essentialism—may condemn themselves to repetition, with or without difference, by virtue of this very trait). And impossible, as well, because the rejection is, of necessity, uttered from within history. It is in this context, moreover, that one may wonder about the impact of earlier critiques of history (if such is the way to understand the "crisis of historicism" and the so-called postmodern, i.e., postcolonial, "challenge").[77] Finally, and more important, it may well be that the least appropriate response is attempting to come up with yet another *novelty* (and yet, as Ranajit Guha recognizes, "the pursuit of things goes on, the pursuit of novelty for its own sake").[78] In the face of Catastrophe—the mourning of mourning—what novelty, what mourning is possible? What contribution, in other words, could still be made to the archive? Marc Nichanian—writer, translator, literary critic, philosopher—looks after the impossible. On the one hand, he tends to "keep silent with (and about) a certain silence."[79] On the other, he looks after monuments of mourning that, irreceivable from within historical time, are not simply outside it. These monuments cannot be fashioned either (not constructed, made, produced, or invented), nor can they surrender to the demands of the historical age. They are, strictly speaking, *unfashionable*.

DENIALS

One well-known adversary did put historians on the defensive, of course, attempting—or so it would seem—a proximate assault on history.[80] The word *negationism*, used throughout this translation to refer to this adversary, is not quite an English word. In the original French (*négationisme*), the word refers to a specific kind of denial, most prominently to Holocaust denial.[81] Yet the word acquired currency when it became clear that the label, applied to those who wanted to revise the historical record (namely, *révisionnistes*), could grant them legitimacy and credit. They might be perceived as participating in a wider, and not illegitimate, movement of historical revisionisms.[82] Indeed, historians are in many ways professional revisionists. They interrogate the veracity of the biblical account of the Exodus, the significance of the French revolution, or the history of objectivity. They debate and change their mind regarding what constitutes a historical document, the value of evidence, and the limits of the archive. Over time, they have expanded the definition of the historical object and participated in the transformation of the concept of event. Insofar as the discipline of history is itself historical, it is always open to *revision*. Surely historical disputes antedate the institution of history as a modern discipline, and it is a matter of further debate whether professional historians have managed to restrict the range of potential discord or exacerbated it and to what effect. Still, as I have already suggested, the importance of historical questions, the arguments surrounding them, and the public echo they receive in museum exhibits and the erection of memorials and monuments, in television programs and the making of blockbuster movies, in newspapers and magazines and even on the pages of numerous books, as well as, finally, in politicians' statements (from slavery to Vietnam, from colonialism to genocide), cannot be gainsaid, even if the measure of significance of all this is itself open to discussion. Are historical disputes, reconstructions, and revisions truly about history or are they epiphenomenal, displacements of, even screens for, contemporary agendas, struggles, and conditions?

Negationism is, or should be, a different matter. It crosses beyond the legitimate dispute and claims that a particular event did not take place. In a manner that is deemed anything but thought provoking or plausibly playful (think, for arguable contrast, of Jean Baudrillard and his *The Gulf War Did Not Take Place*), negationism seeks to assert that the *factuality* of an event has not been established and that the historical record, here too, is open to revision. Negationism is usually met with strenuous opposition. In many countries, negationism—the denial of the Holocaust—is punishable by law. Yet, there is nothing obvious about the congruence it seems to occasion between history and law (a congruence that, moreover, exceeds the specific occasion). These are after all two distinct fields of practice, even if they also share much, both historically and methodologically, procedurally.[83] Why should a rebuttal of negationism take this particular form? Why should courts adjudicate on historical events or on their denial? There are many ways of answering these questions, but posing them should suffice to reveal that which Marc Nichanian is most committed to expose and demonstrate in *The Historiographic Perversion*: the fundamental consensus, shared by jurists and historians, over the definition of a historical fact (the more substantial dispute over who wields the power and authority to finally adjudicate is another, if perhaps less interesting, issue). More disturbing, no doubt, is Nichanian's compelling realization that negationists partake of that consensus as well. And so, finally, do the murderers.

As a practical and concrete matter—his argument hardly takes place in some abstract dimension: it engages public figures, state institutions and harsh current debates, changes in legislation and professional standards—Nichanian's argument should not be unexpected (even if it unsettles us). "All sciences," Lorraine Daston and Peter Galison remind us, "must deal with the problem of selecting and constituting 'working objects,' as opposed to the too plentiful and too various natural objects."[84] If all it took to determine the "working object," and to admit an event onto the stage of history, were "just one witness," the science of history would have become no more than a vast field of competing rumors.[85] And perhaps it has. Still, at an institutional level, it would have had too many objects and would never have acquired the rigor, credibility, and respectability worthy of an academic field (as Daston and Galison put it, "the Borgesian archive of all historical information would duplicate history, not explain it").[86] Our very sense of what a fact is (assuming our relation to facts is, primarily, a matter of sense or sensibility) would not only be different. If recognizable at all, it would have a very different practical and institutional shape. As things stand, many factors are necessary in order for a fact to be one, from structures of legitimacy to political decisions, from memory claims to cultural practices. And the congruence of law and science, jurists and historians. Minimally, though, a fact, a historical fact, is that which can be proven—and the language of proof and evidence is here key—by appealing to witnesses and documents, all of which constitute (or fail to constitute) an archive. It is this constellation of elements (witness, proof, document, archive, fact) that brings together the historian and the judge, the witness and the perpetrator.[87] It is on its basis that Marc Nichanian can write "genocide is not a fact."

For the question ultimately involves that which fails to register on the historical scales. And one must contend with "the destruction of that which constitutes the condition of possibility for any destruction to become a historical fact in the eyes of civilized humanity: the archive."[88] Again, as Sigmund Freud famously insisted, a murder that would leave no traces is difficult to carry out. Part of the difficulty has to do with the nature of the deed (the degree to which one could speak of the occurrence of a disappearance), but also with the attributes of the traces, the admissibility of evidence. In however a manner, these are related, with various degrees of proximity, to changes in the norms and comportments of science (forensic or other). If, on the other hand, "the history of scientific objectivity is surprisingly short," it is also because evidentiary objects—traces, evidence, procedure—have been defined anew.[89] To be sure, Daston and Galison trace the history of objectivity "as a new way of studying nature, and of being a scientist" (17). In this specific realm, "objectivity is blind sight," a form of knowledge "that bears no trace of the knower—knowledge unmarked by prejudice or skill, fantasy or judgment, wishing or striving. Objectivity is blind sight, seeing without inference, interpretation or intelligence" (17). Here the archive is supposed to testify, as it were, by itself, as if under the gaze of no one. Without entering into the enduring "conflict of the faculties," it is not hard to recognize that the historical disciplines have also refigured or reinvented their objects and methods in such a manner as to alter reigning notions of what constitutes evidence, and fact, when it comes to historical events. These deploy a different aesthetic perhaps. Nichanian writes elsewhere not of the blind sight of the scholar but of the mute voice of the native who shadows and foreshadows the witness.[90] Martin Harries compellingly formulates a proximate version of this argument when he considers figurations of Lot's wife and speaks of "the formal logic of spectatorship in various disciplines—from histories of theater, from film theory, from psychoanalysis, from art history," and beyond. For Harries, the twentieth century in particular "had a particular investment in a formal logic that placed the spectator in a spot where that spectator had to contemplate her own destruction."[91] Now a murderer does not need to agree with the prevailing norms of justice, evidentiary and testimonial procedures, in order to enact that destruction, in order to adopt a practical behavior that affirms and countersigns the same notion of evidence as the justice system. And such applies to the mass murderer as well: "the murderer himself did not preserve any trace of his crime in his own memory."[92] What then of the witness? One could debate the history of the perfect crime or the (recent or ancient) origins not only of genocide but also of the willful attempt to hide and deny it. Is there nothing new under the sun when it comes to genocide? Nichanian insists that this would be—that it is—a strange assertion for a historian to make; that it would be a bizarre *historical* conception to adopt.[93] More important, however, is that historians have failed to understand (there is a less generous way of phrasing this) that "genocide is not a fact." The singularity of the genocidal will was always already intent on the destruction of spectatorship, on erasing all the traces and all the evidences linked to its murderous actions.[94] Understanding the nature of the archive, the genocidal will was always and precisely intent on leaving no archive (and therefore no witness) behind. Unlike countless historical massacres that were willfully publicized, used as a mark of greatness or meant to instill fear (one thinks of Genghis Khan), genocide is akin to the perfect crime, that is, to a crime intent on leaving no traces. And, like the perfect crime, genocide is therefore perpetrated by first acknowledging, then accepting the same notion of evidence as the historical system, the very notion of fact upheld by historians. And it is this very fact that the genocidal will is bent on destroying.

> History, here, as a discipline, is perfectly powerless. The absence or nonexistence of the archive is not an adjacent fact, secondary in relation to the will to exterminate. Rather, it must be understood that it lies at its core. There can be no archives of the will to exterminate if it is true that this will is founded, in its essence, on the very destruction of the archive. This is also why there can be no memory and, subsequently, no mourning for the extermination. (*WDNR* 14).

Like the historian, the genocidal will knows that reality—the collection of facts in the archive—is fully coextensive with what can be proven, documented, archived. History, in other words, is a revisionism. It is "that affirmation of the nonplace of the event that bears the name revisionism."[95] That nonplace is the archive, and there is no fact but such fact. Nothing outside the fact. Accordingly, it is this shared understanding of the fact—by murderers and historians, by jurists and archivists alike—that makes genocide into what it is. Or, rather, into what it is not. Genocide is *not* a fact.

> The planned murder did not consist in mere killing. The planned murder consisted, however one understands this, in erasing the death of the victims, in eradicating all traces of death and (accessorily) of murder. It consisted not in killing life, but in killing death. This last formulation is, alas, not at all rhetorical. The suppression of death by way of the suppression of the archive is the essence of genocide. (*HP* 55)

Only in this manner can one understand how the same group of French historians who had vocally and vociferously mobilized *against* the negationism of a Robert Faurisson could go on to gather *in support* of the negationism of a Gilles Veinstein and a Bernard Lewis. Nichanian is very clear and finds here the point of departure for his rich and complex demonstration. It is not simply that *this* genocide rather than *that* one share a distinct status in relation to fact. *It is that the notion of fact around which the consensus holds is predicated on the negation of genocide.* A fact is constituted by its traces, by the evidence that emerge from the archive, by the force of documents legitimated by the historian (and the judge). By agreeing with this definition of the historical fact, by having invented it along with its conditions of possibility in the first place, historians produced the necessary background without which genocide could never occur and, simultaneously, that which genocide can never be. A fact. Put another way, which I have quoted earlier, "the power of the archive is what has made possible the genocidal will as such" (*HP* 16). Thus is "an event produced that thereby denies in itself and of itself its belonging to history, that negates and denies its own factuality" (*HP* 73). Therein lies the profound and profoundly disturbing intelligence and power of the genocidal will. And therein the complicity of historians and jurists in the genocidal apparatus, a complicity—this should not have to be said— that goes beyond any intentionality.[96]

The harshness of the indictment, which focuses most directly on historians, their concepts and practices, does not spare those who have tried, with distinct protocols, to uphold the notion of testimony as evidence ("the primary transformation of testimony into a discourse of proof") or, as Nichanian puts it, those who have made testimony into a document for the archive (Nichanian here relies on, but also departs from, the distinction made by Foucault between document and monument).[97] In his earlier work, Nichanian asks about the overwhelming absence of literary texts among Armenian writers after the Catastrophe, as well as the disaster that seems to have been articulated *before* it. The emphasis on testimonial, indeed, testamentary and mournful, writing leads Nichanian to trace the modern figure of the witness to its philological origins (following Foucault, Giorgio Agamben had traced it to more recent linguistic developments).[98] After Edward Said, it is philology that prepares the ground for the historical, documentary, and testamentary thinking here at work. Philology, the unity of a division that made history and literature into mournful accomplices, created the archive, which the genocidal will knew it only had to bypass to produce an event that would not be one. I want to linger on Nichanian's literary trajectory in order to consider what brought him to return to philology, to see in it the condition of possibility of "the witness and the archive" (as Agamben has it), of literature and history.

THE HISTORY OF LITERATURE

The task Marc Nichanian has long set for himself, then, is explicitly to counter history, not simply to criticize it toward an elusive and self-correcting goal. It is a task that, in an early formulation, "does not present itself in the form of a history" for "history is still, despite all renewals of the discipline, the discourse of facts" (*WDNR* 10). That is why "we have first to free this event, the Catastrophe, from everything that weighs against its comprehension, in particular from the ballast that historical and political approaches always introduced into it. It is a question of liberating the Catastrophe of everything that transforms it into an object, an instance, or a fact, that gives a delusory *meaning* to it" (11–12). At an earlier stage, however, there were explicit efforts to write, indeed, to *improve* history, more specifically, "a history of the Armenian language through its ages and usages" (*AULA* 22). *Ages et usages de la langue arménienne* was consciously intended as a history, albeit of a different kind, one that sought to "escape entirely the domain of assured knowledge by focusing the inquiry on the question of 'literarization,'" the becoming-literary of the Armenian language through events and ruptures that define a new periodization . . . to consider contemporary problems through historical aspects that are not, habitually, taken into account (24–25). Appealing to the literary as the other side of history, Nichanian demonstrates his ability to write history, "to produce self-consciously and with the historian's methods," a more expansive and inclusive history, "a history that does not yet exist."[99] Typically extending the dominion of that more inclusive history, he sets out to write the history of a language that would examine

> the meaning of the process of "literarization," which is to say of the *conditions* in which a language becomes "literary" and the *modalities* of this phenomenon. What will hold our attention first and foremost is therefore the series of *ruptures* in the history of this language and the consciousness its speakers had of them. . . . It is the history of conceptions and of receptions: conceptions of the language in general through the ages, as much as one can have access to them; receptions of the spoken language and of its popular usages. (24–25)

But note that the principles Nichanian identifies as making such literarization possible (one, a principle of centralization [76]; two, a setting to work of the community [82]; and, three, a principle of separation from the foreign, a passage through the foreign that is also a foreclosure of it [84–85]) are said to be of a nature that is neither linguistic nor historiographic ("Can a historiographic account bring about the evidence related to the reasons and conditions that enable the birth of a 'literary language'? Circumstantial reasons should not mask *what is actually happening*" [86; emphasis added]). In other words, it is already the case that the notion of an event ("what is actually happening") is marked as that which exceeds (or has exceeded so far) the limits of a *historical* inquiry. Nichanian will go so far as to prefigure his later efforts when underscoring his attempt to refrain from considering literary works as "'archives' that would enable in a way the 'documentation' of the states of spoken language" (139). And yet, at this point, the endeavor remains remedial. It is to critically engage previous historical projects and, indeed, entire bibliographies. Nichanian clarifies that "there exists an entire bibliography of volumes, written essentially in the Armenian language, the object of which is *apparently* the same as the one that occupies us here: to retrace a history of the Armenian language by highlighting the salient epochs of its evolution" (29–30; emphasis added).

And so, subtle reservations notwithstanding, there seems to remain a confident clarity regarding the singularity of literature, at least for a while. There is, in other words, the promise of "another history, very different, and distinct from that of the historians, vaguer and more fluid" (*ATRN* 158). That is why, on several occasions, Nichanian could lament the manner in which writers of undeniable literary talent and stature had transformed themselves into "secretaries of the archive."[100] As he puts it in *The Historiographic Perversion*, "these writers, the greatest of the century among the Armenians, expressed their readiness to become the secretaries of testimony and, in truth, of the archive, to the point that they themselves chose to inflict the fatal blow on literature" (*HP* 15; and see, e.g., *ATRN* 264). The promise (even if rarely) and singularity of literature—literature as standing *aside* or *outside* of history—emerged around the question of whether literature had something else to say, something different regarding and about history, precisely, and the Catastrophe, if not or not only regarding the facts.[101]

> Do writers and poets have more to say about the national revolution and its relatedness to the Catastrophe than, say, the actors themselves or the historians, or, again, the political interpreters of the events? Yes, they have, but not because they are able to see the historical circumstances with more insight or because their interpretations are more accurate. They have more to say because of the power of literature, because literature is primarily, although paradoxically, linked to the work of mourning, and is able to explore the intricacies of mourning in its possibility and, more often, its impossibility. (*WDNR* viii)

The issue is not simply that literature deserves a distinct and separate treatment, then, nor that processes of literarization ("the complex movement whereby a language comes to be written but also becomes a literary language, whereas it had earlier been either simply a spoken language or else a vernacular language in relation to a written, noble, and archaic one") must be attended to by way of a specific inquiry, a distinct history, as it were, that would include "conceptions and receptions: conceptions of the language in general over the course of the ages, to the extent that these are accessible; receptions of the spoken language and of its popular usages."[102] Literature, for Nichanian, demands a philosophically and historically informed reflection, a critical treatment that attends to its singularity, its ruptures and transformations, indeed, its becoming-literature. "The emergence of a literary language is therefore not the cultural product of a natural language. Its emergence constitutes an event of which man is not the master."[103] A critical and studious reading of literature thus requires careful attention not only to internal linguistic differences over time and place, ages and usages of the language/s (audiences and constituencies, dialects, uniformity and/or unification, and so forth) but also to the matter of translation, more generally, to considerations of and relation to "the foreign," which is included or excluded, borrowed and reworked, but always leaving its traces on the language and its sociopolitical and rhetorical formations. Nichanian is himself a devoted and tireless translator of great sensibility (from French and German into Armenian as well as from Armenian and English into French), and his reflections on translation, disseminated as they are throughout his writings, are indispensable for a reading of his work in general and for a proper understanding of his critical interventions.[104] Most important in this context is his attention to internal translations, the possibility and impossibility for Armenians to communicate with each other, to access their textual traditions, based on the various divisions that have marked the Armenian languages, beginning with the distinction between Eastern and Western Armenian.

When it comes to literature, therefore, the task cannot (minimally, it does not) "present itself in the form of a history" (*WDNR* 10). Rather, "the critic's task par excellence is to make visible by other means, means which are not novelistic [*des moyens non romanesques*], that which only literature [*seule la littérature*], or so it seems, could seize and retain within itself; that of which only literature could have the experience" (*WDNR* 246/*ATRN* 278; translation altered). Literature, if one could formulate the matter in this abbreviated form, is thus *against history*. For "history is still, despite all renewals of the discipline, the discourse of facts. In literature, facts are always outside of the thing itself" (*WDNR* 246/*ATRN* 278). Literature is and must be set apart.

> We will not have taken account of literature in its essence, as the specific type of event [*en son événementialité propre*] that it really is. At best we will have transformed it *into an object or a document* for history, which is still possible and which is, unfortunately, the most frequent feature, even in the most modern and best-informed studies. At any rate, the type of event that literature is and is able to narrate does not belong to history. No historical category could give an account of it. In a word, within the horizon of the Catastrophe, there is no history of literature. There is only an experience of its limits, a repetition of its birth, a calling into question of its powers.[105] (*WDNR* 246/*ATRN* 278)

It is only by acknowledging and accepting the singularity of literature, the distinctive sphere of aesthetic action it constitutes, that Nichanian can go on at this point to evoke, and even lament, an absence of literature. The terminology here varies, and this is significant, of course, but whether writing of a disappearance or of a renunciation, even of a certain failure (*la littérature défaille, ATRN* 274), even when asserting that "a work of literature could also appear as an instrument against literature itself, against literature as accomplice, and against the literary determination of nationalism" (*WDNR* ix), what continues to be affirmed is the work of literature, "the power of literature," as we saw, "because literature is primarily, although paradoxically, linked to the work of mourning, and is able to explore the intricacies of mourning in its possibility and, more often, its impossibility" (viii). It is, to repeat, in the name of such literature, in the name of the work of literature, that Nichanian can describe modern Armenian writers (and the greatest among them) as having renounced and failed literature, as having become "no more than the secretaries of the archive" (*WDNR* 233). Theirs was "the terrible experience of a writer's renouncement and self-denial, of *an adieu to literature*" (*WDNR* 233; emphasis added).

Essentially linked to the impossibility of mourning, the end of mourning that the Catastrophe is (for the genocidal will *forbids* mourning, it commands "the interdiction of mourning"), this conversion of literature into testimony, the process whereby "the Catastrophe re-situated every literary testimony in the dimension of the archive and, thus, immediately destroyed the very notion of 'testimony'" also brings about an abandonment of literature, a movement toward "a most un-literary conception of the text" (*WDNR* 245). For "a literary text is no testimony, not a personal account of events, facts, problems, or situations."[106] Literature, famously articulating a demand for a "suspension of disbelief" requires more than that (and so perhaps does testimony). Engaging with the unreal, as that which is beyond documentation and facts (as history and law define them), literature also demands "a suspension of belief," indeed, a "suspension of reality." Nichanian explains that "it is with this—the suspension of faith or belief, with simulation and the simulacrum—that literature in the proper sense of the word begins" (*WDNR* 245).

Against the document, against the archive, Nichanian proposes the monument, literature as monument. I should however point out that there are numerous monuments in Nichanian's work and, in particular, that the phrases "monument of mourning" (*monument de deuil*) and "monument to mourning" (*monument du deuil*) occur throughout his writings. The phrase announces a distinction Nichanian borrows, as we saw, from Michel Foucault, the distinction between document and monument, but it operates before gaining explicit thematization. It occurs either as a descriptive (as in Gurgen Mahari's *Burning Orchards* or Zabel Essayan's *Among the Ruins*) or, more often, as the name of that which is wanting, absent, and missing. There are different kinds of monuments, of course. Indeed, even the native, that formidable invention of philology to which we shall soon turn, even the native is described as a "monument," a monument of (and to) the mourning of philology. Later, Nichanian will express a kind of wish or dream for a monument to come, describing a future time—perhaps not so distant—when the texts written by survivors will be read and commented, rather than used for historiographic purposes. "The narrative of survival will then escape the gravitational field of the historical gaze; it will be offered to the public as a monument. . . . Testimonies as monuments will have, perhaps, a chance to be read. With no spectral presence. Finally rid of the fact and of the historians' history! Finally rid of the reality principle! They will end up achieving the suture between irreconcilables: the lack of the tear in representation and the destitution of the fact in historicity. Is this a dream?" (*HP* 104). As a monument of mourning, a monument to the impossibility of mourning, and beyond anything we have henceforth known under this name, literature emerges as a monument. It is a fragile artifact, always vulnerable to corruption ("the monument has always already been corrupted by the document" [*HP* 123]). Literature emerges as another name for the "monumental historiography" Nichanian repeatedly sets to work, denounces, and still inscribes throughout his writing. Like a poem (in this particular case, "Land of Fire" by Yeghishé Tcharents), a monument of writing that must "be read as a lamentation bearing on the disaster itself, but also of course, as an interpretation of this disaster" (*WDNR* 57), literature as monument is at once history and fiction, mourning and the impossibility of mourning, poetry, and criticism. "Poetry becomes reflection upon itself. It no longer seeks simply to take place, to be pure event. It seeks to reflect on this taking-place, on the occurrence of events in general, on itself and history as event. In the process, poetry already, but secretly reveals itself as that which opens up the place of taking-place . . . as the strange, unsettling event in which the possibility of any event whatsoever—that is, once again, poetry's face to face confrontation with history as such, in an act of mutual recognition— is announced and reflected" (*WDNR* 71–72). As literature and criticism, as "the imbrication of poetry and history," poetry is, it takes, "the place of history" (*WDNR* 71–72).

Literature (or history), in an alternative sense of the term, would therefore be a monument. It promises an act of witnessing that does not aim at documenting but is rather a means "of giving a meaning, of giving a style, of opposing the interdiction of mourning through mourning itself; of rescuing the act of mourning through writing, erecting a monument, and, at the same time, communicating . . . suffering; writing . . .

at the limit of what is utterable, what is tellable, but in a way that allows a great book to emerge from it" (*WDNR* 228). But is literature, so conceived, possible? Can literature, in other words, offer a different testimony? Is there testimony outside of philology? One can see something shifting in Nichanian's work when he turns his attention to philology or, more precisely, when he returns to it. Viewed historically, there would have occurred a sizable *revision* of his earlier work ("la révision est de taille," *ATDP* 17), which transforms and construes anew the work of rigorous philology performed in *AULA*, reviewed and revised, critiqued and reworked over the course of long and terse, even tense, pages. Nichanian says so himself, he testifies to the revision, and explicitly so, but I want to suggest that the consequences for his conception of literature and, undistinguishable from it, a measure of the Catastrophe should be underscored for a more profound difference than—again—a historical one, however operative the latter remains in the work. Not that it was incorrect to phrase it in this manner and according to familiar rules, yet whereas the Catastrophe, and, with and through it, the discourse of history, was seen as putting an end to mourning, it is now philology—that is, the joint invention of history and literature—that is said to block our access to mourning. It is philology, in other words, that forbids mourning, because the invention of philology is the "appropriating event that has made us what we are, that of us which is 'proper' and which, in addition (but is it an addition?) has given us our literary language" (*ATDP* 20). To the extent that literature is "the twin sister of philology" (*ATDP* 15) it partakes in the impossibility of mourning. And, if it is true that "we know nothing today of mourning (that is, of catastrophic mourning)," it is because of philology, because of the philological invention and distribution of art, religion, and literature. For "from the beginning, philology has decided everything with regard to mourning (. . . it has decided everything with regard to the disaster of which it is the mourning). Art would therefore be, in its function as well as in its content, entirely dependent upon this decision of philology" (*ATDP* 15). Ultimately, "that which defines itself as literature does so historically and only as a reaction to the onset of a philological project. . . . Literature [finds itself] in a double dependence vis-à-vis philology" (102).

He invents the art of making the poor speak by silencing them, by making them speak as mutes. . . . Their speech is always filled with sense. Simply, they ignore the sense that makes them speak, that speaks in them. The role of the historian is to deliver this voice.

—JACQUES RANCIÈRE

The minimal signified as the murmuring source of language remains merely itself as long as it does not speak; the stylus comes to its aid.

—FRIEDRICH KITTLER

Philology is the name Nichanian gives to history—the way in which history translates and, indeed, displaces—everything ("every historical object becomes essentially philological," *ATDP* 110). Like literature, as literature, philology is shown in its essential relation to mourning. There would be much to say about mourning and about this attention to mourning in Nichanian's work. In the context that interests us here, one would have to begin perhaps with yet another of Nichanian's singular definitions of *genocide*, namely, the impossibility of mourning and, more precisely, the interdiction of mourning decreed by the genocidal will. Confronted with the failure and lack of mourning—"Gleich fehlet die Trauer," wrote Friedrich Hölderlin, and Nichanian joins those who have tried to take the measure of this statement and perhaps to translate it.[107] More generally, one could assert that Nichanian writes—mourning. That is to say, mourning is the only thing he writes from and about. One might speak of trauma as well, and Nichanian himself does, at times, if with a measure of resistance that should make us pause. After him, for now I too will do no more (if, no doubt, much less) than translate mourning. Yet what I will try to offer in this section, somehow indirectly, is the tracing of some of the inscriptions of the word *disaster* through Nichanian's writings in order to account for the claim I have just put forward, namely, that philology is the name of history. To put it briefly, disaster is that upon which the invention of an originary silence is predicated. And we have begun to see that history needs this silence in order to "make it talk," as the ground of its own operations. History, as Michel de Certeau puts it, "forces the silent body to speak. It assumes a gap to exist between the silent opacity of the 'reality' that it seeks to express and the place where it produces its own speech, protected by the distance established between itself and its object."[108] What remains to be seen is the extent of a structure—historical difference—whereby iterations of silence remain constitutive of a number of discourses (Orientalism, as well as nationalism and colonialism, literature and anthropology, the witness and the archive), all of which "belong" to philology, partaking of its deployment. At the end of a trajectory that begins with disaster (appearing early on in Nichanian's writing and echoing the influence of Maurice Blanchot), one finds another figure, however, that remains determined by its belonging to disaster: the native. What is the native? Nichanian finds the question and the concise summary of his own trajectory in the work of Stathis Gourgouris, who, singularly prefiguring the arguments we have been following, answers that very question by way of the archive. "What is native?" Gourgouris asks.

> This question marks the site where the Nation resides. It designates the archive of (self-)representation, the sacred inventory of idols that make a national history possible. This archive encloses all the place frames and time frames projected by the national imaginary. It is here that the cultural continuity so necessary to the institution of any nation is produced and safeguarded. It is the place upon which the history of a nation's various geographies, its geographical moments remembered and envisioned, is inscribed. It is the navel of the nation's dream, to invoke Freud once again— the very *topos* that enables the cultural *omphaloskopisis* (navel gazing) that fuels every nation's reproduction. The archive is thus ultimately uninterpretable, if only because it itself produces the "ground" of its interpretation.[109]

The native, in other words, is the archive. More precisely, he prefigures the witness: the result of the same hermeneutical and performative operation, standing on and as the same ground, as that which is fashioned and validated by, while legitimizing, history. And the silence the native shares with the archive ("the archive is thus ultimately uninterpretable") is what Nichanian calls disaster. But Nichanian lingers, as it were, *against* national history, by considering the conditions of its emergence in and through the figure of the native. Consider Nichanian's translation of Gourgouris's argument, which brings together a number of threads we have been attending to, beginning with the role played by history as a technology of rule, of power and knowledge.

> One already knows that the native is he who carries disaster within himself. It is the figure of the disaster of tradition. The native is a residue. *The invention of the native, of the obverse of the philologist, as residue is the manner in which Orientalism sets to work the historicization of the object.* For philological thought, the disaster has occurred historically. The native no longer remembers. He no longer remembers his history, nor his own historicity. Such is the will of philology. On the other hand, philology must ignore everything of the fact that it forms one body with the residual and vestigial figure of the native as carrier of disaster. It is thus philology who invented the historical disaster. (*ATDP* 138)

The native is already a witness. He is "the *silent witness*."[110] Better yet, he is already the survivor of a disaster he knows not, having come into being as carrier of this disaster ("survivors of an ancient disaster that does not speak its name," 172). He is an invention that does not simply come about in history, but is the condition of history, its ground and source of legitimation. History is defined, in fact, "according to the manner in which it will treat this event/nonevent of a speech whose subject does not have the capacity to guarantee the reference of what he says."[111] That is why he is like the archive, indeed, himself an archive, "a ruin and a monument" (123), a tomb or a document waiting to be read, interpreted, and made to talk.[112] Jules Michelet describes his condition in precise terms: "Guardian of the earth, man's monument, the tomb contains a silent witness who would speak as needed."[113] The native speaks, therefore, yet he is mute, unable to hear himself, having lost access to his own voice, a voice he not only never knew he had, but one to which he continues to have no access. He is master and inhabitant of "the kingdom of the mute, the unreal, and the 'illiterate.'"[114] The native is thus forbidden to mourn that which he knows not he has lost. What had to be ensured was

> for these people to hear themselves, enter into a relationship with themselves. . . . One had to give voice to that which until then had been void of voice, to return speech to those whose speech had been cut at the root, since it could not reach their own ear. Such is muteness. Muteness is what is most proper to the "native." One had to put his own speech back into his mouth and ear. (71)

To think this muteness is to think disaster, to think muteness as disaster (72).

But the native does speak, I have said. In and through his muteness, he speaks. He speaks "the archives of an ancient speech, constituted by pure internal necessity, and precisely because of the presumed antiquity of the native's speech. . . . The speech of the living is perceived as 'antiquities.' The speech of the native is an antique, much as inscriptions on tombstones and colophons on forgotten manuscripts" (83). The native speaks therefore, and his is the voice of ancient times, weakened and erased. Listening to his speech—a speech he, strictly speaking, does not own or understand—and rendering unto him that which he cannot hear and does not know he says, the philologist *historicizes* him (82). The native is granted depth, thereby, historical depth. He is divided as being of history but not in it.[115] And the operations of history will therefore always be to return him to history, and most particularly his own. Much like the maps of sites void of inhabitants that budding archaeologists had begun to draw ("the first works of philology were of an archaeological and geographical nature" [130]), the native is there to be read, granted his own voice and meaning. He is like a geographical space in need of discovery, "a space that now carries its own history, on the very surface of its body, as it were. . . . [One must] 'read' the temporal depth on the objects of geographical space, open these objects to their historical temporality" (137). Reading so, philology introduces historical differ-ence as that which divides the land from itself (and ultimately, the native from himself), as it were, removing it from under the feet of its inhab-itants, the natives, at the same time as the latter too are divided: from their voice (which they cannot hear) and from their ears (which cannot understand). The site of this division, also the beginning of history, is the disaster.

It is, as we have begun to see, a historical disaster. And Nichanian, long familiar with the plots of history and its narratives, confesses: "I have always asked myself how it was that the ethnographer always man-aged to arrive to the site at the very moment of a definitive vanishing . . . precisely at the moment when tradition reached a point of disintegra-tion that only older women had access to it, and no longer the youth" (146). What if the philological scholar had not come? What if he had not arrived at that very moment? The disaster would have occurred, and it would have been, for the native, another loss without mourning. For it is the native himself, of course, who is always already incapable of interpretation. He is a sign for which "all deciphering has become impossible, having lost the key of his original language, the world in which he was significant" (148). Dead on arrival and unaware of the dis-aster that befalls him, what native could have gathered, within himself, his own disaster, the disaster that is constitutive of his being (that is, his being-native)? The loss of the native (double genitive) is a loss without mourning. "The native is he who has lost mourning" (149). Such is "the disaster of the native" (153). Such is the *historical* source of "catastrophic mourning," the possibility, or rather, impossibility, that comes about *as* history (165). History, in other words, shares with the genocidal will the edict in which the capacity to mourn is denied.

Yet the task of the historian and the function of historical difference will always be to render onto the native his own history (for he will teach the natives how to mourn, what to mourn—a mourning that is not one). And it matters little whether this history is universal or fragmented. It is the gesture whereby one grants access to what is, by any account, absent from itself, unavailable to itself, indeed, a ruin and a tomb. What one finds, therefore, at the origin of the philological project that is history is a civilizing mission that refigures mourning by denying it, "the violent threat of a definitive silence in one's rapport to oneself and thus the strange necessity of a mediation in order for the native to hear anew his own voice at its epico-mythical source" (71). As Marx's famous phrase has it (which Edward Said reactivated in *Orientalism*), the native cannot represent himself. He cannot be described or thought, except as having survived a disaster ("the end has already occurred," 72), which divides him from himself and, more important, gives birth to him as what he never was: a native (Orientalism, Robert Young demonstrated, is a historicism). That which was "before" the native is therefore not conceivable as history, which is why history, rupture, or continuity inevitably cuts the native off from any dwelling, speech, or practice, forever, and constitutively, remaining outside the archive. To include this outside, to archive *everything*—the historical gesture par excellence—alters little the dominion of history.[116] Indeed, it expands it every further, if also falsely. What history can include, the only elements it can recognize, are natives, witnesses, and documents, indeed, archives. There is no history without natives, much as there is none without archives. No history, in other words, without disaster. History grounds the native in disaster—it announces and produces it—as it grounds itself in the archive (the destruction of the archive or, as Derrida puts it, *archive fever*). And so, perhaps, it was never a matter of being against history (as if it were possible), much less against historians. Only to contend with that nonfactual fact that history is against us. This may begin to explain why one finds in Armenian literature prefigurations of the Catastrophe (prophecy was not speaking there. History was. And it was telling the natives what had already been coming to them).[117] It also makes clear the constitutive and devastating role played by philology in the project of erecting a national literature—testimonies and documents catering to the archive. It explains finally why, since the beginning of his work on modern Armenian literature, and preceding by far the Catastrophe, Nichanian was constantly attending, along with the texts he has been reading, to iterations—indeed, to translations—of the disaster.[118]

NOTES

INTRODUCTION

1. Jean-François Lyotard, *The Differend: Phrases in Disputes*, trans. Georges Van Den Abbeele (Minneapolis: University of Minnesota Press, 1988), 57.

2. The reference here is to Jean-François Lyotard, "Discussions, ou: 'Phraser après Auschwitz,'" which was published in Philippe Lacoue-Labarthe and Jean-Luc Nancy, eds., *Les fins de l'homme: À partir du travail de Jacques Derrida* (Paris: Galilée, 1981), 281–310. The original lecture was followed by a debate, reproduced on pp. 310–315. The transcription of the debate was done by Lyotard himself. It is therefore certified and countersigned.

3. Ibid., 287.

4. Ibid.

5. The only exception is perhaps *1915*, which has long served the role of proper name for the event, at least in Armenian. It is important to know that the first part of the extermination of the Armenians of the Ottoman

Empire (in the form of systematic deportation and murder in the open in situ and on side roads) took place between the spring and fall of 1915. In the spring of 1916, however, there were still too many survivors. The second part therefore took place from the spring to the fall of 1916, this time in the deserts of Mesopotamia. One of the characteristics of the extermination of the Armenians is thus that, from beginning to end, it entirely took place under the open skies.

6. Cf. Marc Nichanian, "The Style of Violence," *Armenian Review* 38 (Spring 1985): 1–26. This was already an essay on the treatment of the Catastrophe in the work of Hagop Oshagan.

7. Trans.: The French term *négationisme* has gained currency in the specific context of Holocaust denial. Historians who had declared themselves "révisionistes" were in this case renamed "négationistes." Although the term's semantic field has expanded quite a bit, it still covers a much narrower range than *denial* or *denegation*. Its use in English, moreover, is by now sufficiently widespread to justify its being deployed here as well.

8. Jacques Derrida, "Force of Law," trans. Mary Quaintance in Jacques Derrida, *Acts of Religion*, ed. Gil Anidjar (New York: Routledge, 2002), 296.

9. Carlo Ginzburg, "Just One Witness" in Saul Friedlander, ed., *Probing the Limits of Representation: Nazism and the "Final Solution"* (Cambridge: Harvard University Press, 1992), 82–96.

10. Lyotard, *The Differend*, quoted in Ginzburg, "Just One Witness," 96.

11. Giorgio Agamben, *Remnants of Auschwitz: The Witness and the Archive*, trans. Daniel Heller-Roazen (New York: Zone, 2002), 164. This extraordinary argument against refutation (and therefore about the function of the archive and the status of testimony) occurs at the very end of Agamben's book. I shall return to it, in a more circumspect manner, at the conclusion of chapter 3 (on refutation) and in chapter 4 (on testimony), as well as in my conclusion (on shame).

I. THE LAW AND THE FACT

1. Let me remind the reader that this text was written in 1995, published in September of that year in the journal *Lignes*, under the editorship of Michel Surya. It was the first time I had understood anything about the destitution of the fact and the historiographic perversion. I have therefore left the text as it was written, in the present of its enunciation.

2. The interview with Bernard Lewis was published in *Le Monde*, 16 November 1993. His response to the "heated reactions" was published in the same newspaper on 1 January 1994.

3. The official plaintiff was the Armenian community of France, supported by the Ligue Internationale Contre le Racisme et l'Antisémitisme (LICRA).

4. Jay Winter has recently published a collective volume, entitled *America and the Armenian Genocide of 1915* (Cambridge: Cambridge University Press, 2003), where he fails to revisit his 1994 assertions, which suggests that he has not renounced them.

5. This argument about "belligerence" was taken up by Marthe Robert in an article published in *Passages* (April-May 1995), to which I shall return in the next chapter. It had already been defended by Lewis at the time he was speaking of an Armenian "Holocaust"; cf. B. Lewis, *The Emergence of Modern Turkey* (Oxford: Oxford University Press, 1961), 356. Robert Melson criticized Lewis with an ironic tone in his *Revolution and Genocide: On the Origins of the Armenian Genocide and the Holocaust* (Chicago: University of Chicago Press, 1992), 67–69.

6. In Jay Winter's words: "It is important to note that this chapter in the history of the Great War, as ignoble as it is, is very different from those of Auschwitz and Treblinka." Whoever doubted it?

7. On the question of uniqueness and its use, as absolute and as argument, I refer the reader to my "L'empire du sacrifice" in *L'intranquille* 1 (1992).

8. Here is the exact phrasing of the court's conclusions: "Given that Bernard Lewis had the right to contest the value and significance of such affirmations, it was incumbent upon him to consider and analyze the circumstances likely to persuade his readers of their lack of relevance; at any rate he could not occlude the elements of an opposed evaluation, such as those upheld by international organizations and revealing that, contrary to the arguments criticized, the thesis concerning the existence of a plan aiming at the extermination of the Armenian people is not only defended by the latter."

9. Hagop Oshagan (1883–1948) is one of the greatest Armenian writers of the twentieth century. In his work, and in his novels in particular, he has taken the experience of the Catastrophe to its utmost limits. It is there that he encounters the ineluctable, definitive character of our entry into the era of the archive. I quote from volume 9 of his monumental *Panorama of Western Armenian Literature* (in Armenian) (Antelias, 1982), which contains one of the only critical essays he dedicated to another writer of the Catastrophe, Andonian. To the best of my knowledge, Oshagan is also one of the only writers

to have cogently spoken of the Jewish Holocaust (in 1948, the last text he published while still alive). Awaiting a better treatment, one can nonetheless read my "Hagop Oshagan tel qu'en lui-même" in *Dissonanȝe* 1983 and also "L'écrit et le mutisme: Introduction à la literature arménienne moderne" in *Les Temps Modernes* (Summer 1988). I return to Oshagan in the last chapter.

10. One should read the remarkable book by Yves Ternon, *Enquête sur la negation d'un génocide* (Marseille: Parenthèses, 1989). It is the first instance of an explicit demonstration of the negation and denegation at work in the very acts of the executioner.

11. I shall return to Andonian in the final chapter, where the reader will find brief biographical details as well as a reflection on his testimonial, literary, and historiographic activities.

12. There exists no accessible French translation of these 1919 trials and no scientific edition of the original minutes. Historians have here failed at their task. The supplements of the *Takvimi Vekayi*, the official Turkish journal, covering the period of the trials, were discovered and studied in the sixties by an Armenian scholar who signed his work (written in Armenian) by the name Krieger (an acronym of Krikor Guerguerian). More recently, Vahakn Dadrian as finally devoted an exhaustive study to the trials, written from the juridical point of view, in the *Yale Journal of International Law* 14.2 (1989). A French version of this study is available: *Autopsie du genocide arménien* (Bruxelles: Complexe, 1995), trans. Marc Nichanian and Mikaël Nichanian.

13. Maggiori's text was published in *Libération*, 28 April 1994.

14. *Le monde des débats*, February 1994. The article is entitled "Faussaires de l'histoire" (Counterfeiters of history).

2. BETWEEN AMPUTATION AND IMPUTATION

1. On the Veinstein affair, one can now read Yves Ternon, *Du négationisme: Mémoire et tabou* (Paris: Desclée de Brouwer, 1999). Thanks to this book, I do not need to elaborate on the unpleasant details of the affair.

2. Yves Ternon, *L'état criminel* (Paris: Seuil, 1995).

3. Trans.: The Gayssot law was voted on July 13, 1990, at the French parliament. Its stated aim was to intensify the struggle against racism and anti-Semitism. Its main contribution was an addendum to article 24 of the July 29, 1881, law on the freedom of the press. The new article, "article 24 bis,"

provides the basis for the punishment of any one who would "contest the existence of one or more crimes against humanity" (http://www.jura.uni-sb.de/france/Law-France/l90–615.htm, accessed June 17, 2007). It is the first law of a now longer series adjudicating on the matter of historical events related to racism and anti-Semitism and to crimes against humanity.

4. Now that I reread this sentence, "testimony can only testify to the facts," I notice that it calls for an observation. The sentence is obviously written *from the perspective of the historiographic perversion*, as befits the prejudice adopted in this entire chapter. One must wait until the next chapter to see the difference thematized between the witness according to the fact and the witness according to the sign.

5. Since then, the famous historian of nationalism has published the original version in a book entitled *On History;* see Eric Hobsbawm, *On History* (London: Weidenfeld and Nicolson, 1997).

6. The reading of the original English enables one to appreciate the elegance of the French translation ("toute conclusion reste ambiguë quant aux différentes versions de l'événement"), there where Hobsbawm opposes interpretation and, therefore, qualification to brute fact.

7. Hannah Arendt, *Eichmann in Jerusalem: A Report on the Banality of Evil* (New York: Penguin, 1994 [1964]), 254–259.

8. Philippe Lacoue-Labarthe, *Heidegger, Art and Politics: The Fiction of the Political*, trans. Chris Turner (Oxford: Blackwell, 1990), 35.

9. Ibid., 35–36.

10. Ibid., 37.

11. Ibid., 42.

12. Ternon, *Du négationisme*, 139–150.

13. Pierre Vidal-Naquet, *The Jews: History, Memory, and the Present*, trans. David A. Curtis (New York: Columbia University Press, 1996); the French original was published in 1981; *Assassins of Memory: Essays on the Denial of the Holocaust*, trans. Jeffrey Mehlman (New York: Columbia University Press, 1992), French original 1987.

3. REFUTATION

1. Saul Friedlander, ed., *Probing the Limits of Representation: Nazism and the "Final Solution"* (Cambridge: Harvard University Press, 1992).

2. Saul Friedlander, "Introduction," ibid., 4–5.

3. Paul Ricoeur, *Memory, History, Forgetting*, trans. Kathleen Blamey and David Pellauer (Chicago: University of Chicago press, 2004), 253.

4. Ibid., 253–254; for the full account of the debate on generalized rhetoricity and the confrontation between White and Ginzburg, see pp. 248–261.

5. Hayden White, "The Politics of Historical Interpretation: Discipline and De-Sublimation," *Critical Inquiry* 9.1 (1982), reprinted in Hayden White, *The Content of the Form* (Baltimore: Johns Hopkins University Press, 1987), 58–82. The book opens with an epigraph from Roland Barthes: "The fact has none but a linguistic existence." Earlier, White had published, among other works, *Metahistory: The Historical Imagination in Nineteenth-Century Europe* (1973), which will remain his major achievement, then *Tropics of Discourse: Essays in Cultural Criticism* (1978), and later *Figural Realism: Studies in the Mimesis Effect* (1999), all at Johns Hopkins University Press.

6. White, "The Politics of Historical Interpretation," 72.

7. See the extract of my letter to Vidal-Naquet in the appendix to the previous chapter.

8. Let there be no misunderstanding. It is not an enormity to seriously interrogate the conditions under which a truth is established by consensus, the reciprocity between diverse instances, senders and recipients, or the social reception upon which the factuality of a fact is, in general, dependent. It is an enormity for other reasons—let us call them moral reasons—and because the analogy presupposes in an absurd manner, I repeat, the existence of *subordinate or subaltern groups* with an interest in the rewriting of history on the matter of the Holocaust.

9. Trans.: *mise-en-intrigue* and *mise-en-narrativité* are French translations for Hayden White's "emplotment." Nichanian choses instead to emphasize the *plot* of *emplotment* by using the French *complot* (plot or conspiracy). With this word, he is playing with the English language as well, since the English *plot* translates both the French *récit* or *narration* and *complot* or, indeed, *intrigue*.

10. Trans.: What the French word *complot* makes visible is that the plot or emplotment is the result of a collective action. A plot, in Nichanian's usage, is therefore a common plot, a plot in common or, indeed, a com-plot.

11. Jean-François Lyotard, *The Differend: Phrases in Dispute*, trans. Georges Van Den Abbeele (Minneapolis: University of Minnesota Press, 1988), 106. Gil Anidjar brought my attention to this sentence, so terrible in its brevity. Here is the whole passage: "Between the SS and the Jew there is not even a differend, because there is not even a common idiom (that of a tribunal) in which even damages could be formulated, be they in place of a wrong. . . .

One does not dare think out Nazism because it has been beaten down like a mad dog, by a police action, and not in conformity with the rules accepted by its adversaries' genres of discourse (argumentation for liberalism, contradiction for Marxism). It has not been refuted." There is no tribunal of history, no common idiom, no possible presentation of a wrong, nor of a damage, no speculative result, no concept *Auschwitz* (which is only a contingent name, not the name of a concept, as Lyotard says earlier [103]).

12. Ricoeur, *Memory, History, Forgetting*, 257–258.
13. White, "The Politics of Historical Interpretation," 74; and Carlo Ginzburg, "Just One Witness," in Friedlander, *Probing the Limits of Representation*, 92. White's sentence continues: "Something like Schiller's notion of the historical sublime or Nietzsche's version of it is certainly present in the thought of such philosophers as Heidegger and Gentile and in the intuitions of Hitler and Mussolini." It is the only time White mentions Gentile. I must admit that I do not understand very well what might have been Hitler's "intuitions" on the historical sublime.
14. Ginzburg, "Just One Witness," 93.
15. Ibid., 95.
16. This is volume 4 (1927) of the massive *Filosofia come scienza dello spirito*, which I read in the 1948 edition, Benedetto Croce, *Teoria e storia della storiografia* (Bari: Laterza, 1948). There the reader will find the 1912 essay in the chapter on universal history, especially pp. 41–45.
17. Renato Serra, *Scritti letterari, morali et politici*, ed. Mario Isnenghi (Turin: Einaudi, 1974), 279–288.
18. Renato Serra, *Epistolario*, ed. Luigi Ambrosini, Giuseppe de Robertis, and Alfredo Grilli (Firenze: Le Monnier, 1953), 459–460.
19. Serra, *Scritti letterari*, 287.
20. Ginzburg, "Just One Witness," 96.
21. Jacques Derrida, *Archive Fever: A Freudian Impression*, trans. Eric Prenowitz (Chicago: University of Chicago Press, 1996), 94. We are therefore offering some elements in abeyance, again, taking our point of departure in the work of reelaboration conducted by Derrida on the concept of archive. In question will be the death drive, the destruction drive, as it appears in Freud's *Civilization and Its Discontent* in 1926. "It is at work, but since it always operates in silence, it never leaves any archives of its own. It destroys in advance its own archive, as if that were in truth the very motivation of its most proper movement. It works *to destroy the archive: on the condition of effacing* but also *with a view to effacing* its own 'proper' traces—which

consequently cannot properly be called 'proper.' It devours it even before producing it on the outside . . . It will always have been archive-destroying, by silent vocation" (Derrida, *Archive Fever*, 10).

22. Ibid., 92–93. The Freudian reference to those stones that speak is from the 1896 text entitled "The Aetiology of Hysteria" in Sigmund Freud, *The Standard Edition of the Complete Psychological Works of Sigmund Freud*, ed. James Strachey (London: Hogarth Press and the Institute of Psycho-Analysis, 1953–1974), 3:187–221.

23. Lyotard, *The Differend*, 56–57.

24. Ginzburg, "Just One Witness," 96.

25. Lyotard, *The Differend*, 57–58.

26. Giorgio Agamben, *Remnants of Auschwitz: The Witness and the Archive*, trans. Daniel Heller-Roazen (New York: Zone, 2002), 164.

27. If Lyotard and Agamben (and before them Hayden White, in spite of the ambiguities and insufficiencies of his argument) are correct in their "irrealist" but "significant" treatment of reality and in their nonhistoricizing approach to testimony, one understands why one of the most recent investigation on the modern concept of testimony, conducted by a sociologist, goes entirely astray; see Renaud Dulong, *Le témoin oculaire: Les conditions socials de l'attestation personelle* (Paris: EHESS, 1998). It goes astray in wanting to ground what it calls "the probative value [*la valeur probante*]" of testimony by taking into account (and constructing) a new conception of the social space, without much concern for the dimension of the archive and thus for the "metareality," that is, the destruction of reality and thus, in the final analysis, for the irreducible ruptures, the catastrophic wounds at the heart of this same social consensus that founds and makes possible, Dulong claims, the factuality of the fact. It is strange how sociology is often a philosophy that does not say its name, and a marked philosophy, historically *dated*.

28. Lyotard, *The Differend*, xiii.

29. Ibid., 162.

30. Ibid., 164.

31. Ibid., 165.

4. TESTIMONY

1. Freud first made this remark in a 1925 letter, then in one of his last articles in 1937; see Sigmund Freud, *The Standard Edition of the Complete Psycho-*

logical Works of Sigmund Freud, ed. James Strachey (London: Hogarth and the Institute of Psycho-Analysis, 1953–1974), 19:273 and 23:248.

2. These two citations of Anne-Lise Stern are extracted from Annette Wieviorka, *The Era of the Witness*, trans. Jared Stark (Ithaca: Cornell University Press, 2006), 135 and 128–29.

3. Giorgio Agamben, *Remnants of Auschwitz: The Witness and the Archive*, trans. Daniel Heller-Roazen (New York: Zone, 2002), 158; I return to Agamben's extraordinary effort to "save" testimony from the archive in my essay "Témoigner. Traduire. De Hölderlin à Primo Levi," in *Lianes* 23–24 (Novembre 2007); 209–243.

4. I obviously borrow the term *monument* from Michel Foucault who had himself borrowed it from Canguilhem. "I shall call an *archive* . . . the series of rules which determine in a culture the appearance and disappearance of statements, their retention and their destruction, their paradoxical existence as *events* and *things*. To analyze the facts of discourse in the general element of the archive is to consider them, not at all as *documents* . . . but as *monuments*"; Michel Foucault, "On the Archaeology of the Sciences: Response to the Epistemology Circle," in *Essential Works of Foucault 1954–1984*, vol. 2: *Aesthetics, Method, and Epistemology*, ed. James D. Faubion (New York: New Press, 1998), 309. One knows that it is from this definition of the archive that Agamben finds his starting point in chapter 4 of *Remnants* ("The Archive and Testimony"). The paradox, obviously, is that the archive is also the sedimented traces left by a culture after the disaster. By invoking this term, Foucault thus uses *the same word* in order to describe the general element in which monuments appear, in which they exist as such, as well as the archived collection (the postcatastrophic one, at least) of documents. Such an ambiguity has profound reasons and contains, we can see, many dangers. The entire question deserves to be revisited in detail in another context.

5. This section is a revised version of my introduction to the special issue of the *Armenian Review*, vol. 49, nos. 1–4, which I edited and dedicated to *Art and Testimony: Around Atom Egoyan's* Ararat.

6. See François Niney's introduction to the study workshop of Valence entitled "Méduse, ou comment montrer ce qu'on ne saurait voir (Medusa, or How to Show What Could Not Be Seen)" (December 2004), www.crac .asso.fr. The reflection on the relation between history and image was significantly broached in the work of Sylvie Rollet on Rithy Panh and on Atom Egoyan.

7. I refer of course to the so-called archaeological films codirected by Yervant Gianikian and Angela Ricci Luchi, most particularly the trilogy of war images and tortured and decomposed bodies: *Prigioneri della Guerra* (1995), *Su tutte le vette è pace* (1998), and *Oh! Uomo* (2004).

8. Scene 58 of the published screenplay: "Celia is in front of the painting. She takes out a knife and slashes the painting. . . . The painting is damaged." *Ararat*, screenplay and introduction by Atom Egoyan (New York: Market, 2002), 69.

9. These lines are extracted from an article published in *Les Temps Modernes*, no. 395 (June 1979). The article was republished in *Au sujet de Shoah* (Paris: Belin, 1990), and the quoted lines appear in a prominent location, p. 308. Does the reader understand that Lanzmann is here cruelly mocking the Armenians?

10. Shoshana Felman's article was first published in French in *Au sujet de Shoah*, pp. 55–145. It was translated by Lanzmann himself (in collaboration with Judith Ertel), something that should give some sense of the importance it had for him. The English version, "In the Era of Testimony: Claude Lanzmann's *Shoah*," was first published in *Yale French Studies* 79 (1991): 39–81. It was finally republished in Shoshana Felman and Dori Laub, *Testimony: Crises of Witnessing in Literature, Psychoanalysis, and History* (Routledge: New York, 1992). The citation is from p. 41 in *Yale French Studies*.

11. Felman, "In the Era of Testimony," 45.

12. Ibid.

13. Ibid., 53.

14. Ibid; of course, by "decanonization," Felman means that the event no longer belongs to the order of the sacred, that the silence of the witnesses ceases to be venerated as such, that it is henceforth broken and represented, which enables the historicization of the event.

15. Jean-Luc Nancy, "Forbidden Representation" in Nancy, *The Ground of the Image*, trans. Jeff Fort (New York: Fordham University Press, 2005), 47.

16. The only exception I know of is the testimony of Vahram Altounian, whose survival narrative, written in Turkish, has a public existence thanks to the care of his daughter Janine Altounian. She not only translated it into French and published it in her first book but also produced a magnificent commentary. Janine Altounian, *L'intraduisible: Deuil, mémoire, transmission* (Paris: Dunod, 2005). It is the first time, I believe, that a survivor narrative was the object of a literary or psychoanalytic study and could reach the gaze of the "civilized world." This commentary convinces me that testimony is per-

haps about to enter into the era of the monument, in spite of its originary and irreversible "corruption by the document."

17. Yervant Odian, *Anitseal Tariner, 1914–1919 (Andznakan Hishatakner)* (Cursed years, 1914–1919 [personal memories]), ed. Grigor Hakopyan (Yerevan: Naïri, 2004), 531–532.

18. Grigor Hakopyan (1959–2005) died without seeing the publication of this book, on which he worked tirelessly during the last months of his life. In Armenia he was the single most knowledgeable person on the literature of the Armenian diaspora.

19. *Levon Shanti Yerkerë* (*Works of Levon Shant*), vol. 9 (Beirut: Hamazkain, 1954), 371. Levon Shant (1869–1952) is the greatest playwright in Western Armenian. He was also a teacher and a politician. The ten volumes of his complete works were published in Beirut in the early 1950s.

20. Ibid, 377.

21. The content of this paragraph is developed in my essay on Zabel Essayan, published in my *Writers of Disasters: Armenian Literature in the Twentieth Century*, vol.1: *The National Revolution* (Princeton: Gomidas Institute, 2002), 187–242. The preface to Toroyan's testimony is reproduced in its entirety on pp. 221–222.

22. Aram Andonian, *Mets Vochirë* (Boston: Hayrenik, 1921), 9. Between 1919 and 1922 Andonian was prolifically active as a historian-journalist, concerned with the telling of the event in all its aspects. After 1922 he devoted his life to a possible history of the extermination on the basis of testimonies, which he never stopped collecting throughout his life. The entirety of the Andonian dossier remains, to this day, unpublished.

23. The first book, Aram Andonian, *Ayn Sev Orerun* (Boston, 1919), reports on horror scenes that were either seen or heard by Andonian during his second deportation. This book has just been translated into French by Hervé Georgelin, cf. Aram Andonian, *En ces sombres jours* (Genève: Métis, 2007).

24. Hagop Oshagan, *Hamapatker Arevmatahay Grakanutean* (Panorama of Western Armenian literature), vol. 9 (Beirut: Hamazkain, 1979), 272.

25. Ibid., 278.

26. The 1931 interview was first published in March and May 1932, in the journal *Haïrenik* in Boston. It was published in book form in 1983, in Beirut, under the title *Mayrineru Shuk'in Tak* (In the shadow of the cedars). The sentence I quote is on page 19.

27. For a very long time, none of these books (with the exception of Andonian's *The Great Crime*) had ever been translated into English. Now, at least,

we have an English version of Shamdanjian's book (Los Angeles: Hagop Manjikian, 2007).

28. Oshagan, *Hamapatker*, 8:429.

29. Agamben, *Remnants of Auschwitz*, 161.

30. It seems to me that it is in the same sense that Derrida writes, on the "question of the archive" that "it is a question of the future, the question of the future itself.... The archive, if we want to know what that will have meant, we will only know in times to come"; Jacques Derrida, *Archive Fever: A Freudian Impression*, trans. Eric Prenowitz (Chicago: University of Chicago Press, 1996), 36.

CONCLUSION

1. This conclusion is a reworked version of an essay entitled "De l'archive: La Honte," which was read in French at the conference "L'histoire trouée: Négation et témoignage" organized by Catherine Coquio and the International Research Organisation on Crimes Against Humanity (AIRCRIGE) in September 2002 at the Sorbonne and published in the proceedings (Nantes: L'Atalante, 2003). It was also presented in English at Columbia University during a conference with and around Jacques Derrida, which was organized by the Center for Comparative Literature and Society in 2003.

2. Giorgio Agamben, *Remnants of Auschwitz: The Witness and the Archive*, trans. Daniel Heller-Roazen (New York: Zone, 2002), 104.

3. Ibid.

4. Ibid., 65.

5. On the ignoble character of the word *genocide*, one can also read my conversation with David Kazanjian, "Between Genocide and Catastrophe" in *Loss*, ed. David Eng and David Kazanjian (Berkeley: University of California Press, 2002). Were one to put aside the constant ignominy of uttering the word *genocide*, one could even keep the same name. As Lyotard puts it, "the damages are not the wrong, the property to be demonstrated is not the event to be told, and I understand this even in the case when they bear the same name"; Jean-François Lyotard, *The Differend: Phrases in Disputes*, trans. Georges Van Den Abbeele (Minneapolis: University of Minnesota Press, 1988), 30.

6. On this parable by Kafka, one should read Avital Ronell, *Stupidity* (Urbana: University of Illinois Press, 2002), 287–294; the context there is an explora-

tion of the uncertain and dangerous limit zone that separates literature from philosophy, where reason and stupidity sometimes exchange their values.

AGAINST HISTORY

1. In what follows, I refer to the writings of Marc Nichanian by way of abbreviations:

AULA   *Ages et usages de la langue arménienne (Paris: Entente, 1989)*
WDNR   *Writers of Disaster: Armenian Literature in the Twentieth Century,*
vol. 1: *The National Revolution* (Princeton: Gomidas Institute, 2002)
ATRN   *Entre l'art et le témoignage: Littératures arméniennes au XXe siècle,*
vol. 1: *La revolution nationale* (Geneva: MetisPresse, 2006). This is the
French version of *WDNR.*
ATDP: Entre l'art et le témoignage: Littératures arméniennes au XXe siècle,
vol.2: *Le deuil de la philologie* (Geneva: MetisPresse, 2007)
HP: The Historiographic Perversion (this volume).

Although I do quote from the English translations, I have relied mostly on the original French, which I proceeded to translate myself. In engaging these writings, it should be obvious that I make no claims to exhaustiveness. I leave aside, in fact, most of what Nichanian writes from and about: Armenian literature, obviously (Zabel Essayan, Hagop Oshagan, Daniel Varoujan, in particular), but also philosophy (Schelling, Heidegger, Benjamin, Derrida, Lacoue-Labarthe) and, most important, the question of translation, whence, I would have wanted to argue, emerges the entirety—and the powerful originality—of his work. Neither is this, not by any means, a summary of Marc Nichanian's work, as it spans books and languages, fields and texts (literary, historical, philosophical), themes and problematics. My own attempt serves only as a boundary stone of sorts, setting bibliographic markers on the side of a path, *un partage des voies, sinon des voix* ("Être voie—c'est-à-dire chemin de passage—et non pas voix" writes Robert Harvey in *Témoins d'artifice*). Not quite a translation either, but a marker of friendship and gratitude as well, however poorly expressed. My gratitude as well to Nauman Naqvi, Rebecca Herzig, Nina Caputo, and George Hoffmann for their reading and commenting on this afterword.

2. As Rolf Tiedemann recalls from the title of the anthology he edited, Adorno himself had a more pointed formulation or question: "It is a question whether one can *live* after Auschwitz"; Theodor W. Adorno, *Can One Live After Auschwitz? A Philosophical Reader*, ed. Rolf Tiedemann, trans. Rodney Livingstone et al. (Stanford: Stanford University Press, 2003), xi and 435.

3. I quote here from Dipesh Chakrabarty, *Provincializing Europe: Postcolonial Thought and Historical Difference* (Princeton: Princeton University Press, 2008), xii. Nichanian shares with Chakrabarty a major concern with translation and a sense of its necessity as an alternative mode of thought and practice ("The problem of capitalist modernity cannot any longer be seen simply as a sociological problem of historical transition . . . but as a problem of translation, as well" [17]), although it leads him, I think, to distinct conclusions. For both, at any rate, translation offers distinct resources to address historical difference—the difference history makes—without privileging it.

4. As Robert Young puts it, "why, after all, 'history' at all? Why . . . not the class struggle, or economics, the state, or social relations?" Robert J. C. Young, *White Mythologies: Writing History and the West*, 2d ed. (London: Routledge, 2004), 55. Pierre Hadot recalls that ancient philosophers often neglected to grant any positive value to the past. "The fundamental philosophical attitude consists in living in the present, to possess the present and not the past"; Pierre Hadot, *Exercices spirituels et philosophie antique* (Paris: Albin Michel, 2002), 328. Norman Brown extends the interrogation to its furthest reaches: "Why does man, alone of all animals, have a history?" Norman O. Brown, *Life Against Death: The Psychoanalytical Meaning of History* (Middletown: Wesleyan University Press, 1985), 15. But another, more pointed, version would be Blanchot's question: "How is it possible to say: Auschwitz has happened?" Maurice Blanchot, *The Writing of the Disaster*, trans. Ann Smock (Lincoln: University of Nebraska Press, 1995), 143. The phrase "the transcendance of its dignity" (*la transcendance de sa dignité*) is Jacques Derrida's, whose *Speech and Phenomena* and its interrogation of the voice informs, directly and indirectly, Nichanian's reflections on history; Jacques Derrida, *Speech and Phenomena and Other Essays on Husserl's Theory of Signs*, trans. David B. Allison (Evanston: Northwestern University Press, 1973), 77.

5. Michel de Certeau, *The Writing of History*, trans. Tom Conley (New York: Columbia University Press, 1988), 85.

6. Friedrich Nietzsche, *Unfashionable Observations*, trans., with afterword, Richard T. Gray (Stanford: Stanford University Press, 1995), 143.

7. I borrow the expression of a scientific signature ("the signature of science") from Jacques Rancière, *The Names of History: On the Poetics of Knowledge*, trans. Hassan Melehy (Minneapolis: University of Minnesota Press, 1994), 8. Rancière—I mention this in passing—suggests that historical difference is nothing else but a neutralization of the past (49), the site of "the death drive inherent in the scholarly belief in history" (41).

8. Michael Taussig, "History as Commodity: In Some Recent American (Anthropological) Literature," *Critique of Anthropology* 9:1 (1989) 16.

9. Michel-Rolph Trouillot, *Silencing the Past: Power and the Production of History* (Boston: Beacon, 1995) 49; and recall Joan Scott's formulation that "gender is a primary way of signifying relationships of power"; Joan Wallach Scott, *Gender and the Politics of History* (New York: Columbia University Press, 1988), 44, where gender is ultimately subsumed under historical difference.

10. Talal Asad, *Genealogies of Religion: Discipline and Reasons of Power in Christianity and Islam* (Baltimore: Johns Hopkins University Press, 1993), 264; thus "peoples without history" were negotiated through the management of differential categories, marked with marks that did not apply to those studying and ruling them: ethnicity and race, race and religion. David Chidester elaborates on the way in which peoples without history were also "without religion"—an essential absence for missionary and colonial rule; David Chidester, *Savage Systems: Colonialism and Comparative Religion in Southern Africa* (Charlottesville: University of Virginia Press, 1996). Elsewhere, they were found to have *only* religion, "proving," albeit in divergent ways, that, much like ethnicity and race (or caste), religion served as a differential marker vis-à-vis history and civilization.

11. Trouillot, *Silencing the Past*, 28.

12. Rancière, *The Names of History*, 29.

13. Nicholas Dirks, *Castes of Mind: Colonialism and the Making of Modern India* (Princeton: Princeton University Press, 2001), 8–9. I am quoting Dirks on caste, not on history, and yet it is difficult to ignore that caste—"the single and systematic category to name, and thereby contain, the Indian social order" (13)—was derivative of a deeper and more significant difference. Caste was "one of the major reasons why India has no history, or at least no sense of history" (3). Behind the difference caste makes, then, there is the difference history makes (although one might also consider, in

another context, the differential function of the word *cultural* in the phrases cited). That this history—the history of India as a geographic entity of unquestionable historical integrity—is colonial and, moreover, contingent on the (imperial) archive is what Dirks goes on to show and, surprisingly, to historicize. History is thereby opposed to anthropology, constructivism opposed to essentialism. Yet is not colonialism the very institution of a difference between history and anthropology? Their ambivalent alliance? With his otherwise compelling critique of "the ethnographic state," Dirks omits to target "the historiographic," indeed, "the historical state" that rules over it—or constitutes its other face. Indeed everything is as if history had to be affirmed as the last and only protection available against essentialism, rather than its uninterrogated condition of possibility. As Ann Stoler puts it, "colonial archives were both sites of the imaginary and institutions that *fashioned histories* as they concealed, revealed, and reproduced the power of the state"; Ann Laura Stoler, "Colonial Archives and the Arts of Governance," *Archival Science* 2.1–2 (March 2002): 97 (emphasis added).

14. Nietzsche, *Unfashionable Observations*, 140.

15. Amos Funkenstein, *Perceptions of Jewish History* (Berkeley: University of California Press, 1993), 15.

16. According to Peter Burke, "the historical revolution associated with Ranke was above all a revolution in sources and methods, a shift away from the use of earlier histories, or 'chronicles,' to the use of the official records of governments. Historians began to work regularly in archives"; Peter Burke, *History and Social Theory*, 2d ed. (Ithaca: Cornell University Press, 2005), 5. They have not stopped since. Archives remain "sacred places where one culls from documents 'facts' about the past" (Scott, *Gender and the Politics of History*, 8). Interestingly, a recent survey of the philosophy of history, which does mention the archive, if in passing, fails to treat it as a problem worthy of interrogation, much less as a concept; Mark Day, *The Philosophy of History: An Introduction* (New York: Continuum, 2008). The emergence of "the conjectural paradigm of semiotics" described by Carlo Ginzburg is predicated on an "evidential paradigm," that is to say, on what qualifies as a reliable sign, beginning with animal tracks; Carlo Ginzburg, "Clues: Roots of an Evidential Paradigm," in Carlo Ginzburg, *Myths, Emblems, Clues*, trans. John and Anne C. Tedeschi (London: Hutchinson Radius, 1990), 118.

17. Mary Poovey, *A History of the Modern Fact: Problems of Knowledge in the Sciences of Wealth and Society* (Chicago: University of Chicago Press, 1998), 18.

18. Ibid.

19. As theorists of the archive put it, the archive remains "the basis for and validation of the stories we tell ourselves, the story-telling narratives that give cohesion and meaning to individuals, groups, and societies"; Joan M. Schwartz and Terry Cook, "Archives, Records, and Power: The Making of Modern Memory," *Archival Science* 2.1–2 (March 2002): 13. It includes, virtually or practically, the sources validated by historians, institutions (e.g., legal and scientific) and cultural production (archives in this sense are the sources grounding history, such as discussed, for example, in Martha Howell and Walter Prevenier, eds., *From Reliable Sources: An Introduction to Historical Methods* (Ithaca: Cornell University Press, 2001). It might be important to note that in her discussion of the modern fact Mary Poovey registers her own historical project as being out of bounds, open to disqualification by historians, for objects such as the fact, she writes, "leave none of the traces that historians recognize as *documentable evidence*" (Poovey, *History of the Modern Fact*, xiv; emphasis added). She therefore seeks to challenge the notion of "documentation by conventional means," if not the archive as such; yet what she documents is precisely the constitution of the modern archive, "particulars . . . interpreted as evidence" and "valuable enough to collect" (9). Trouillot, for his part, locates the archive in a seemingly even continuum of production (sources, archives, narratives, history), but he grants archives a unique, *necessary* role. For him, archives are "the institutions that organize facts and sources and *condition the possibility of existence* of historical statements" (Trouillot, *Silencing the Past*, 52; emphasis added). The rest, one might want to say, is mere commentary.

20. Trouillot, *Silencing the Past*, 19.

21. There is much that echoes Benjamin here and that deserves a separate, extended study. For now, the claim could be succinctly demonstrated by reading Nichanian together with Cadava's *Words of Light*, and here in particular, the section entitled "Danger"; Eduardo Cadava, *Words of Light: Theses on the Photography of History* (Princeton: Princeton University Press, 1997), 47–59. Cadava elaborates on connections with Ernst Jünger and suggests later parallels with Paul Virillo and Friedrich Kittler.

22. "But why should they not add a supplement to history?" is the question asked by Virginia Woolf and by many a feminist historian after her; Virginia Woolf, *A Room of One's Own* (San Diego: Harcourt Brace Jovanovich, 1989), 45. Woolf's own, well-known, answer is Shakespeare's sister: "I prefer, therefore, to put it in the form of fiction" (113). Ranajit Guha's wish

for history to "emulate literature to look afresh at life in order to recuperate the historicality of what is humble and habitual" can be located along the same lines; Ranajit Guha, *History at the Limit of World-History* (New York: Columbia University Press, 2002), 94.

23. I am therefore unsure of the necessity to clarify the use of the word *history* (and its numerous homonyms) in attempting to comment, as I do here, on Nichanian's position. One could adopt a number of gestures, beginning with the suspension of the word *history* within quotation marks. Hayden White already addressed this gesture when he argued that "conventional distinctions between 'history' and 'historicism' are virtually worthless"; Hayden White, "Historicism, History, and the Figurative Imagination" in *Tropics of Discourse: Essays in Cultural Criticism* (Baltimore: Johns Hopkins University Press, 1978). Alternatively, one could maintain the famous distinction operative in the German language between *Historie* and *Geschichte* and argue only about the latter (the narration and interpretation of the former, of the bare facts, as it were). This too is not Nichanian's choice. He is perhaps closest to Michel de Certeau, who, by "history" means "a practice (a discipline), its results (a discourse), and the relation between them"; de Certeau, *The Writing of History*, trans. Tom Conley (New York: Columbia University Press, 1988), 102n2. But the operations of "discourse" in de Certeau's own argument seem to me to exceed by far the "results" of the discipline. Instead they provide a relatively autonomous context within which the discipline functions. With this caveat, and recalling the affirmation of homonymy deployed by Jacques Rancière (in *The Names of History*), one approaches, I think, Nichanian's position.

24. Cited here is Michel Foucault, *The Archaeology of Knowledge and the Discourse on Language*, trans. A. M. Sheridan Smith (New York: Pantheon, 1972), 129; and see Rancière, who explains that "in a sense, the document is identical to the event itself" (Rancière, *The Names of History*, 44).

25. On the way "silences enter the process of historical production," see Trouillot, *Silencing the Past*, esp. 26, 28, 48ff. But the interrogation of silence that occupies historians implicates, once again, a much larger field, and one would have to attend to those whom Nichanian describes as "unable to hear themselves" as produced by the discourse of a tradition that places "the voice that keeps silence" at its center (Derrida, *Speech and Phenomena*, 70–87) or in the archive as a voice that is "the place of the negative," as "the voice of death"; Giorgio Agamben, *Language and Death: The Place of Negativity*, trans. Karen E. Pinkus and Michael Hardt (Minneapo-

lis: University of Minnesota Press, 1991), 39 and 47; Agamben writes that "it is important to observe here how the 'conscience' of Western philosophy rests originally on a mute foundation" (91). The questioning of history here at work (cf. Derrida, *Speech and Phenomena*, 102–103; Agamben, *Language and Death*, 103–104) implicates much more than a professional or provisional inclination.

26. As Carlo Ginzburg phrases it "documents (defendants, witnesses) do not speak by themselves . . . to make documents speak, we must interrogate them"; Carlo Ginzburg, *The Judge and the Historian: Marginal Notes on a Late-Twentieth-Century Miscarriage of Justice*, trans. Antony Shugaar (London: Verso, 1999), 35. Elsewhere, Ginzburg will make explicit the darker aspects of the expression *make it talk*, referring specifically to torture; Carlo Ginzburg, *History, Rhetoric, and Proof: The Menahem Stern Jerusalem Lectures* (Hanover: University Press of New England, 1999), 23; and see also Shoshana Felman on "the task of the historian," which is "to reconstruct what history has silenced, to give voice to the dead and to the vanquished and to resuscitate the unrecorded, silenced hidden story of the oppressed," in *The Juridical Unconscious: Trials and Traumas in the Twentieth Century* (Cambridge: Harvard University Press, 2002), 34. Jacques Rancière, on the other hand, recognizes in his commentary on Percennius's speech (in Tacitus's *Annals*) that some testimonies might be "made to talk" *as nonevents*, as the absence of speech, and therefore without need for falsification or refutation. The historian quotes these (or invents them), but he "does not comment on them, does not refute them. They are not said to be either true or false. They have, more fundamentally, no relation to the truth," that is, to the facts (Rancière, *The Names of History*, 26; and see also the operations involved in letting documents "speak for themselves," 44ff.). "To make survivors talk," Nichanian says somewhere, "is criminal."

27. Scott, *Gender and the Politics of History*, 138; the concern "with the legitimating social coordinates of epistemologies, how people imagine they know what they know and what institutions validate that knowledge, and how they do so" is part of a recent "archival turn," which Ann Stoler has well described and summarized (Stoler, "Colonial Archives," 95). What continues to be emphasized throughout is perhaps best indicated by the proliferation of a rhetoric of production, of making and fashioning, a language of potentiality and ability.

28. Attending to Derrida's work on the archive, which Nichanian also reads, the archivist Brien Brothman pertinently asks: "does preservation not in-

trinsically carry within it the seeds of destruction? Does it not disturb—appropriate—the past, making it (a) present, a material 'presentness,' and achieve perdurable effects that destroy finiteness? Is not the presiding effect of archival transmission the restoration—that is, destruction—of presence?" Brien Brothman, "The Limits of Limits: Derridean Deconstruction and the Archival Institution" in *Archivaria* 36 (Autumn 1993): 209. Surprisingly, Brothman never quite revisits these questions, nor does he address the destruction of the archive in his extended reading of Derrida and, particularly, of *Archive Fever;* see Brien Brothman's book review, *Archivaria* 43 (Spring 1997): 189–192, and his "Declining Derrida: Integrity, Tensegrity, and the Preservation of Archives from Deconstruction," *Archivaria* 48 (Fall 1999): 64–88; and see how destruction and erasure also elude David Bell's otherwise rich reading of Derrida, most specifically in his comparing of Derrida's work with Friedrich Kittler's; David F. Bell, "Infinite Archives" in *SubStance* 105, 33.3:148–161.

29. Nietzsche, again, wrote of this destructive dimension of (antiquarian) history and, by implication, of the archive as destructive of life ("a blind mania to collect . . . a restless gathering of everything that once existed") (Nietzsche, *Unfashionable Observations*, 105). Kittler describes how Nietzsche places "the medium of the soul against a background of emptiness or erosion"; Friedrich A. Kittler, *Discourse Networks, 1800/1900*, trans. Michael Metteer and Chris Cullens (Stanford: Stanford University Press, 1990), 207. Amos Funkenstein insisted on the destructive nature of some forms of history writing, describing them as well as being "self-destructive of necessity" (Funkenstein, *Perceptions of Jewish History*, 48–49). Kittler brings us back to the "making it talk" and extends the diagnostic to "every medium that brings the hidden to the light of day and forces the past to speak" as contributing "by gathering evidence, to the death of Man" (Kittler, *Discourse Networks*, 286). More modestly, for Nichanian, the archive is destructive and, indeed, of necessity self-destructive, destructive of death and partaking of the interdiction of mourning.

30. Foucault, *The Archaeology of Knowledge*, 129–130. Giorgio Agamben insists on the positive dimension of the archive as a space of possibility and actuality: "the archive," Agamben writes, "is situated between *langue*, as the system of construction of possible sentences—that is, of possibilities of speaking—and the *corpus* that unites the set of what has been said, the things actually uttered or written"; Giorgio Agamben, *Remnants of Ausch-*

witz: The Witness and the Archive (Homo Sacer III), trans. Daniel Heller-Roazen (New York: Zone, 2002), 143–144).

31. Foucault, *The Archaeology of Knowledge*, 130.

32. Ginzburg, *History, Rhetoric, and Proof*, 24. Trouillot adds much to Ginzburg's account, most notably perhaps when he attends to the archive and describes "archival power" as determining "the difference between a historian, amateur or professional, and a charlatan" (Trouillot, *Silencing the Past*, 52). But those *made* or *unmade* by the archive (the hegemony of a language of production and making endures) would seem to move exclusively in the professional orbit. What about witnesses? Surely, their making and unmaking is not of the same nature. And what, finally, not of silence or even obliteration *in* the archive but of active destruction *by* the archive?

33. Ginzburg, *History, Rhetoric, and Proof*, 25; Ginzburg strangely confines the ability to make reality appear and disappear to television's remote control; Kittler will more broadly write that "technologically possible manipulations determine what in fact can become a discourse" (Kittler, *Discourse Networks*, 232). And though Ginzburg discusses the matter of sources at length, he seeks to articulate "the point of view of those who work in contact with documents, in the broadest sense of the term" (Ginzburg, *History, Rhetoric, and Proof*, 2). Never interrogating the availability of documents (and lack thereof) and its meaning for "history, rhetoric, and proof," Ginzburg thus entertains no more than the question of "access" to the archive, which is presumably given and awaiting its unearthing and interpretation. No question is raised about the constitutive role of destruction in the making of the archive—and of the fact. Yet, as Joseph Mali points out, Ginzburg is one among recent historians who has countered the dismissal (read: destruction) of *mythistory*, thus demonstrating an acute understanding of the destructive force of the archive—and of those who claim to make it speak; Joseph Mali, *Mythistory: The Making of Modern Historiography* (Chicago: University of Chicago Press, 2003), 25–26.

34. "Traces thus produce the space of their inscription only by acceding to the period of their erasure," writes Derrida of an early archival apparatus. "From the beginning, in the 'present' of their impression, they are constituted by the double force of repetition and erasure, legibility and illegibility"; Jacques Derrida, *Writing and Difference*, trans. Alan Bass (Chicago: University of Chicago Press, 1978), 226. The phrase "apologists of the factual" is Nietzsche's (in *Unfashionable Observations*, 144). Joan Scott offers a

milder, but no less pertinent, formulation. She speaks of records, archives, as "ways of establishing the authority of certain visions of social order, or organizing perceptions of 'experience'" (Scott, *Gender and the Politics of History*, 115).

35. Jacques Derrida, *Archive Fever: A Freudian Impression*, trans. Eric Prenowitz (Chicago: University of Chicago Press, 1996), 7.

36. A striving for all-inclusiveness could almost be said to be the trademark of historians, and particularly those who seek to transform the field. As Peter Burke describes them, the Annales historians, for example, wanted to replace political history "with what they called a 'wider and more human history,' a history which would include all human activities" (Burke, *History and Social Theory*, 14). Jack Goody makes strikingly manifest the persistence of this inclusive dream in *The Theft of History*. Here inclusiveness is not only predicated on the claim that "history" is found elsewhere than in the West. Rather, all these "achievements" that were inflicted on "the rest" by the West are reclaimed as a kind of universal heritage (from love and democracy to market capitalism, from freedom to individualism and even ethnocentrism). See Jack Goody, *The Theft of History* (Cambridge: Cambridge University Press, 2006).

37. "Right on that which permits and conditions archivization, we will never find anything other than that which exposes to destruction, and in truth menaces with destruction, introducing *a priori*, forgetfulness. . . . The archive always works, and *a priori*, against itself" (Derrida, *Archive Fever*, 12).

38. De Certeau, *The Writing of History*, 101; translation altered.

39. "The One guards itself of, and from, the other" (*l'Un se garde de l'autre*) is Derrida's striking formulation in *Archive Fever*, but one should hear as well echoes of Rancière, who describes a "territorialization" of historical speech in terms of an interment, "a placing of speech in reserve" (Rancière, *The Names of History*, 54). The archive is a tomb, and the historian a "necrophile" (74).

40. Ginzburg, *The Judge and the Historian*, 20; both Ginzburg and de Certeau attend, albeit in very different ways, to the collusions and divisions of law and history, with one significant difference, however. By focusing on the isolated person (the judge, the historian) in a limited sphere (the court room, the writing desk), Ginzburg drastically reduces the range of operations and mechanisms under consideration (thus excluding the archive). Following Hannah Arendt, Shoshana Felman also explores the particular

configuration whereby "legal institutions undertake to put on trial history itself" (Felman, *The Juridical Unconscious*, 112), although she does not thematize the production (and destruction) of the archive except as a problem of reception ("we do not hear" [30], "the jurors look but do not see," 81), which, guaranteeing that "the evidence will fail or will fall short" (96), might nonetheless be palliated by expansion, by way of the literary record (100); for an example of what a different comparative account might look like, see Bruno Latour, "Scientific Objects and Legal Objectivity" in Alain Pottage and Martha Mundy, eds., *Law, Anthropology, and the Constitution of the Social: Making Persons and Things* (Cambridge: Cambridge University Press, 2004), 73–114; and see also Mark Cousins, "The Practice of Historical Investigation" in Derek Attridge, Geoff Bennington and Robert Young, eds., *Post-structuralism and the Question of History* (Cambridge: Cambridge University Press, 1987), 126–136.

41. Yosef Hayim Yerushalmi, *Freud's Moses: Judaism Terminable and Interminable* (New Haven: Yale University Press, 1991), 85; and see Derrida, *Archive Fever*, 64ff. Derrida goes on to argue that "instead of signifying, as [Yerushalmi] believes he can claim, that if the murder did not leave any archive it is because it did not take place, it suffices to read the texts he himself cites to conclude the contrary" (66). Raising the possibility of "an archive of the virtual" Derrida is not calling for inclusiveness, but for a transformation of the concept of the archive.

42. Cadava, *Words of Light*, 22.

43. "The genocidal will" is Nichanian's phrase. One is reminded of Fred A. Leuchter Jr., to whom Errol Morris dedicated his documentary *Mr. Death*. Leuchter's logic is that murder itself, more precisely, the killing of a human being, is difficult to achieve, and requires therefore much effort. "It's a tough job, to execute several hundred people at once. We have a hard job executing one man" (see www.errolmorris.com/film/mrd_transcript.html, accessed July 14, 2008). Looking for traces of this effort, and failing to find them, Leuchter draws what appeared to the Harvard students selected for an early screening to be an impeccably historical conclusion: there was no murder (see http://errolmorris.com/content/interview/moma1999.html, accessed July 14, 2008).

44. One can therefore say about the discourse of the archive that it functions like the discourse of the alibi, as Shoshana Felman describes it: "the discourse of the alibi speaks . . . precisely *not to know* and especially *not to acknowledge*" (Felman, *The Juridical Unconscious*, 98). Robert Pogue Harrison

accurately describes the mechanism at work here as what occurs "when history turns against its own memorializing and self-conserving drive, when it is perceived to have become a force of erasure rather than of inscription, of assault on the earth rather than humanization of the earth." Then, he adds, "images of an apocalyptic sea inevitably surge up in the human imagination"; Robert Pogue Harrison, *The Dominion of the Dead* (Chicago: University of Chicago Press, 2003), 16; later on, Harrison describes again "this loss of historicity," claiming that one of its "manifestations is in fact overhistoricization" (86). There are remarkable parallels here with what Renée Bergland describes as "one specific discursive technique of Indian removal," namely, the extraordinary proliferation in American literature of representation of Native Americans as ghosts—as archives of a past long dead and gone, and constantly so. Archivization is spectralization; Renée L. Bergland, *The National Uncanny: Indian Ghosts and American Subjects* (Hanover: Dartmouth College and University Press of New England, 2000), 3.

45. Kittler, *Discourse Networks*, 52–53.

46. Ibid., 222, resonating with Carlo Ginzburg's "conjectural paradigm of semiotics" in Ginzburg, "Clues." There are Benjaminian echoes as well, which are compellingly spelled out in Eduardo Cadava's *Words of Light*.

47. Implicitly exonerating history (or at least historians), Shoshana Felman testifies to a crisis of legal, but not historical, meaning. She therefore attributes exclusively to law the power to destroy evidence, to "nullify its visibility" (*The Juridical Unconscious*, 79). Felman asks, "Has history not taken place to register at least a legal difference?" (83), but not whether law and history would have to interrogate ("register") historical difference (one could say that this interrogation is nonetheless the very thing with which Felman struggles throughout; see, e.g., pp. 12–13). "Verdicts," she continues, "are decisions about what to admit into and what to transmit of collective memory. Law is, in this way, an organizing force of the significance of history" (84). This is precisely parallel to what Nichanian (who finds inspiration in Felman on more than one occasion) argues, with one major caveat, which could be phrased as follows: making similar decisions as to the record and evidence to admit, history too is an organizing force of the significance of law.

48. Nietzsche knew this well who wrote of the task of the historian in the following terms: "It almost seems as if the task is to watch over history so that nothing will ever come of it but history stories—but certainly no events!"

(*Unfashionable Observations*, 118). Nietzsche then turns to the wider matter of "the historical sensibility" as that which "uproots the future because it destroys illusion and robs existing things of that atmosphere in which alone they are able to live." As well, "historical justice" (the judge and the historian) is that which "undermines and destroys living things; its verdict is always a death sentence" (Nietzsche, *Unfashionable Observations*, 131).

49. Christopher Lasch, *The Culture of Narcissism: American Life in an Age of Diminishing Expectations* (New York: Norton, 1979), xviii; on "historical time," see Reinhart Koselleck, *Futures Past: On the Semantics of Historical Time*, trans. Keith Tribe (New York: Columbia University Press, 2000); on the extensive reach of "the thematic awareness of history," see Trouillot, *Silencing the Past*, 19ff.

50. Lee Edelman, *No Future: Queer Theory and the Death Drive* (Durham: Duke University Press, 2004), 11; on the survivor, see Elias Canetti, *Crowds and Power*, trans. Carol Stewart (New York: Farrar, Straus and Giroux, 1984); the phrase "the poverty of history" is Karl Popper's.

51. The question "has history come to an end?" was hardly a challenge to the historical profession. If at all, it was a challenge to Marxism. Moreover, the question retains a hyperbolic sense of history, as Jacques Derrida makes clear in his critique of Fukuyama in *Specters of Marx*, trans. Peggy Kamuf (New York: Routledge, 1993). Historians, and historical consciousness, never lost their object—certainly never admitted to having lost it; for example, Lutz Niethammer, *Posthistoire: Has History Come to an End?* trans. Patrick Camiller (London: Verso, 1992).

52. Peter Burke, "Overture: The New History, Its Past and Its Future," in Peter Burke, ed., *New Perspectives on Historical Writing* (University Park: Pennsylvania State University Press, 1992), 1.

53. Georg G. Iggers, *Historiography in the Twentieth Century: From Scientific Objectivity to the Postmodern Challenge* (Hanover: Wesleyan University Press, 1997), 7.

54. Karl Löwith, *Meaning in History* (Chicago: University of Chicago Press, 1949).

55. Giambattista Vico, *The New Science of Giambattista Vico*, trans. Thomas Goddard Bergin and Max Harold Fisch (Ithaca: Cornell University Press, 1968), 425; like Marx after him, Vico recognized the limits of this assertion when he stated that "this world without doubt has issued from a mind often diverse, at times quite contrary, and always superior to the particular ends that men had proposed to themselves" (ibid.).

56. As Chakrabarty puts it, with consequences that carry over to the present attempt, "an antihistorical consciousness" maintains history as "precisely the site where the struggle goes on" (37). It should be noted, however, that Chakrabarty seeks not simply to fragment but to divide history from itself, which explains his intermittent use of scare quotes around the term (see, e.g., p. 41). One could venture that a version of "the politics of despair," once affirmed, then disavowed, by Chakrabarty (45–46), is still operative in Nichanian's work. For a proximate, and compelling, interrogation of Chakrabarty, see Qadri Ismail, "(Not) at Home in (Hindu) India: Shahid Amin, Dipesh Chakrabarty, and the Critique of History," *Cultural Critique* 68 (Winter 2008): 210–247.

57. See, e.g., Delphine Gardey's striking *Écrire, calculer, classer: Comment une revolution de papier a transformé les sociétés contemporaines (1800–1940)* (Paris: La découverte, 2008), esp. 147–184; significantly, Gardey concerns herself with the very same period Nichanian attends to.

58. http://www.historians.org/perspectives/issues/2006/0610/0610new1 .cfm.

59. Young, *White Mythologies*, 68. Somehow apologetic about writing an impressive chapter in the history of antihistoricism, David Myers describes in limpid terms the "remarkable success story" of historicism in the scholarly and popular imagination. "As a mode of cognition," he writes, historicism "has come to dominate our way of thinking about the past"; David N. Myers, *Resisting History: Historicism and Its Discontents in German-Jewish Thought* (Princeton: Princeton University Press, 2003), 5. Myers's sophisticated sense of "historical difference" locates that difference on a contained grid that includes memory and theology (the state and the law, in other words), yet he shows very well—indeed, he affirms—that both memory and theology (along with symptoms of and laments over historical ignorance) have all fallen under the rule of history. And so has antihistoricism. As Dipesh Chakrabarty has reiterated after Foucault, historicism is the only history we know; the only history with which or from which we expect salvation and emancipation, along with the state, perhaps, if preferably cosmopolitan; Dipesh Chakrabarty, "Postcoloniality and the Artifice of History: Who Speaks for 'Indian' Pasts?" *Representations* 37 (Winter 1992): 1–26.

60. Gayatri Chakravorty Spivak, *Death of a Discipline* (New York: Columbia University Press, 2003).

61. Talal Asad, *Anthropology and the Colonial Encounter* (Atlantic Highlands, NJ: Humanities Press International, 1973); see also Johannes Fabian, *Time*

and the Other: How Anthropology Makes Its Object (New York: Columbia University Press, 1983); and David H. Price, *Threatening Anthropology: McCarthyism and the FBI's Surveillance of Activist Anthropologists* (Durham: Duke University Press, 2004). The "historical turn" in anthropology is hardly incidental in this context; cf. Stoler, "Colonial Archives,"especially 88–92.

62. Edward W. Said, *Orientalism* (New York: Vintage, 1978).

63. What follows in this section is by no means a substitute for the deep engagement by Beatrice Han-Pile with the place of history in Foucault's work. I merely try to take a measure of this problem in Foucault insofar as it pertains to Nichanian's work; B. Han-Pile, "Is Early Foucault a Historian? History, History, and the Analytic of Finitude," *Philosophy and Social Criticism* 31.5–6:585–608.

64. Michel Foucault, *The Order of Things: An Archaeology of the Human Sciences* (New York: Vintage, 1970); hereafter abbreviated as *OT*.

65. Gary Gutting, *Michel Foucault's Archaeology of Scientific Reason* (Cambridge: Cambridge University Press, 1989), 213.

66. A few pages later, Foucault writes that "all knowledge is rooted in a life, a society, and a language that have a history; and it is in that very history that knowledge finds the *element* enabling it to communicate with other forms of life, other types of society, other significations" (*OT* 373).

67. Gutting, *Michel Foucault's Archaeology*, 179; emphasis added.

68. Amos Funkenstein refers to the irruption of history, what he calls "the discovery of history as *contextual reasoning*," as constituting "a profound revolution in historical thought in the sixteenth and seventeenth centuries." He describes its result as "a conception of every historical fact, be it a text, an institution, a monument, or an event, as meaningless in itself unless seen in its original context"; Amos Funkenstein, *Theology and the Scientific Imagination from the Middle Ages to the Seventeenth Century* (Princeton: Princeton University Press, 1986), 206.

69. G. W. F. Hegel, *Philosophy of Right*, trans. T. M. Knox (Oxford: Oxford University Press, 1967), 11.

70. Walter Michaels has argued along these lines for an understanding of the alleged disappearance of an imposed determinism of race transformed into the chosen inescapability of culture. Mobility remains contingent on an unmovable realm of whatever nature; Walter Benn Michaels, "Race Into Culture: A Critical Genealogy of Cultural Identity," *Critical Inquiry* 18.4 (Summer 1992): 655–685.

71. Gutting, *Michel Foucault's Archaeology*, 220–21.

72. Ashis Nandy, *The Romance of the State and the Fate of Dissent in the Tropics* (New Delhi: Oxford University Press, 2003), 90.

73. Beatrice Han, *Foucault's Critical Project: Between the Transcendental and the Historical*, trans. Edward Pile (Stanford: Stanford University Press, 2002), 38. Han describes how "in the progression from archaeology to genealogy the tension swings between the transcendental and the historical and back again" (9). As she makes clear, much hangs on the understanding of the transcendental in Foucault and whether "the historical a priori" is reducible to the Kantian, empirico-transcendental, scheme (38–69).

74. The notion of a "return to history" is constitutive of Zionist thought and policy, as Amnon Raz-Krakotzkin has demonstrated. Its implications, resonating with Chakrabarty's concerns, reach much wider; Amnon Raz-Krakotzkin, "Jewish Memory Between Exile and History" *Jewish Quarterly Review* 97.4 (Fall 2007): 530–543.

75. The promise of history (the sense of "a redeemed mankind," as Walter Benjamin cuttingly describes) was recently reiterated by Ranajit Guha, who dreams of an inclusiveness whereby the writing of history "would have a subject-matter as comprehensive as the human condition itself. The world would open up with all of its pasts ready to serve for its narratives. No continent, no culture, no rank or condition of social being would be considered too small or too simple for its prose. . . . It would be the world of the prose of the world itself. And what stories it would have to tell!" (Guha, *History at the Limit of World-History*, 22). To be sure, Guha recognizes as well that this "hope of making historicality coextensive with the human condition itself did not materialize" (73). Shoshana Felman pursues a similar trajectory, without the final caveat, when she answers in the affirmative to the question "Can literature be viewed as the *record* of what has remained *out of the legal records?*" (Felman, *The Juridical Unconscious*, 100). And the archive grows.

76. Koselleck, *Futures Past*, 3.

77. I do not mean to underestimate this challenge, which has been compellingly demonstrated by Robert Young and others. Indeed there is no doubt that Nichanian's work is indebted to the very sources attended to by Young and others after him. There remains, however, the question of history's enduring symbolic capital.

78. Guha, *History at the Limit of World-History*, 65.

79. Derrida, *Writing and Difference*, 36. I have altered the translation on the basis of the French, which reads: "se taire d'un certain silence" and means

both, as I have tried to render it, "to keep silent about a certain silence" and "to keep silent in a certain manner, with a particular kind of silence"; Jacques Derrida, *L'écriture et la différence* (Paris: Seuil, 1967), 58.

80. Under Nichanian's guidance, one is better equipped to perceive the irony of a gesture that conflates philosophical responses to the Holocaust with apology for it (or some other bizarre version of retrospective historiography, whereby that which had not yet come about—say, postmodernism—could be seen as a kind of enabler for what happened under distinct, historical, and, indeed, darker skies). Instead of placing the discipline of history under interrogation—minimally, as a significant actor in the production of the modern (and totalitarian) state—the Holocaust serves to buttress undisturbed notions of history and of historical methods.

81. The need has generally been felt to deploy a new vocabulary with regard to this phenomenon. Thus Colin Tatz opts "for denialism and denialist rather than the conventional denial and denier for this genre of genocide negation or disavowal"; Colin Tatz, *With Intent to Destroy: Reflecting on Genocide* (London: Verso, 2003), 185n1. The French word *négationisme* has however begun to appear in English.

82. The word *revisionism*, which the OED traces to the nineteenth century, emerges with a negative charge (relying on the objectivism of history) in socialist circles and is prominently used within political contexts. *Historical revisionism*, which would come to label Holocaust deniers, occurs in a more neutral context around the 1950s.

83. Although he asserts that "law and history, it seems, have different rules and different epistemological foundations," Carlo Ginzburg goes on to affirm "the connection among proofs, truth, and history," emphasizing the status of both witness and "reality"; Carlo Ginzburg, "Just One Witness," in Saul Friedlander, ed., *Probing the Limits of Representation: Nazism and the "Final Solution"* (Cambridge: Harvard University Press, 1992), 85–86; and see Ginzburg's extended meditation on the subject in *The Judge and the Historian*, esp. 12–18, 110–119, where he surprisingly seems to suggest that in contradistinction with those of the judges, the errors of historians have less "immediate" or "serious consequences" (119).

84. Lorraine Daston and Peter Galison, *Objectivity* (New York: Zone, 2007), 19.

85. I am referring again to Carlo Ginzburg's title, "Just One Witness," which Nichanian discusses at length in chapter 3.

86. Daston and Galison, *Objectivity*, 50.

87. In addition to a historicization of the historical fact (offered, for example, by Mary Poovey), one could no doubt argue against the nature of the historical fact as Nichanian (or my rendering of him) engages, that it should be interrogated along the lines of "objectivity," as drawn by Daston and Galison. They explain, "current usage allows a too easy slide among senses of objectivity [and therefore of fact] that are by turns ontological, epistemological, methodological and moral. Yet these various senses of the objective [and of the fact] cohere neither in precept nor in practice" (Daston and Galison, *Objectivity*, 51). This might be true, but note there is a *legal* dimension that Nichanian underscores, which is absent from Daston and Galison's account. And what else but law could make "precept and practice" cohere?

88. Nichanian, *HP* 12; Nichanian finds his inspiration, here and elsewhere, in Jacques Derrida's *Archive Fever*.

89. Daston and Galison, *Objectivity*, 27.

90. Nichanian, *ATDP*. I return to this matter further on in the text.

91. Martin Harries, *Forgetting Lot's Wife: On Destructive Spectatorship* (New York: Fordham University Press, 2007), 9; Harries is careful not to simply equate spectatorship and testimony, yet the distinction is a difficult one to maintain, particularly in the face of trauma. Hence the apposition, at times, of "the spectator's position, the witness's position" (58, and see also 72).

92. Nichanian, *ATRN* 22.

93. See his discussion of Ginzburg and the latter's claim that "memory and the destruction of memory are recurrent elements in history" (Ginzburg, "Just One Witness," 96). The destruction of memory, the death of death and the erasure of all traces, of all archive would thus be nothing new for the historian. More than that, the very notion and status of the witness would be unchanged for all eternity, something that does not cease to astonish Nichanian.

94. My colleague Courtney Bender reminds me that *génocidaires* are often compulsive record keepers and archive producers. But this goes to show precisely their deep understanding of the rule of the archive: its destructive efficacy being predicated upon the very affirmation, and operations, of preservation.

95. Rancière, *The Names of History*, 31, and see also 37.

96. "The complicity between imperialism and World-history," writes Ranajit Guha, "is therefore not merely a question of the expropriation of the pasts of the colonized by colonizers. It stands also for the globalization of a

regional development specific to modern Europe—that is the overcoming of the prose of the world by the prose of history" (Guha, *History at the Limit of World-History*, 45).

97. Archaeology, Foucault writes, referring to the short-lived "method" he advocated, "does not treat discourse as *document*, as a sign of something else, as an element that ought to be transparent, but whose unfortunate opacity must often be pierced if one is to reach at last the depth of the essential in the place in which it is held in reserve; it is concerned with discourse in its own volume, as a *monument*. It is not an interpretative discipline: it does not seek another, better-hidden discourse. It refuses to be 'allegorical'" (Foucault, *The Archaeology of Knowledge*, 138–139). Nichanian quotes a 1968 text in which Foucault credits Canguilhem with the idea of using the term *monument*. Here, and elsewhere, one should also listen to Benjaminian echoes, which leave no reprieve to any "document of civilization" in its relation to barbarism.

98. Agamben, *Remnants of Auschwitz*.

99. Chakrabarty, *Provincializing Europe*, 20 and 42.

100. Writing of the spirit of literature circa 1900, Kittler writes that it "became a dictator giving dictation, followed by young men who killed off what was real in them and recorded by secretaries" (Kittler, *Discourse Networks*, 167). Later on, Kittler attends to Bram Stoker's 1897 *Dracula*, describing Mina Harker as the ultimate archivist/secretary, thematizing the literary as secretarial: "She who dreamed of doing what she saw lady journalists do uses her typewriter to transcribe every diary entry, every phonograph roll, every relevant newspaper clipping and telegram, every document and log book. She makes copies of her transcriptions; she delivers these daily to all the investigators, and so on and on" (354). Interestingly, Kittler mentions, but does not comment on, the destruction of the archive, indeed, on its role in the extermination of that enemy from "the very frontier of Turkey-land." And one would have to wonder as well on the manner in which the destruction is affirmed by the witness in *Dracula*. Indeed, those who faced the apocalypse also confront the destruction of the archive and *affirm* it: "we want no proofs; we ask none to believe us!" Bram Stoker, *Dracula*, ed. John Paul Riquelme (Boston: Bedford/St. Martin's, 2002), 369. Kittler revisits the issue in his "Dracula's Legacy," where he acknowledges the destruction of the archive (double genitive). Hence "the Count no longer merely burns secret documents, but also the apparata that go with them." And yet what remains of the archive is described by way of a

strange unilaterality, even denegation. "Secretaries" of the archive, Kittler says, "do not merely collate and distribute information, each evening they bring the neutralizing and annihilating signifiers together into safety. The destruction of the Count begins with paper money and typewriter paper, *as they survive indestructibly*"; Friedrich A. Kittler, "Dracula's Legacy" in John Johnston, ed., *Literature, Media, Information Systems* (Amsterdam: G+B Arts International/Overseas Publishers Association, 1997), 74; emphasis added).

101. For Nichanian, there is only "one Armenian work written in the twentieth century in which testimony succeeded in transforming itself into literature [*se faire littérature*] or succeeded at least in turning literature to its own benefit, by rendering problematic the very concept of literature in its confrontation with the Catastrophe" (*ATDP* 189). The reference is to Zabel Essayan's *Among the Ruins* (*Averaknerun mej*).

102. Such is the project articulated in Nichanian's first book, *Ages et usages de la langue arménienne;* see *AULA* 24–25; there Nichanian distinguishes his literary critical project from linguistics and from history and historiography, doubting that the last could ever account for "the reasons and the conditions that govern the birth of a 'literary language'" (86). The phenomenon of literarization, he writes, "escapes entirely the conceptuality of linguistics" (151; cf. also 201).

103. Nichanian, *AULA* 170–171.

104. Whether related to historical conceptions as in *AULA*, especially 130–138, 300–301, or to discussions on the works of Walter Benjamin or Antoine Berman, both of whom Nichanian also translated into Armenian.

105. Nichanian, *WDNR* 10; I have altered the translation to approximate the later French version (*ATRN* 27).

106. Nichanian, *WDNR* 245; here again the translation is altered on the basis of the French text (*ATRN* 277).

107. Nichanian speaks of "le défaut du deuil" (*ATDP* 168, and see also 148 and 243–44). Derrida attends to the impossibility of mourning and discusses, among others, Hölderlin's *Mnemosyne*. There Derrida cites Michael Hamburger's English translation: "Mourning is in default"; Derrida, *Memoires for Paul de Man*, trans. Cecile Lindsay et al. (New York: Columbia University Press, 1989), 6, although another version gives "mourning is at fault." For a more extended discussion, see Marc Nichanan, "Avons-nous vraiment perdu la langue à l'étranger?" in *TTR* 14.2:161ff.; and Hanselm Haverkamp, "Error in Mourning—A Crux in Hölderlin: 'Dem gleich feh-

let die Trauer' ('Mnemosyne')," trans. Vernon Chadwick in *Yale French Studies* 69 (Fall 1985): 238–253.

108. De Certeau, *The Writing of History*, 3.

109. Stathis Gourgouris, *Dream Nation: Enlightenment, Colonization, and the Institution of Modern Greece* (Stanford: Stanford University Press, 1996), 45.

110. The phrase is Jules Michelet's, as discussed by Rancière, *The Names of History*, 54ff., yet the context of national history adopted by Rancière should be widened, along the lines suggested by Nichanian in the wake of Edward Said, in order to include philology—history—as an Orientalist and colonial enterprise. And one should take into consideration structural and political parallels with what Friedrich Kittler describes as "the Woman as the Mother's Mouth," who has "every right to be a Voice, but no right to have one." Akin to the native, "the Mother neither speaks nor writes, but from the depth of her soul arise the unembellished accents that the author rescues by writing" (Kittler, *Discourse Networks*, 66–67). Not surprisingly, the Schlegel brothers are at the center of Kittler's and Nichanian's analyses. Incidentally, Kittler explicitly relates the figure of the Mother to the archive and its technological reproduction (e.g., 110, 117).

111. Rancière, *The Names of History*, 24.

112. "The witness is . . . a figure of the archive," writes William Robert in his extended discussion of Derrida and Agamben; William Robert, "Witnessing the Archive: In Mourning," in Oren Baruch Stier and J. Shawn Landres, eds., *Religion, Violence, Memory, and Place* (Bloomington: Indiana University Press, 2006), 46.

113. Michelet, quoted in Rancière, *The Names of History*, 57.

114. Trinh T. Minh-ha, *Woman, Native, Other: Writing Postcoloniality and Feminism* (Bloomington: Indiana University Press, 1989), 57; Minh-ha expands and explains that the native "always stands on the other side of the hill, naked and speechless, barely present in its absence" (67). That is why the goal of the philologist (here the anthropologist) will always be the expansion of the archive or, as Clifford Geertz puts it, "the enlargement of the universe of human discourse" (quoted in Minh-ha, 72).

115. As de Certeau writes, invoking Lacan, the subject of history, the native, is seized by a "constituent division" (de Certeau, *The Writing of History*, 102).

116. Norman Brown puts it succinctly and graphically, commenting on Nietzsche: "Man's ability to promise involves an unhealthy (neurotic) constipation with the past (the anal character!); he can 'get rid of' nothing"; Brown, *Life Against Death*, 267).

117. Cf. *ATDP* 35 and 94–95; one is reminded of the infamous justification for extermination that had already cast natives into oblivion before offering to assist and accelerate the matter; cf. Sven Lindqvist, *"Exterminate All the Brutes,"* trans. Joan Tate (New York: New Press, 1996).

118. Cf. *AULA* 327–330; 346–351; 365–369; 372, 381–383, 391–397; and *ATRN* 306.

INDEX

Archive(s) (*continued*)
93, 112–13, 115, 122, 145; in U.S., 122;
validation and, 25, 26, 128; violence
of, 129; witness and, 146; writers as
secretaries of, 15, 17, 148, 150

Arendt, Hannah, 48–49, 50, 51, 52, 54,
55, 137

Armenian, 3, 7, 8, 11, 19, 26, 33, 36, 47,
49, 52, 54, 95, 99; language, 146, 147,
149; literature, 107, 159; survivors, 93;
testimony, 104; writers, 15, 17, 103, 113,
115, 145

Armenian Golgotha (Balakian), 113

Art, 3, 14, 15, 74, 153; cinema and, 98;
representation of atrocity and, 107–8;
testimony and, 94–95, 100, 101, 102,
104; witness and, 100

The Assassins of Memory (Vidal-Naquet),
56, 57, 71

Atrocity, 98; art and representation of,
107–8

Auschwitz, 2, 5, 6, 9, 17, 23, 81, 83, 125, 127;
proof of, 85; reality of, 89; as sign, 87

Balakian, Grigoris, 113
Baudrillard, Jean, 141
Belief, 51, 151
Blanchot, Maurice, 10, 82, 155
Bosnia, 13, 20
Burning Orchards (Mahari), 151

Cadava, Eduardo, 129
Cahen, Michel, 34, 35, 40
Camps: concentration, of Mesopotamia,
109; extermination, 17; Nazi, 16;
Soviet, 5; testimonies of survivors of
Nazi, 91–92
Captanian, Ms., 113

Catastrophe, 7, 8, 9, 15, 26, 53, 84, 102,
127, 150, 151, 159; impossibility of
representation of, 79, 103; invisibility
of, 99; liberation of, 146; natural, 20;
see also Genocide

Certeau, Michel de, 126, 133, 155
Chakrabarti, Dipesh, 133
Christendom, 49
Chuvin, Pierre, 34, 35, 40
Cilicia, massacre of, 109
Collège de France, 3, 4, 33
Colonialism, 48–49, 83, 159, 175*n*13,
193*n*110
Complicity, 145, 150
"Conflict of the Philosophy Faculty with
the Faculty of Law" (Kant), 88
Consensus, 43, 145, 168*n*27; fact and, 96;
truth as, 121
Coquio, Catherine, 33, 42
Court(s): civil, 3, 19, 30; conclusion of,
in Lewis trial, 163*n*8; historians and,
41; international, 20; methods of, 38;
military, 28; Paris high, 20, 23–25, 27,
29, 32, 34, 48
Crime(s): collective, 49; of genocidal
denial, 34; of genocide, 23, 24, 26;
against humanity, 29, 48–49, 50, 51, 52,
54; perfect, 143; of silence, 56; without
trace, 129; unmotivated, 49; war, 21
Critique of Judgment (Kant), 89
Croce, Benedetto, 16, 74, 75, 76
Cursed Years (Odian), 113

Daston, Lorraine, 141, 142
Death: circumstances of, 26; drive,
167*n*21, 175*n*7; suppression of, 55, 144
Denegation, 27, 28, 30, 55, 112; by Turkey, 22

Historical difference, 125–26, 186*59*

Historical discipline, 60, 63, 70, 85, 140; expansion of, 132

Historiography, 14, 133; crisis of, 9, 10, 14, 16, 60, 67, 73, 76, 84, 93, 99, 139; of denial, 57; of extermination, 60; fact and, 13; limits of, 92; perversion of, 12, 13, 45, 107, 112, 115; refutation and, 17; state, 56, 57, 60, 64, 65, 70, 71, 175*n*13; truth and, 12; Turkish, 57

History: all-inclusiveness of, 188*n*75; archive and, 86, 127, 159; barbarism of, 131, 139; chaos of, 88, 89; of conceptions/receptions, 147, 148–49; contribution/significance of, 131–32, 133; definition of, 72, 145, 178*n*23; definition of fact of, 145; as empirical science, 135–36; erasure of, 137; fact and, 81, 145, 146; fiction and, 62; function of, 66, 127; ideological abuse of, 31; image and, 169*n*6; of India, 175*n*13; interpretation through, 61, 65; justice and, 183*n*48; law and, 4, 141, 189*n*83; literature and, 127–28, 145, 149–50; loss of, 184*n*44; meaning and, 126; in media, 132; national, 155, 156; native and, 158, 159; objectivity and, 66, 86, 142; opposition to/critique of, 133, 134, 135, 139; oral, 76; of Ottoman Empire, 51; philology and, 154; philosophy and, 76; position of, 135, 136, 137; postmodern approach to, 61; power and, 126, 156; reality and, 81; renunciation of, 54; representation and, 97, 103; return to, 134, 138; ruling over human/social sciences, 127, 135, 138, 186*n*56; as science, 81, 88, 126; as series of massacres, 99; sign of, 88; silence and, 154–55; state,

56, 57, 60, 64, 65, 70, 71, 175*n*13; on trial, 182*n*40; truth and, 1, 3, 4, 59–60, 62, 65, 68, 71, 72, 86, 93; turning against itself, 183*n*44, 184*n*48

Hitler, Adolf, 99

Hobsbawm, Eric, 31, 42, 43, 44, 45, 48, 57

Hölderlin, Friedrich, 154

Holocaust, 6, 20, 50, 61, 62, 64, 67, 73, 100, 101, 140, 189*n*80; banalization of, 99; historical context of, 92; interpretations of, 65; uniqueness of, 23

Houssaper, 113

Humanity: civilized, 12, 13, 19, 28, 112, 120, 128; civilized, as witness, 95, 96, 97; crimes against, 29, 48–49, 50, 51, 52, 54

Identity, 49, 118

Ideology, 50, 61, 72, 74; distortion of, 65, 68; extermination and, 21–22; history and, 31; massacre and, 51–52; superficial, 22, 23

Image, 97, 98, 101, 102; history and, 169*n*6

Impossibility: of mourning, 110, 139, 144, 148, 150, 151, 152, 153, 158; of representation of TKCatastrophe, 79, 103; of testimony, 85, 119, 121–22

"In an Era of Testimony: Claude Lanzmann's *Shoah*" (Felman), 100

India, history of, 175*n*13

Insult, 57; of realism, 8, 14

Intention, 30, 49; archives and, 41; of genocide, 21, 26, 37; testimonies and, 40

Interpretation, 36, 43, 45, 48, 49, 50, 62, 64, 68, 69, 70; archive and, 155; emplotment and, 72; genocidal, 37; historical, 61, 65; of Holocaust, 65;

Interpretation (*continued*)
humanitarian, 13; lack of, 47; law and,
38, 39; proof and, 39, 41; reality and,
16; truth and, 65, 66, 72; violence of, 86
In These Dark Days (Andonian), 123
Israel, 65
Istanbul trials (1919), 28

Jews, 20, 23, 26, 50, 52, 60, 99, 100; geno-
cide of, 51, 57, 59
Jews: History, Memory, and the Present
(Vidal-Naquet), 56
Justice, 4, 7, 82; historical, 183*n*48; nega-
tionism and, 20; for victim, 97
"Just One Witness" (Ginzburg), 16, 61,
74–75

Kafka, Franz, 123
Kant, Immanuel, 81, 87, 88, 89, 90, 94
Kapiguian, Garabed, 113
Kittler, Friedrich, 130
Koselleck, Reinhart, 139

Lacoue-Labarthe, Philippe, 5, 49, 50, 51,
52, 54
"Land of Fire" (Tcharents), 152
Language, 83, 93, 121; Armenian, 146,
147, 149; becoming literary, 147; limita-
tion of, 79
Lanzmann, Claude, 95, 99, 100, 101, 102
Lasch, Christopher, 131
Laub, Dori, 92
Law, 55, 82, 88, 94, 130; archive and, 86;
destruction of evidence and, 184*n*47;
fact and, 11, 29, 39, 41; French, 29;
Gayssot, 38, 87, 164*n*3; genocide and,
45; historians and, 29, 34; history
and, 4, 141, 189*n*83; international, 87;

interpretation and, 38, 39; truth and, 3;
Western philosophy of, 48
Legitimacy, 127, 128, 140, 142
Lemkin, Raphael, 87
Levi, Primo, 16, 74, 85
Lewis, Bernard, 4, 21, 36, 51, 57, 145; argumentation of, 22, 23, 25, 31; court's
conclusion in trial of, 163*n*8; trial of, 3,
11, 19–20, 23–24, 29, 30, 48; verdict of
trial of, 34; *see also* Court
Libération, 33, 42
Linguistics, 61, 69, 74
Literarization, 146, 147
Literature, 15, 103, 104; absence of, 145,
150; American, 183*n*44; archive and,
147; Armenian, 107, 159; facts and, 150;
history and, 127–28, 146, 149–50; language and, 147; as monument, 151–52,
152; mourning and, 148, 150; national,
159; negationist, 22; philology and, 153;
postcatastrophic, 145; power of, 148;
suffering and, 111; testimony and, 17,
107–9, 112, 114, 151, 153, 192*n*101; *see
also* Writers
Logic, 49, 50, 54, 55, 56; of executioner,
95; of murderer, 47; of proof, 47; of
shame, 117
Lyotard, Jean-François, 2, 5, 6, 7, 8, 9, 14,
17, 24, 39, 45, 72, 81, 82, 83, 85, 94

Maggiori, Robert, 29, 30
Mahari, Gurgen, 151
Massacre(s), 130; of Cilicia, 109; history
as series of, 99; ideology and, 51–52;
possibility of, 127; publicized, 143; war
and, 51
Meaning, 32, 46, 132; absence of, 47–48,
49; historians as guardians of, 42; his-

tory and, 126; reality and, 48; witness giving, 152; *see also* Sense

Media, 92, 140; history in, 132; validation through, 25, 26

Memories of an Armenian Deportee (Captanian), 113

Memory, 3, 13, 14, 20, 66, 70, 77, 80, 92, 93, 111, 130, 134, 144; destruction of, 83–84; disowning of, 28; fact and public, 97; idolatry of, 76; national, 95; preservation of, 128; survivor deprived of, 112; testimony and, 122

Mesopotamia, concentration camps of, 109

Metareality, 82, 83, 84, 168*n*27

Mets Vochirë (Andonian), 111

Michelet, Jules, 156

Microhistory, 76, 133

Mnatsortats (Oshagan), 7, 113

Modernity, 132, 135, 139

Le Monde, 19, 40, 49, 54, 56

Le Monde des Débats, 42

Monument, 105, 139, 140, 169*n*4; literature as, 151–52, 152; of mourning, 151; testimony as, 94–95, 104, 107, 109, 114, 152

Morality, 13, 89

Motive, 22, 49, 56; crime without, 49; genocidal will and, 12; proof by, 48, 50, 51, 52, 53, 54

Mourning, 25, 111; archive and, 114; denial and, 47, 159; genocidal will forbidding, 151, 154; impossibility of, 110, 139, 144, 148, 150, 151, 152, 153, 158; literature and, 148, 150; monument of, 151; native and, 157, 158; philology and, 153, 154; rescuing act of, 152

Murder(er), 53, 55, 79, 102, 112, 123, 129, 141, 142, 144; archive and, 183*n*41;

effort of, 183*n*43; logic of, 47; mass, 21, 127, 143; proof of, 47; reason for, 49, 51; *see also* Executioner

Muselmann, 17, 85, 121

Muslims, 16–17

Muteness: disaster and, 157; of native, 143, 156–57

Name: emblematic, 2, 5, 6, 7, 8–9, 14, 17, 93, 94, 114, 126; generic, 6, 8–9, 14, 93; proper, 7, 8–9, 23

Nancy, Jean-Luc, 5, 6, 54, 102, 114

Narrative, 43, 77, 78, 104, 105; archive and, 26; as grave, 25; proof and, 28; reality and, 31; of survivors, 27, 103, 106, 152, 170*n*16; testimony and, 84

Native, 193*n*114; archive and, 155, 156; definition of, 155, 156; disaster and, 156, 158; history and, 158, 159; mourning and, 157, 158; muteness of, 143, 156–57; speech of, 156, 157; witness and, 155, 156

Native Americans, 183*n*44

Nazi(s), 11, 49, 59, 64, 166*n*11; camps, 16; testimonies of, camp survivors, 91–92

Nazi genocide, 29, 30

Negationism, 10, 12, 21, 27, 28, 29, 30, 32, 33, 51, 68, 90, 145, 189*n*81; definition of, 140–41, 162*n*7; denial of, 11; forms of, 56; genocidal will and, 72–73; justice and, 20; in literature, 22; perversion of, 23; state, 60, 64, 65, 70, 71; truth and, 74; *see also* Denial

"Negationism at the Collège de France" (Coquio), 33

Nietzsche, Friedrich Wilhelm, 125, 131, 132

Niney, François, 96

Testimony(ies) (*continued*)
112; documentation and, 16, 17, 93; erasure of, 101; as evidence, 145; fact and, 13, 16, 75, 76, 86, 165*n*4; first published, 109; function of, 14; genocidal will and, 121; historian and, 92; impossibility of, 85, 119, 121–22; insufficiency of, 79; intention and, 40; literature and, 17, 107–9, 112, 114, 151, 153, 192*n*101; memory and, 122; as monument, 94–95, 104, 107, 109, 114, 152; narrative and, 84; of Nazi camp survivors, 91–92; possibility of event/possibility of, 101; postcatastrophic, 90; proliferation of, 76, 77; proof and, 39, 48, 112, 123; realism and, 15; realist/emblematic option of, 17, 94; reality and, 79–80; as refutation, 17; shame and, 118, 119, 120, 121; sign and, 86; status of, 1, 4, 91–94, 97, 99, 100; of survivor, 4; totality of, 37, 39, 40, 41, 43, 44; truth and, 92

Tolstoy, Leo, 75, 79, 83
Toroyan, Hayg, 109
Tradition, 134; disaster of, 156; disintegration of, 158; Western, 99, 101
Translation, 149, 159, 173*n*1, 174*n*3
Trial(s): court's conclusion in Lewis, 163*n*8; history on, 182*n*40; of Istanbul (1919), 28; Lewis, 3, 11, 19–20, 23–24, 29, 30, 48; political, 57; verdict of Lewis, 34
Tribute to Armenian Intellectuality (Shamdanjian), 113
Trojan genocide, 13
Trouillot, Michel-Rolph, 133
Truth, 16, 69, 103, 106; as consensus, 121; emplotment and, 72; establishment

of, 166*n*8; facts and, 30, 66; historians and, 41; historiography and, 12; history and, 1, 3, 4, 62, 65, 68, 71, 72, 86, 93; interpretation and, 65, 66, 72; law and, 3; negationism and, 74; standpoints of, 72–73; status of, in history, 59–60; testimony and, 92
Turkey, 49, 54, 99; denegation by, 22; EU and, 12, 13; government of, 42, 43; historiography of, 57; publications of, 57
Twentieth century, 91, 107; genocidal will in, 99; genocide in, 1, 5, 11, 84

UN, *see* United Nations
Undecidability, 28, 31, 44, 45
United Nations (UN), 24
United States (U.S.), 12, 57, 60, 99, 138; archives in, 122; literature in, 183*n*44
U.S., *see* United States

Validation, 29, 30, 43, 44, 78; of annihilation, 84; of archive, 25, 26, 128; through archives/media, 25, 26; of facts, 24–25, 86; of sense, 81
Veinstein, Gilles, 3–4, 11, 12, 13, 33, 36, 56, 64, 145; defense of, 34, 35; writings of, 57
Victims: justice for, 97; perpetrators and, 35; relativity of innocence of, 51
Vidal-Naquet, Pierre, 34, 57, 60, 64, 65, 66, 68, 71, 72, 81; letter to, 56
Violence: of archive, 129; of interpretation, 86; segregational, 99; style of, 9, 10; system of mythical, 11
Visibility, 94–95, 97, 101, 103, 115, 149

War: cold, 91; crimes, 21; massacre and, 51; *see also* World War II

War and Peace (Tolstoy), 79

Western philosophy, of law, 48

Western tradition, 99, 101

White, Hayden, 12, 14, 16, 72, 73, 77, 87, 90, 133; attack on, 60–61; critique of, 68–70; discussion of article by, 62, 63–64, 65, 66, 67; Ginzburg on, 67, 68, 74–75, 78

Wieviorka, Annette, 91, 92

Winter, Jay, 21, 23

Witness, 67, 105, 142, 181n32; archive and, 146; art and, 100; authority of, 93; civilized world as, 95, 96, 97; erasure of, 101, 102; event without, 101, 114, 115; fact and, 90, 94; meaning and, 152; native and, 155, 156; origins of, 145; postcatastrophic, 90; proof and, 40; refutation of, 115; sign and, 90, 94; status of, 77–78, 84, 85; sublime and, 89

Wittgenstein, Ludwig, 88

World War II, 29

Writers: Armenian, 15, 17, 103, 113, 115, 145; as secretaries of archive, 15, 17, 148, 150; *see also* Literature

Yale University, 92

Yerushalmi, Yosef Hayim, 46

Young, Robert, 133, 159

Young Turks, 28

Zola, Émile, 3